ARIS Design Platform

Rob Davis

ARIS Design Platform

Advanced Process Modelling and Administration

 Springer

Rob Davis
BT OneIT
British Telecommunications plc
UK

ISBN: 978-1-84800-110-7   e-ISBN: 978-1-84800-111-4
DOI 10.1007/978-1-84800-111-4

British Library Cataloguing in Publication Data
A catalogue record for this book is available from the British Library

Library of Congress Control Number: 2008926119

Printed on acid-free paper

9 8 7 6 5 4 3 2 1

Springer Science+Business Media
springer.com

DEDICATION

**For Sally,
who makes this all worthwhile.**

Acknowledgements

I would like to thank all my colleagues at BT, many of whose ideas have contributed to the store of knowledge I have built up and which has enabled me to write this book. In particular to Ordelia Sansford for reviewing some of the chapters.

Also thanks to the staff at IDS Scheer in Germany and the UK who have provided much help and assistance. In particular Andrea Albrecht and Britta Hilt for arranging for people to review parts of the book and especially to reviewers including: Christina Reinshagen, Philipp Lahmé and Hans Maas. Further thanks to Britta Hilt for providing previews of ARIS 7.1.

Thanks also to Eric Brabänder for working with me on the previous book. He didn't join me on this book and I missed his support and our late night voiceconferences.

I would like thank Springer-Verlag for the opportunity to publish the book. In particular Beverley Ford for her continued enthusiasm for ARIS books; to Catherine Brett for all her help and support, and to Frank Ganz for his assistance on the book layout.

I would also like to thank IDS Sheer AG for permission to reproduce screen shots of the ARIS Platform and to use figures and text from ARIS promotional and technical documentation.

Finally I would like to thank Sally for putting up with me for a second year of book writing.

Rob Davis

Contents

Chapter 1   Introduction

This chapter gives an overview of the ARIS Platform and the ARIS products. The structure of the book is described with advice for different reader groups.

1.1   Introduction to the ARIS Platform

The ARIS products are aligned to the Business Process Management (BPM) lifecycle and offered in an integrated software solution grouped into four ARIS Platforms:

- **The Strategy Platform**,
- **The Design Platform**,
- **The Implementation Platform**,
- **The Controlling Platform**.

The system architecture of the ARIS Platform allows globally distributed organisations to set up common scenarios for designing, analysing, and optimising processes, IT, and software architectures.

Web-based products such as *ARIS Business Optimizer*, *ARIS Business Architect*, *ARIS Business Designer*, and *ARIS UML Designer* can access a centrally managed *ARIS Business Server* from anywhere in the world via a three-tier architecture. These products are designed to use utilise low bandwidth connections (e.g. dial-up, ISDN, etc.). Web-based clients can be started directly from within a Web browser or, alternatively, they can be installed as a desktop application manually or by automated software distribution. In both cases, any necessary client updates can be set up and controlled centrally to facilitate the rollout process.

The integrated software solution of the ARIS Platform has two key characteristics:

- Central data repository,
- Common language and semantics.

ARIS is based around a central database for all modelling items (e.g. models, objects, connections, etc.) and all administration information. Everything described, designed and analysed within the different ARIS products is stored in this central data repository. All ARIS clients access the database server via the *ARIS Business Server* and thus work with a common database.

ARIS
Controlling Platform

ARIS Process Performance Manager
ARIS Audit Manager
...

ARIS
Strategy Platform

ARIS BSC
ARIS Business Optimizer
...

ARIS
Implementation Platform

ARIS for SAP NetWeaver
ARIS SOA Designer
ARIS UML Designer
ARIS BI Modeler
...

ARIS
Design Platform

ARIS Business Architect
ARIS Business Designer
ARIS Toolset
ARIS Easy Design
ARIS Simulation
ARIS IT Architect
ARIS Business Publisher
ARIS Web Publisher
...

Fig 1.1 ARIS Platform – Major Products

All the ARIS products have been developed by IDS Scheer without the need to integrate any external software not based on the central repository concept. Integration also means everything you model and describe using the ARIS Platform products is based on common language and semantics that can be understand by all users. The semantics of describing process models and enterprise information is based on the underlying concept which gave ARIS its name.

"ARIS – Architecture of Integrated Information Systems"

The ARIS Platform offers a high level of system scalability and availability. For instance, the majority of modellers can use *ARIS Business Designer*, while a smaller number of expert users can provide central administrative functions (e.g. management of access privileges, available reports, conventions/filters, etc.) using *ARIS Business Architect*. It is these expert users that this book is intended for.

1.2   What's in this Book

After the success of my first book on ARIS Toolset:

"Business Process Modelling with ARIS – A Practical Guide",

I teamed up with Eric Bräbender from IDS Scheer to work together on a new book:

"ARIS Design Platform: Getting Started with BPM".

In this book we provided a practical 'how-to' guide to using the *ARIS Design Platform* and gave an introduction to starting out on Business Process Management (BPM) based on ARIS modelling. We covered the basic principles of using *ARIS Business Architect* and *ARIS Business Designer* to design processes and introduced many of the key concepts, models and objects including:

- How to establish BPM with ARIS,
- Background to modelling and the ARIS Method,
- Basic instructions for using *ARIS Business Designer*,
- Selected information on using *ARIS Business Architect*,
- How to structure a business process architecture,
- How to set and use standards,
- Hints and tips on *ARIS Business Architect* and *ARIS Business Designer*.

Following on from that, this latest book complements the *ARIS Design Platform*, updating some material from the original *ARIS Toolset* book while adding new material on topics such as the Matrix Editor, Database Administration and Configuring the ARIS Method. In particular, it covers in detail the following topics aimed at more expert users:

- Issues to consider before starting a modelling project,
- Advanced modelling concepts and tools,
- Database administration and configuration.

This book is not a substitute for attending any of the ARIS training courses offered by IDS Scheer Academies worldwide (which are strongly recommended). However, using the guidance in this book you should be able to use *ARIS Business Architect* effectively in complex modelling situations and be able to administer ARIS to support enterprise-wide modelling projects.

There are several target groups for this book:

- People familiar with *ARIS Business Architect* who wish to use some of the more advanced modelling concepts and tools,
- People who need to manage ARIS modelling projects,
- People who need to Administer ARIS databases for projects and organisations,
- People who need to define and configure the ARIS Method and modelling conventions for their organisation,
- People who wish to use the *ARIS Design Platform* for the development of organisation-wide BPM systems,
- People with experience and knowledge of *ARIS Toolset* or *ARIS Easy Design* who want to migrate to the web-based ARIS products.

For all these groups the book provides a practical 'how-to' guide to what are complex topics, however plenty of space is given to providing lots of hints and tips regarding the practical use of *ARIS Business Architect*.

I have been using ARIS in British Telecommunications plc for more than ten years and was responsible for implementing ARIS in BT. I introduced ARIS, both to process modellers familiar with other tools, and to people with little experience of tools or modelling. My colleagues and I had to work out what standards to define, how to publish them, how to review them and how to overcome natural resistance to change. Although most users had been trained, what they needed above all was an easy-to-understand guide to how to apply the tool for modelling their business.

I have tried to mix detailed advice about how to operate key aspects of *ARIS Business Architect*, along with guidance on how to go about process modelling using ARIS in your organisation and wherever possible I have stuck to the ARIS Method. My approach won't suite everyone, but if you use it as a starting point you can develop your own style and techniques as you progress.

Inevitably, this is *my* pragmatic approach to modelling *your* business in ARIS based on my experience. It is not intended to replace the published information on the ARIS Method or the ARIS product range, the ARIS help files, or any training you may receive from IDS Scheer.

I have described and illustrated *ARIS Business Architect* version 7.02 (as of December 2007). There may be small differences with later versions of ARIS, but nevertheless the basic principles of modelling with *ARIS Business Architect* should remain the same. Where I have indicated 'bugs' or 'limitations' with the current release, these have be reported to IDS Scheer and may well have been fixed by the time you read this book.

I have prepared this book with due care and attention, but can take no responsibility for the consequences of any actions readers take as a result of reading this book. If in doubt, consult IDS Scheer AG.

1.3   How to Use this Book

Unlike the previous book, which was intended be read through from beginning to end, this book is more of a reference manual of the more advanced *ARIS Business Architect* facilities. You should be able to read a chapter on any topic that interests you in isolation. However there is a great deal of interaction between some topics (i.e. Database Administration and User Administration) so you may find yourself having to refer to other chapters to get a full understanding of what you need.

I would not recommend anyone to try to read the book in one go. Using ARIS successfully is based on practice and experience. It is best to read a few chapters and try out the techniques described, moving on to more complex material as you become more familiar and confident.

Depending on your interest you may wish to concentrate on chapters in the following areas:

- **Issues to consider before starting a modelling project:**
  - Chapter 2 – Before You Start Modelling,
  - Chapter 3 – Process Capture and Modelling.
- **Advanced modelling concepts and tools:**
  - Chapter 4 – The Matrix Editor,
  - Chapter 5 – Find and Query,
  - Chapter 6 – Model Generation,
  - Chapter 7 – Modelling in Rows and Columns,
  - Chapter 8 – Modelling Process Variants,
  - Chapter 9 – ARIS Evaluations.
- **Database administration and configuration:**
  - Chapter 10 – Database Administration,
  - Chapter 11 – User Administration,
  - Chapter 12 – Configuring the ARIS Method,
  - Chapter 13 – The Symbol Editor,
  - Chapter 14 – Method Filters and Evaluation Filters,
  - Chapter 15 – Defining and Using Templates,
  - Chapter 16 – Administration Reports,
  - Chapter 17 – Model Verification,
  - Appendix A – ARIS Admintool Commands.

1.4 References

Davis R (2001) Business Process Modelling with ARIS: A Practical Guide,
Springer-Verlag, London.

Davis R, Brabänder E (2007) ARIS Design Platform: Getting Started with BPM,
Springer-Verlag, London.

1.5 Icons Used in This Book

To draw your intention to hints and tips, and to make you aware of possible problems, I have used the following icons:

 Warning – this is a warning symbol. These warnings should not be ignored, otherwise dire effects will be experienced which will influence your work with ARIS. You have been warned so there is no excuse if you go ahead and do so. I take no responsibility for any subsequent loss or damage.

 Hint – hints will help you to work more efficiently with *ARIS Business Architect*. Following these hints will speed up your daily work or, at the very least, will allow you to impress your colleagues!

 Expert Tip – these tips will give you examples of more detailed, and sometimes more complex, facilities you may wish to try once you have mastered the basics.

 FAQ – I have often heard the same questions from different people working with ARIS. I have tried to identify the most common '*Frequently Asked Questions*' and provide you with some answers.

 ARIS 7 – this highlights new facilities available in *ARIS Business Architect* that weren't available in ARIS prior to release 7 and new facilities that may be available in release 7.1 due in 2008.
ARIS 7

1.6   Conventions Used in this Book

I have described the use of the keyboard and the mouse to operate *ARIS Business Architect* in plain English wherever I can. I have used the English spelling of words like 'reorganise' in the main body of the text, but show the actual spelling and capitalisation used in *ARIS Business Architect* (e.g. US English – "reorganize") in command strings. In order to save space when listing commands, I have used the conventions shown in Table 1.1 and Table 1.2 as shortcuts for complex commands.

Table 1.1 Text Formatting Conventions Used in this Book

Description in Text	Action Required
'*ARIS term*'	Highlighting the use of a specific ARIS term or tool.
Designer Window	Reference to one of the ARIS windows.
"*relationship*"	An ARIS relationship.
Userinformation	Text to be entered as shown.
<Alt+B>	Keyboard shortcut for a command.
Objectname	The name of an ARIS object, database or model as shown in an example.
Menuitem 1	Item on menu to be selected.
Dialog Box	Name of a dialog box.
Attribute	Name of ARIS attribute in which data can be viewed or entered.
Field	Name of menu field in which data should be entered or an option chosen.
{MenuGroup}	Label for items grouped in a dialog box.

Table 1.2 Command Descriptions Used in this Book

Description in Text	Action Required
Click <u>B</u>utton	Hover the mouse over the button on the displayed window and click the left mouse button. The underlined character shows the shortcut for the button (i.e. Alt+b).
Select <u>M</u>enuitem	Hover the mouse over the item on the *Main Menu* or pop-up *Right-Click Menu* and click the left mouse button.
Select <u>M</u>enuitem1> Menuitem<u>2</u>	Hover the mouse over item1 on the *Main Menu* (if necessary, click the left mouse button). When a submenu appears click the left mouse button on item2.
Select ***Object***	Hover the mouse over the object and click the left mouse button. The object should appear selected.
Double-Click ***Object***	Hover the mouse over the object and rapidly click the left mouse button twice. This will normally open up a new window.
Select *Tab*	On window bar, select the tab by hovering the mouse over the tab title and clicking the left mouse button.
Right-Click > Menuitem1 [*Dialog Box / Sub Dialog Box*]	With an object already selected, hover the mouse over the selected object and click the right mouse button. When a floating menu appears, hover the mouse over item1 on the menu and click the left mouse button. When the dialog box appears, select the sub-dialog box from the list on the left-hand side of the dialog box.
Right-Click > Menuitem1 [*Dialog Box* {fieldname}] enter givenvalue	Enter the value given into the text field called fieldname in the dialog box.

Chapter 2   Before You Start Modelling

This chapter looks at the issues you need to consider before starting to model with ARIS. Of particular importance is the need to define your objectives and viewpoint.

2.1   Objectives for Modelling

Before starting any modelling project it is important to be clear about why you are modelling. It is surprising how many people start modelling without any idea of what the model is for, who will use it, what type of information is required and in what format the output will be needed. Remember, a process model is not a replica of the real world; it is merely a representation – a viewpoint. It is essential the viewpoint is tailored for its intended use and the people who will view it. Different viewpoints may be needed for different purposes. One of the key strengths of ARIS is its ability to produce different viewpoints based on common underlying data. Some views can be produced automatically (e.g. using Model Generation), while others are constructed manually.

The objectives of your modelling may change during the life of the project. This may be due to changing requirements, discovery of new opportunities or planned enhancement of the model. Do not assume that models created to meet one set of objectives will be suitable for other objectives. Sometimes models developed with one viewpoint may even conflict with models produced for other purposes. For instance, a high-level abstract model of the business may over-simplify interactions between business units and appear to conflict with what actually goes on. Ideally, we would like to create a set of hierarchical models which provide increasing levels of detail about our business, but sometimes we must be aware that a high-level abstract model will not 'cleanly' decompose into more detailed models because its viewpoint is very different.

It is strongly recommend you explicitly write down your objectives, agree them with your stakeholders and document them in the database (you can use the *Objectives Diagram*). Below is a list of some of the key questions you should ask yourself:

- Why are you modelling?
- What are you modelling?
- Who are you modelling?
- When are you modelling?

2.1.1   Why Are You Modelling?

What is the main purpose of the modelling work? Table 2.1 shows some possible reasons.

Table 2.1 Why Are You Modelling?

Reasons for Modelling	Aspects to Consider
Business Planning	Concentrate on business objectives, customer needs and metrics. Use *Value-added chain diagrams*, *Balanced Scorecard Models*. Look at the high-level business functional breakdown.
Business Restructuring	Concentrate on the organisations carrying out tasks and the hand-offs between them. Look at the value added by each task. Use *EPC (row display)* to provide organisational swim-lane view.
Baseline the Business	Usually impractical in all but the simplest and static businesses. It takes too much time and the world moves on in the meantime. Concentrate instead on key processes that need to change or where you already know there are problems. "Don't model the Universe."
Operational Process Design	Concentrate on getting the flow of the process correct. Use *EPCs* and *FADs*. Identify the key decisions being made. Look for failure paths as well as the normal process flow. Identify inputs and outputs for all tasks. Identify key documents and sources of information.
Systems Development	Requires very detailed logic flow to be modelled. Exception handling is very important. Detailed data models, data flow and systems interfaces should be modelled.

2.1.2   What Are You Modelling?

You may be modelling a process, an organisation, the data or the many other aspects of an organisation that ARIS can represent. Normally you will be modelling several of these. However you should decide the main viewpoint from which you will be modelling. Typical viewpoints are shown in Table 2.2.

In the middle of a process capture or design exercise it is very easy to become confused about the viewpoint you are using. The worst offence is to mix up viewpoints as this leads to confusing models that omit or gloss over key elements. Particular care has to be taken when a process 'hands-off' to another organisational unit. Do you follow the process into the other unit or ignore the detail of what happens and wait for that unit's response?

Table 2.2 What Are You Modelling?

Modelling Viewpoint	Approach
Follow a business entity	Possibly the easiest approach to take. Select a key business item (e.g. a customer order) and follow it through the process. See what actions are performed on it, who handles it and where it ends up. This is also useful for testing other model viewpoints.
Model the business	Modelling what the whole business does is one of the hardest approaches. It can normally only be done at high levels of abstraction and it is often difficult to identify the triggers and outcomes.
Model a business function	The most common approach is to model a particular business function (e.g. order-handling, fault-reporting, etc). This will normally involve many different organisational units. Modelling organisational hand-offs will be essential. Can lead to very 'company oriented' models that don't focus on the customer.
Model a business process	The most useful approach (but not often done) is to model the end-to-end processes a business performs. Particularly valuable when done from a customer perspective. Better than the business function approach as it helps ensure the whole process fits together to deliver a good customer experience. Helps identify failure modes.
Model an organisation	Another common approach is to model what an organisation does. This may not necessarily be the most useful approach. Organisations change over time and the range of tasks an organisation performs may have evolved historically.
Model an organisational unit	This model just focuses on what a single unit does. The model shows the interfaces with other units, but doesn't worry about how they accomplish their tasks. Provides a very focused model, but can over-simplify what is going on. It may also encourage an out-of-sight, out-of-mind approach, which doesn't spot gaps and failure points in the end-to-end process.

The choice of where you follow the process depends on the viewpoint you are taking. If you are modelling the end-to-end process, then you must follow the process wherever it goes. If you are just modelling the processes operated by a particular unit, then you do not. Keeping track of your modelling objectives and viewpoint is essential. It is worth pausing occasionally, standing back from your model and checking you are still on the right path.

2.1.3   Who Are You Modelling?

Related to the choice of viewpoint, you also need to think about what level of organisation you are considering, as shown in Table 2.3.

Table 2.3 Who Are You Modelling?

Modelling Viewpoint	Things to Consider
Business unit	Business units (e.g. Sales, Manufacture, etc.) provide a pragmatic modelling abstraction. They are well understood and have major significance to the business. They do not change frequently, but when they do they have a significant impact on business processes.
Line management team	To be avoided at all costs. Have very little business significance, change frequently and have little impact on processes when they do.
Operational centre	A very useful modelling abstraction. Normally have a very significant impact on process, change infrequently and fit within business units. Consider whether it is sufficient just to nominate the operational centre that does a task (e.g. Sales Office) or whether it is necessary to be more explicit about the roles within the centre (e.g. Sales Office Customer Service Advisor).
Management layer	Many business sectors have functional layers. For instance in Telecommunications we talk of Service Management, Network Management, etc. They can provide a useful level of abstraction, but can be problematic because often there is no clear definition of what they mean. Useful when modelling 'to-be' scenarios, but business units are better for 'as-is' models.
Roles	The lowest practical level of organisational unit. If used in process models you should make sure they are unique. The role 'Customer Service Advisor' or 'Planner' when attached to a task doesn't convey very much as many operational centres will have such roles. You can model their parentage in an *Organizational chart*, but it is better to make the names unique and meaningful (e.g. Sales Office – Customer Service Advisor).

2.1.4   When Are You Modelling?

It is important to consider both the time-frame within which you are modelling and also the granularity of time that is important to you (Table 2.4).

Table 2.4 When Are You Modelling?

Timeframe	Things to Consider
'as-is'	The process as it is now. But be careful to define what 'now' means. Does it mean what should be happening now, as documented now or as actually operated now? If you know the documented process is not being followed and a 'work-around' is being used, you need to decide which you are going to model. If changes are being made while you are capturing the process, will you include them or freeze the model at a certain point in time?
'to-be'	How far in the future are you considering? Are you starting from scratch with a new business model or re-engineering what you already have? How radical can you be? What constraints have you got?
Time-scale	Complex processes can sometimes complete within seconds, while simple processes can often last for weeks. What time-frame is important to your model?
Delays	Are potential delays in the process important to you? Populating Function attributes with process times may not make delays explicit to people viewing the model. Consider explicitly modelling delays as additional steps in the process if you want to draw attention to them.
Simulation	Simulation can be used to analyse process delays and optimise performance. A very powerful tool, but requires good quality models and good quality data. Models must conform to certain rules. Consider seeking advice from specialist simulation experts.

Again it is important not to get confused about the time-frame. If you have decided to model the process as it is currently documented, don't get tempted into altering things you know are wrong. If you want to capture errors and issues, create a separate model. If you are modelling a future 'to-be' process, then think about how much freedom you really have. There is not much point modelling a radical new world at the high-level and then trying to decompose it into detailed processes constrained by old ways of working. Think about the ground rules before you start.

2.2   Modelling Requirements

We will have already captured some requirements by considering our modelling objectives and thinking through the viewpoints we wish to take. However, we need to think further about how our models are to be used. For instance:

- Who are our customers for the models?
- What are they expecting the models to tell them?
- Do they want to see the models or just the results?
- How are they going to view the models?
- How much time will they spend viewing the models?
- How widely will models be promulgated?
- Will different groups of people require different views?
- Will they use ARIS themselves?
- Will they want printed reports?
- Is this a one-off exercise or will the models be maintained?
- How will models be validated?
- Will the models be used for system, workflow or software design?
- Will the models be used for analysis or BPR?
- Is simulation required?

These are important questions and you may find it more difficult than you expect to find the answers; it is quite common for people to ask for models to be built without any clear idea of what they are going to do with them. You may go through the objectives-setting exercise described above and quite clearly define what models are required, but still be no wiser about what the customers plan to do with them. This is often because people are tempted to believe that, simply by having a process (or business) model, this will solve all their problems and the business will automatically operate as described in the model.

Of course it is not fair to blame the customer; the onus is on process modellers to work with customers to 'tease' out exactly what the models are for and to suggest innovative ways in which the models can be used. However, don't take at face value what the customer initially asks for. A good example is the use of ARIS Reports to generate printed documents. Business teams often start by stating a key requirement is that ARIS should automatically generate printed documents in the same format as they currently use. When asked why, typically they reply:

- Senior managers only want documents,
- Operational people wouldn't understand the ARIS models,
- ARIS models are too big,
- People needed to read the documents when out of the office.

Of course, in reality senior managers never read the documents and operational people are much happier with the flowchart approach of *EPCs*. It seems strange people should object to printed *EPCs* that run to several pages, but seem quite happy with documents of 100 pages or more! While there is some argument for having information in document form when 'off-line', in practice there is rarely a need to create reports that exactly replicate existing documents.

The most successful teams are usually those are innovative in their use of ARIS and change the way they work. Typically, they publish their models on the Intranet and use Microsoft NetMeeting (or similar approaches) to validate ARIS models in their electronic form through virtual workshops. Of course you cannot achieve this overnight. Most teams have to gradually move to these new ways of working and you need to consider the business culture in which you are operating. You will need to demonstrate what can be done with ARIS and give people time to realise how it may benefit them.

Some requirements can have significant impact on how you go about modelling. For instance, using ARIS Simulation places certain constraints on the structure and format of your models, and requires particular data (e.g. task processing times) to be captured. It is important to be clear about these requirements at the start, as having to go back to capture and model missing data can be costly and time-consuming. You also need to be clear about what sort of analysis you may wish to perform. For instance, if you wish to be able to ask questions such as "Tell me all the *Functions* executed by this *Organizational unit*?", then you must model the *Organizational unit* that executes every *Function*. There is no value in populating part of the model with *Organizational units* and not the rest, because the analysis would be inaccurate. This is particularly important when you have several people working on process design or capture. If they don't all follow the same rules, your model will be inconsistent.

Increasingly people want to publish the results on the corporate Intranet. It is very likely the vast majority of the people who view your models will not use or see ARIS at all. This significantly affects the way you need to model. Web users have expectations that they can navigate between models using 'hyper-links' so it is essential to create a fully linked model structure using model assignments. You also need to be aware that viewing models on the Intranet may be slower than using ARIS itself. Large models (and hence large web pages) are not handled well by most browsers and slow access links. Conversely, if you have many small models (e.g. lots of *FADs*), people will have to spend a considerable amount of time navigating up and down the hierarchy. Getting the correct compromise between model size and navigation complexity is no easy task, and modellers need to be constantly aware of how their models may appear on the Web.

2.3   Key Principles

All the while you are developing your models, either at the conceptual level or during detailed design, keep in mind some key principles:

- Stick to the ARIS Method (well mostly),
- Don't model the universe,
- Know when you have done enough,
- Keep it simple – clever models often confuse,
- Define standards and stick to them,
- Don't re-invent the wheel; re-use wherever you can,
- If it looks sensible it *probably* is sensible – if it looks silly it *definitely* is silly.

The 'keep it simple' rule is of particular importance. The more you learn about ARIS, the more intellectually stimulating it becomes to find really clever ways to model various aspects of the business. Sometimes this may produce 'clean and elegant' models that provide real clarity and insight. More frequently, however, it creates highly complex models that no one can understand. Always ask yourself: "If I had to hand over all my modelling work to another ARIS user, would that person be able to easily carry on using the same approach?" If you can't answer "yes" to this question, then you need to review the way you are working. The closer you stick to the ARIS Method and agreed standards, the easier it will be to achieve this.

References

Davis R, Brabänder E (2007) ARIS Design Platform: Getting Started with BPM, Springer-Verlag, London.

Chapter 3   Process Capture and Modelling

This chapter describes approaches for process capture and modelling. It
discusses some of the issues that must be considered, the models you might
use and the roles and responsibilities involved.

3.1   Introduction

In the last chapter we looked at the issues to consider before starting modelling,
particularly the need to define your modelling objectives. Once you are clear
about your objectives you can start detailed capture and design. The actual way
you go about this will very much depend on the nature of the project, what information is already to hand and how many people are involved in the modelling activity. Some key issues to think about are discussed below.

3.2   Modelling in Teams

If you have teams of modellers working on a project, it is much easier if they all
share the same ARIS database located on a networked server. You can appoint
people to the roles described in Section 3.7; in particular appointing a Model Librarian (see Section 3.7.5), to create a library of resource objects and insisting that
modellers use them. If modellers need new objects, not currently in the library, either they must ask the Librarian to create a new object, or they create it themselves and then submit it to the Librarian for approval. When using an ARIS
server, the *Group Access Privileges* for library objects and groups can be controlled so that some groups of people can create and change objects, while others
can use them, but not change them.

    If you have teams of modellers working on the project who are not sharing the
same database it is still possible to create a central library and distribute it to individual users who can use the *ARIS Merge* facility to add the library into their own
database. Using the same technique they can also send potential library objects
back to the Librarian. Although this is technically straightforward, it requires a
great deal more project management and administration to ensure success.

    More difficult is combining the individual databases together as the project
reaches conclusion. Again the *Merge* facility can be used to combine the databases. If library objects from a common database have been used in the individual
databases, ARIS will automatically identify these and ensure they are consolidated
into a single object. What ARIS cannot do, is to automatically work out whether
different objects with the same name are in fact the same item or are genuinely
different. Neither can it spot when modellers have each used a different object
with a slightly different name for what in fact should have been the same thing.

These issues can only be resolved manually although, as mentioned above, ARIS does have tools to help you. See Chapter 10 for more detail on database administration including merging databases and consolidating objects.

Modelling in teams is a complex issue, but as a general rule, it works better if there is significant and continual interaction between the modellers and administrators as the project progresses. It is a recipe for disaster to allow everyone to work by themselves for most of the project and then try to bring everything together at the end. Even if server-based working is not feasible, it is still essential to create a master database. You should partition each modeller's work into small well-defined segments and provide them with a copy of the library from the master database and any models with which they need to interact. When they have finished their (small) element of the work, merge it into the master database and resolve any conflicts and issues. Then allocate them a new piece of work and provide them with an update of the relevant parts of the master database.

Working this way places a lot of responsibility and work on the Database Administrator and the Model Librarian, but it does ensure that issues are resolved as the project progresses rather than being left to the end. It also provides the Database Administrator and Project Manager with an evolving view of how the model and the project are progressing.

3.3   Modelling Standards

Before undertaking any serious modelling you must agree and set standards. This is important, even if you are the only modeller, but it is absolutely essential if you have a team of people modelling. In ARIS there is no single way of doing things and hence, if you start a number of people modelling processes, they will all choose to use different models and different ways of using them. We can apply corporate modelling conventions and standards through:

- Structure:
    - Architecture,
    - Hierarchies,
    - Frameworks,
- Use of ARIS:
    - Group structure,
    - Access rights and permissions,
    - Object libraries,
- ARIS Method:
    - Method changes,
    - Method Filters,
    - Font Formats,
    - Templates,
- Training and Coaching:
    - ARIS Guide Sheets.

For a detailed discussion of implementing process standards see *"Ch16 - Standardised Modelling with ARIS"* in Davis and Brabänder 2007.

Not only do you need to agree on the major standards topics, but even trivial tasks like grid settings, use of colour, etc. are worth agreeing in advance. It gives a much more professional appearance if all the models produced by the team have the same look and feel. The use of ARIS Method Filters and Conventions is extremely valuable in establishing corporate modelling conventions. We will look at these in more detail in later chapters of this book.

3.4 Process Modelling

3.4.1 Model Structure

As we saw above, an important aspect of creating a standardised approach to process modelling, especially when modelling in teams, is the structure of your process models. Deciding upon and creating a model structure raises some key questions:

- Should you create you structure first and then create your models?
- Should you create all your models and then try and work out a structure?
- Should you work 'top-down' or 'bottom-up'?

In an ideal world you would create your structure using a top-down approach. Then you would create models containing increasing levels of detail that fit into the structure. This would be very similar to the way software is designed (at least in theory). In practice it is very difficult to do this. You may start with high-level models which show relatively simple interfaces between key business functions, but it is only when you start to model in more detail you discover the real complexity of the interactions between business functions. This means you may have to re-visit your high-level models to adjust their structure. For more information on structuring ARIS models see *"Chapter 13 - Modelling your Business Structure"* in Davis and Brabänder 2007.

The same situation occurs in software design, but it is much more prevalent in process design. Why is this? The reason is mainly due to the optimisation of design for performance. In software engineering, systems are broken down into a large number of well-understood 'atomic' tasks or components with simple and well-defined interfaces. Vast numbers of these components are combined to form a working system. Despite the vast number of components, today's high-performance systems can execute each component very quickly providing a high level of performance.

By contrast, in complex manual business processes moving from task to task can be time-consuming, may incur delay and always carries the risk of generating errors. In addition, people (unlike computers) tend to object to performing simple, repetitive operations. Hence processes tend to have fewer tasks (components) and fewer interfaces, but those interfaces tend to be more complex and more highly interconnected. Moreover, whereas in software systems it is easy to re-use components whenever they are needed, it is much harder to re-use process tasks. A task in one part of the process may superficially look the same as another, but is often done by different people in a different location using different systems. Re-engineering the process to make the tasks truly common is by no means easy.

So we find developing process models in a truly hierarchical manner is not that straightforward. The big danger is having created a structure; people may spend a lot of time trying to force the process models to fit the structure.

It seems natural to conceive a hierarchical structure and then segment each layer of the hierarchy into a number of separate models, perhaps representing functional areas. If you really can achieve this, that's excellent, go right ahead. But most people can't visualise the structure they need sufficiently well at the outset to be able to do this. In practice, you have to proceed using a more trial-and-error approach.

The best approach is to create an initial structure to provide a rough framework to build on. Then decide on the level of detail you need to model to achieve your main objectives. You may have to go down to more detail later to achieve the remainder of your objectives, but you will usually find there is a level of detail at which it seems natural to work. Start creating your model in an *EPC*. Don't worry initially about trying to segment the model into a number of separate *EPCs*. Just create one big model and see how it turns out. As you progress you should start to see the structure of the process emerging, and you can decide how to break the large model up into smaller segments. You can then revise your original rough structure and start to fit new models into it. Don't spend too long fiddling about with high-level structures. Once you start detailed modelling, you will probably find you have to change it all.

Try and be consistent about the level of detail at which you model. This can also be hard to achieve. There are no hard and fast rules. Sometimes you will want to mix trivial, but highly significant, tasks at the same level as complex tasks that may have several layers of decomposition. Just use your common sense. Ask yourself: "Does it look right?"

3.4.2   Libraries and Processes

In Section 3.2 we saw the important of creating a library of frequently reused objects. There are essentially two approaches you can take to modelling new processes: build up a library of key information (e.g. organisation, systems, data, etc) and use these as you model the processes or start modelling processes and build the library as you go. The first approach is the ideal, as it is easier to implement naming standards, keep control and avoid duplication. The latter approach is more practical; it gets you started more quickly, but requires more administration, especially with teams of modellers. It may lead to later rework, for instance to remove duplicate resource objects, but ARIS has administration tools to help you do this;

for instance, the Find > Objects with Identical Name and Consolidate facilities described in Chapter 10.

A lot will depend on the degree of detail to which you model systems, organisation and data. If you have a complex structure of these objects that you need to use in your *EPCs*, it is worth modelling the structure first to ensure it is well understood. In practice, a mixture of the two is required, but the more up-front work that can be done, the better.

3.4.3 What Models to Use

Deciding what models to use can be somewhat of a black art. The *EPC* and *FAD* are the obvious models to use, typically supported by *Organizational charts, Entity Relationship Models* and *Application system type diagrams*.

In more complex business models the choice is not so straightforward. Some models are more useful than others, some objects are only available in certain types of model and the relationships between objects differ between models. A degree of experimentation is often necessary to decide which objects and models best suit your needs before you start modelling in earnest.

Even in basic process design you have the choice of whether to create organisational charts, whether to use swim-lane models, and so on. Table 3.1 summarises the ARIS model types which are most useful and what they should be used for. For more information on ARIS models and objects see Davis and Brabänder 2007.

Table 3.1 Important ARIS Models

Model Type	Use
Application System Type Diagram	At the simplest level, defines a library of the systems used by the business. At a more detailed level, models the structure of systems and their constituent modules or provides a hierarchical classification of system types.
EPC	Detail modelling of processes at various levels in the hierarchy.
EPC (column display)	For modelling the interfaces between separate processes running in parallel. Typically for modelling interfaces between processes running on different application systems.
EPC (row display)	Modelling processes in swim-lanes. Typically at a fairly high level to show how a process moves from organisational unit to unit or system to system.
Event Diagram	For defining how a single Event (typically a process trigger) modelled at one level in the hierarchy can be broken down into more detailed Events when modelled at more detailed levels in the hierarchy.

Model Type	Use
Function Allocation Diagram (FAD)	For defining the relationship between a Function and the resources needed to execute it and the data it transforms.
Function Tree	Models the functional structure of a business in a hierarchical way.
Entity Attribute Diagram	Models the decomposition of data entities showing the attributes they are comprised of.
Entity Relationship Model	A formal model of the data entities used by the business and the relationships between them. Typically used for representing data used by databases or other systems.
Knowledge Map	Models the knowledge held by different business units.
Knowledge Structure Diagram	Hierarchical definition of the knowledge held by the business.
Objective Diagram	Models a hierarchy of business objectives along with their critical success factors, and the Functions and Products that support achievement of those objectives.
Office Process	A form of the *EPC* model using pictorial symbols aimed at presenting process flows to people less familiar with standard ARIS models.
Organisation Chart	A hierarchical model of the business organisation.
Product/Service Tree	Models the hierarchy of the products and services produced by the business, the Functions that deliver them and the Business Objectives their production achieves.
Technical Terms Model	Models the hierarchical and relational structure of information used by the business.
Value-added Chain Diagram	Models a hierarchy of high-level Functions that add value to the business along with the Organisational Units that have a role in those Functions.

3.5   Process Capture

3.5.1   Process Capture Using ARIS

Frequently it is necessary to go out into the business and gather information from which to build ARIS models. This raises a question: "Should you do this as two separate phases (e.g. capture and then model) or should you use ARIS 'in the field' to capture the information and build the model at the same time?"

The rigour of using the ARIS *Event-driven process chain* approach creates realistic and consistent process models and so, wherever possible, you should always make use of ARIS for process capture. The exercise of having to think about what Event and Function objects actually represent helps you identify the real process flow, the actual outcomes and the failure modes. Extending this by adding resource allocations focuses attention on the systems, the people, the data and other resources involved in the process. If you can use these techniques when talking to the process users and experts it will help to articulate what is really happening.

Of course you must be well skilled in the use of ARIS and feel confident about using it in front of other people before attempting to do this. Some people feel either this is too hard or that showing people ARIS is a distraction from the information gathering task. While this may certainly be true in some circumstances, the advantages to be gained in the rapid development of more realistic models can far outweigh the disadvantages.

It is worth making sure beforehand that the process users are aware you intend to work this way. A good approach is to meet them on an earlier occasion and give them a brief demonstration of ARIS. They will then have an appreciation of what you are trying to do and will not be distracted by the tool on the process capture day. They will also have the opportunity to gather any appropriate supporting information beforehand.

The alternative is to collect the necessary information by taking notes and by obtaining documents and other information. However, as soon as you start to use ARIS to create the model, you will find its rigour will cause you to ask questions you can't answer from the information you have gathered. You will then have to go back to the process users and ask additional questions. This is time-consuming, prone to error and does not promote a professional image.

A compromise is to manually collect information and produce a rough ARIS model. Then make a return visit to the process user and 'walk-through' the ARIS model with them. If you explain beforehand this is how you intend to work, it reinforces a professional image and makes them feel continually involved in the process capture exercise.

3.5.2   A Two-Stage Approach to Process Capture

The best method for using ARIS for process capture is to use a two-stage approach. In the first stage, walk through the process with the user and capture the basic process flow. Keep in mind your modelling objectives and remain focused on 'what you are modelling' (i.e. follow the progress of a specific order). Pay particular attention to decision points and branches in the process.

Once you have a first draft of the process flow, walk through the process again and start to identify the key resources used by the process (e.g. data, systems, documents, etc) and who carries out the process (e.g. departments, roles, etc).

Frequently, asking questions about organisation, systems and data helps to clarify how the process actually operates. Quite often when you ask: "What information is the input for this task?" users will suddenly realise that there was in fact an additional step preceding the current step that acquired the necessary information. So this second phase not only collects additional information about the process, it also verifies the process flow is correct.

Our captured process model will now represent:

- The structure of the business process,

- The resources needed to execute it,

- The environment in which it will be used.

It is also important to ensure that when you have finished, you present the results back to the people who provided the information, even if they are not the customers for the work. Not only does this ensure good relations are maintained (you may want to go back to them during future work), but they may also directly benefit from the findings of your modelling and analysis.

The two-stage approach to process capture using ARIS is summarised in Table 3.2. If you can achieve all of this, you will have a pretty good first draft model. It will be quite hard work and you should not try and do too much in one session. It is useful to collect any documents and forms used in the process so that you can produce data models of these later if required.

You will need to decide to what level of detail you model the failure modes of the process. If a failure significantly changes the process flow, it should be modelled. If a failure stops the process and creates an 'exception' that is handled by separate manual intervention, it may be sufficient to note this in a remark and model the exception-handling routine as a separate process.

While undertaking process capture you must always keep in mind the culture of your organisation. The people from whom you capture information may feel threatened by the process capture exercise, either by you as a 'technical expert', by the fear of losing their job, or by being 'de-skilled'. They may tell you what they think you want to hear or what they think their boss wants them to say. Conversely, they may burden you with all their problems and moan about every other department in the organisation. Their goals and mindset will also be different from yours. If you are planning a radical new process, their practical knowledge can often bring you back down to earth and ensure the process will work. However, sometimes they will be set in old ways of thinking and you will have to ignore their objections and press on anyway. Your interpersonal skills will be just as important, if not more important, than your ARIS skills.

Table 3.2 A Process Capture Approach

Step	Things to Consider
Stage 1 – Capture the Process Flow	
1	Work through a segment of the process, task by task.
2	Identify the trigger and outcome Events for each Function: – ensure the triggers are necessary and sufficient, – check the effect of multiple triggers, – ensure all the outcomes are identified, – ensure failure modes are identified.
3	Identify key decision points in the process: – make sure there is a Function representing the decision, – identify the correct Rule (usually an XOR).
4	Identify branches and links to other processes: – identify if branches are actually simultaneous, – identify if links to other processes return to the modelled process, – model 'out-of-scope' processes where appropriate.
Stage 2 – Capture Process Resources and Details	
5	Identify the systems, organisation and resource supporting each Function: – ask how the process is handed-off from one organisation to another, – ask how the process is handed-off from one system to another, – if hand-offs are important to the process, model them explicitly.
6	Identify the data input and output for each Function: – identify information carriers, – identify where data inputs are created (should they be earlier outputs?), – identify where data outputs are used, – ask for copies of the documents or forms the data objects represent, – ask for data definitions or data models.
7	Ask how the people executing the Function know what to do: – identify key roles and responsibilities, – identify special skills, – identify documented knowledge or procedures, – ask for copies of relevant documents (link electronic versions to the model).
8	Define relevant attributes: – add task descriptions, – identify and enter processing times (process, set-up, wait), – enter other supporting information.
9	Review all the organisational and system objects: – check if the relationships between them are clear, – create a simple Organisational Chart to make relationships explicit, – create an IT systems model.

3.6   Verification and Validation

Producing models is not enough in itself; it is essential to ensure they are consistent, correct and fit-for-purpose. Verification and validation are the techniques used to ensure this:

*   **Verification** – ensures the models meet the customer's specification, they are consistent and conform to specified standards,

*   **Validation** – ensures the models meet the customer's requirements and are fit-for-purpose.

The difference between verification and validation is subtle and often confused. However, we can think of them as 'inward looking' and 'outward looking'.

Verification is 'inward looking'. It is all about checking you have done what you said you would do; that you have modelled what was asked of you, you have used the ARIS Method correctly, your models are consistent and they reflect the information you were given. This is the responsibility of the modelling team. If you find you can't deliver what was asked or the information you have been given is inconsistent and incorrect, then it is the team's responsibility to raise these issues with the customers. You must also ensure any issues are resolved, so that at the end of the project you can demonstrate to the customer you have met their specification. Ensuring you meet the specification, and being able to demonstrate that you have met it, is the function of your quality management system. We will discuss techniques for verifying that models are logically correct, consistent and conforms to the ARIS Method in Chapter 17.

Validation, on the other hand, is 'outward looking'. It is about checking that your models are an appropriate and effective representation of the real world, that they meet the customer's actual requirements (as opposed to the specification) and are fit for the defined purpose. It has to be done with the collaboration of end-users, the customer and other interested parties. The degree to which the models are fit-for-purpose will largely depend on how well the project objectives and requirements were articulated in the specification. In well-conceived and well-managed projects, validation will be seen as the joint responsibility of the customer and the modelling team. Customers will often try and take a very hard line and put all the responsibility on the modelling team. However, if the customer's requirements were poorly defined or have changed, the modelling team will never be able to validate their work to the satisfaction of the customer. There are only two ways to run a project: the formal way, where everything is precisely defined and you deliver exactly what is defined; or as a partnership, where customer and implementers take joint responsibility, sharing the risks and the benefits.

3.7 Roles and Responsibilities

While undertaking process capture and modelling you will require, and interact with, a number of different roles and responsibilities. Some of these will be within the process team and people will need to be assigned to them, other roles will be external to the team. Some roles will be formal roles that people will be aware they have, others will be unofficial roles people play during the process capture or design. People may have multiple roles and if you are a lone modeller, you will have to do many of them yourself! Typical roles include:

- Process Stakeholder,
- Information Gatherer,
- Process Designer,
- Process Modeller,
- Model Librarian,
- Model Verifier,
- Model Validator,
- Process Architect,
- Corporate Process Architect,
- ARIS Technical Consultant,
- ARIS Database Administrator,
- ARIS Server Administrator,
- ARIS Configuration Administrator,
- IT System Administrator,
- ARIS Model Publisher,
- ARIS Trainer.

The following sections give a brief overview of these roles. There is some overlap between them (see Fig. 3.1) and many roles require a good deal of collaboration with other role holders.

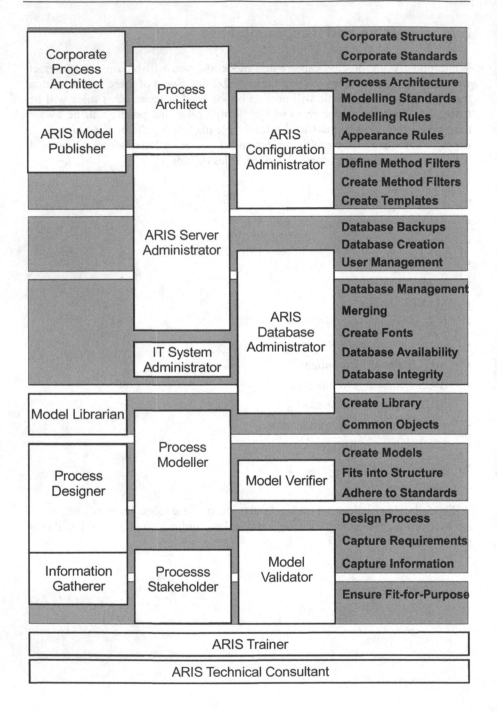

Fig. 3.1 Roles and Responsibilities

3.7.1   Process Stakeholder

The *Process Stakeholder* role represents all the people who have an interest in the process and will typically be consulted during process capture and design. They may be actual users of the process, the owners of the process or people who have some knowledge or expertise in the process. Some Process Stakeholders may just provide information while others may have a formal role in validating and agreeing process designs.

Where you have a number of stakeholders it is usual to carry out a RACI analysis to understand their roles in more detail:

- R – responsible for (does the work),
- A – accountable for (formally agrees the work),
- C – must be consulted,
- I – must be informed about.

 Expert Tip – you can model RACI in ARIS using *Positions* connected to *Functions* with different relationships (e.g. *"carries out"*, *"decides upon"*, *"has consulting role in"* and *"must be informed about"*).

3.7.2   Information Gatherer

This *Information Gatherer* will talk to the Process Stakeholder to collect all the information necessary to build the process model. Ideally they will be a Process Modeller as well so they can build the model at the same time as undertaking process capture.

- **Responsibilities** – collecting complete and accurate information. Resolving queries from modellers,
- **Skills** – good interpersonal skills, good analytical approach.

It may be beneficial for the Information Gatherer to have some domain knowledge so they understand the basic technical terms and know what questions to ask. However, too much knowledge may bias the information they collect and the model that is developed.

3.7.3   Process Designer

The *Process Designer* will design the process to meet the specification and the project objectives. Ideally, they will also be a Process Modeller so they can build the model as a natural part of their job.

- **Responsibilities** – produce the design and verify it meets specification,
- **Skills** – extensive domain knowledge, good analytical and design skills.

3.7.4   Process Modeller

The *Process Modeller* takes information from the Information Gatherer or the Process Designer and creates ARIS models representing the information.

- **Responsibilities** – produce a correct and validated ARIS model that represents the captured or designed process. Ensure the models conform to project and corporate modelling standards. Where appropriate, ensure the model fits into the corporate process architecture,
- **Skills** – extensive knowledge of ARIS, process modelling and data modelling skills.

Increasingly Information Gatherers and Process Designers will acquire process modelling skills, so they can create the models as part of their day-to-day job. However, it is likely there will still be the need for a pool of Process Modellers who can supply additional resource to the design and capture team, and who take on more advanced modelling tasks.

3.7.5   Model Librarian

The *Model Librarian* is responsible for maintaining a library of common objects and models used by modellers working on the same project. The Librarian may have an active role in defining and creating library objects and models, or may just administer the library in accordance with standards defined by the Process Architect. The Librarian will need to work closely with the Database Administrator to manage the merging in and out of library models and objects, and in carrying out database housekeeping (e.g. finding objects with the same name). The Database Administrator may delegate these administrative tasks to the Librarian.

- **Responsibilities** – create and maintain a library of common objects and models. Ensure compliance with project and corporate standards,
- **Skills** – knowledge of ARIS and process modelling. Some knowledge of ARIS database administration.

Typically the Librarian and the Database Administrator may be the same person.

3.7.6   Model Verifier

The *Model Verifier* ensures models produced by individual Modellers conform to the project's modelling standards and that they fit into the model structure defined by the process architecture. Typically, the Model Verifier will run visual and Semantic Checks on the models to ensure conformance before they are merged with other models. If a model fails these checks, the Model Verifier will return it to the Modeller. The Verifier will work closely with the Database Administrator and the Model Librarian.

- **Responsibilities** – ensure models meet the customer's specification. Ensures compliance with project and corporate standards and that models fit into the project's model structure,
- **Skills** – knowledge of ARIS and process modelling. Some knowledge of ARIS database administration.

The exact role of the Model Verifier will depend on the size and nature of the project. The Model Verifier may just be responsible for verifying conformance of individual models, or responsible for ensuring the entire database of models meets the specification. The Database Administrator will often do individual model verification.

3.7.7   Model Validator

The *Model Validator* is responsible for ensuring all the models meet the customer's requirements and are fit for purpose. The exact role of the Model Validator will be implementation specific and will be defined by the project plan.

3.7.8   Process Architect

The *Process Architect* is responsible for designing the overall structure into which all the ARIS models will fit. The Architect will work with the Corporate Process Architect to ensure the models fit within an overall corporate structure and conform to corporate standards.

- **Responsibilities** – define process architecture, modelling standards, naming standards, report formats and WWW publishing standards. Ensure architecture and standards conform to corporate standards, and meet project objectives and requirements,
- **Skills** – knowledge of process architecture and modelling, data modelling and ARIS.

On many projects the Process Architect will be the same person as the Database Administrator. Where it is a different person, the Process Architect will need the Database Administrator to create project-specific Method Filters, Templates, Semantic Checks and Reports.

3.7.9   Corporate Process Architect

The *Corporate Process Architect* ensures there is a common set of modelling standards across the business. This will ensure models produced by one part of the business can be understood and used by others. Normally, they will define a common set of tools and standards. They will develop a corporate process architecture based around a set of generic business processes or a business sector model (e.g. the Telecommunications Operations Model) into which specific project models may fit or can relate to.

- **Responsibilities** – define corporate process architecture and modelling standards. Define tools to be used and business sector models,
- **Skills** – knowledge of process architecture and modelling, knowledge of data modelling. Familiarity with the process and data modelling tools.

In some organisations, the Corporate Process Architect may supervise the construction of a complete model of the business. In other organisations the parts of the business may operate more autonomously and the Corporate Process Architect may have more of a co-ordination role.

The Corporate Architect will work with the Database and Server Administrators to create specific Method Filters, Templates, Semantic Checks and Reports that implement the corporate modelling conventions.

3.7.10   ARIS Technical Consultant

The *ARIS Technical Consultant* provides expertise to Process Architects and Process Modellers about how to go about modelling specific business scenarios using ARIS. The consultant will provide advice on which models and objects to use and provide assistance in creating Method Filters, Templates, Semantic Checks and Reports.

- **Responsibilities** – provide ARIS technical advice as required,
- **Skills** – extensive knowledge of ARIS. Knowledge of process architecture and modelling, knowledge of data modelling.

Large organisations may have their own ARIS Technical Consultant while a small organisation would purchase these specialist skills as and when needed.

3.7.11   ARIS Database Administrator

The *ARIS Database Administrator* is responsible for managing the day-to-day operation and consistency of the ARIS database. Typically, a project will use a single database (or small number of databases) to contain the final set of project models. The administrator will take models produced by individual modellers and merge them into a single set of models. Although Process Modellers are responsible for ensuring their models meet project standards, the ARIS Database Administrator will often perform audits and check their models to ensure compliance. When managing a database on a local PC, the ARIS Database Administrator is actually the ARIS Server Administrator and has full rights to all administrative operations.

When using databases on an ARIS Server, the ARIS Database Administrator has more restricted capability. Because some database administrative functions have to be carried out by the ARIS Server Administrator, they will both have to work closely together. In particular, the ARIS Database Administrator and ARIS Server Administrator will need to negotiate and collaborate on setting up project-specific Method Filters and Templates.

- **Responsibilities** – manage the integrity of the database and its models. Ensure the database is consistent and there are regular backups. Liaise with Server Administrator. Define project-specific Method Filters, Templates, ARIS reports and Semantic Checks. Determine database group structure. Jointly responsible with Process Modellers for conformance to standards,

- **Skills** – detailed knowledge of ARIS administration. Knowledge of process modelling.

Often the ARIS Database Administrator will undertake the roles of Model Librarian, Model Verifier and Model Publisher.

3.7.12   ARIS Server Administrator

The *ARIS Server Administrator* is responsible for the integrity and availability of all the databases on the ARIS server. The administrator will: create and delete databases; perform backups; define and allocate new users, Identifiers, Method Filters and Templates. The ARIS Server Administrator may delegate some of these administrative tasks to the ARIS Database Administrator or an ARIS Configuration Administrator. The ARIS Server Administrator will have to perform some aspects of database administration (e.g. reorganisation) on behalf of the ARIS Database Administrator. The ARIS Server Administrator will liaise with the IT System Administrators on computer hardware and network issues.

- **Responsibilities** – manage the integrity of the server and all its databases. Ensure there are regular backups. Define server-specific Method Filters, Templates, ARIS reports and Semantic Checks. Liaise with System Administrator,

- **Skills** – detailed knowledge of ARIS administration.

3.7.13   ARIS Configuration Administrator

The *ARIS Configuration Administrator* has more limited database administration rights. The administrator may create and maintain Configuration Filters (Method Filters), Templates and Font Formats. When working with a database on a local PC, the ARIS Configuration Administrator performs a sub-set of the ARIS Database Administrator's role. When databases are stored on an ARIS Server, then Filters, Templates and Fonts apply to all databases on the server so the ARIS Configuration Administrator performs a sub-set of the ARIS Server Administrator's role.

- **Responsibilities** – create and maintain Configuration Filters (Method Filters), Templates and Font Formats as delegated by Server or Database Administrator. Liaise with Server and Database Administrators,
- **Skills** – knowledge of ARIS administration.

3.7.14   IT System Administrator

The *IT System Administrator* is responsible for the management and integrity of the computer hardware and communications network on which the ARIS server depends.

- **Responsibilities** – manage the integrity of the computer hardware and communications network,
- **Skills** – knowledge of systems administration and communications networks.

3.7.15   ARIS Model Publisher

The *ARIS Model Publisher* is responsible for publishing models produced by the project on the web (usually the corporate Intranet) using *ARIS Web Publisher*. The ARIS Model Publisher will need to collaborate with the Process Architect to define standards for the appearance and structure of models to be exported to the Web.

- **Responsibilities** – publish ARIS models on WWW. Jointly with Process Architect, set standards for model structure and appearance. Create Web Publisher Templates,
- **Skills** – knowledge of ARIS, extensive knowledge of ARIS Web Publisher, knowledge of HTML and WWW publishing in general.

Typically the ARIS Model Publisher will also manage the project's or team's Intranet site. Increasingly, more of the output from ARIS will be published on the Intranet and the role of the Model Publisher will become more and more important.

ARIS 7 – use of *ARIS Business Publisher* rather than *ARIS Web Publisher* simplifies the procedure for publishing ARIS models and may remove the need for the ARIS Model Publisher role.

ARIS 7

3.7.16   ARIS Trainer

ARIS Trainers provide specific training on the use of ARIS, process modelling techniques and corporate modelling standards. The most benefit is gained when project teams are trained together on all of these aspects, tailored to the needs of their project.

- **Responsibilities** – provide ARIS training as required,
- **Skills** – knowledge of ARIS, process architecture and modelling, data modelling, modelling standards.

Large organisations may have their own trainers while a small organisation would purchase these specialist skills as and when needed.

References
Davis R, Brabänder E (2007) ARIS Design Platform: Getting Started with BPM, Springer-Verlag, London.

Chapter 4   The Matrix Editor

This chapter describes how to create, view and edit relationships between selected objects using the Matrix Editor. It looks at how to distinguish between connections made in the editor and those created in ARIS Models and describes how to print a matrix and export it to Microsoft Excel.

4.1   The Matrix Editor

We are familiar with establishing *Relationships* between objects by making a *Connection* between them in the *Designer Module*. We can view the type of relationship by hovering the mouse over the connection and viewing the tooltip that appears, or by selecting an object and viewing its connections in the *Relationships Tab* of the *Properties Bar*. However, when there are large numbers of objects and connections, creating and viewing them in this way is not ideal. Moreover, we are limited to those connection types allowed by the ARIS Method for the specific model we are using.

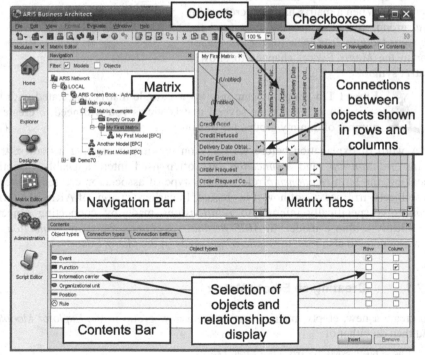

Fig. 4.1 Matrix Editor Window

The *Matrix Editor* (Fig. 4.1) provides an alternative table or matrix view enabling connections to be created and viewed without the need for a graphical model. Furthermore, using the *Matrix Editor* it is possible to create and view sets of connections that cannot be accessed from within a single type of model. You can also export this matrix of connections into Microsoft Excel.

ARIS 7.1 – the *Matrix Editor* will be significantly updated in the ARIS 7.1 release due in 2008. A summary of some of the new, improved features is given in Section 4.14.

ARIS 7.1

4.2   Creating a Matrix

A matrix is created by selecting the range of objects for which you want to view and create connections and then selecting the connection types and the connections required. This can be done by selecting a set of objects and creating a new matrix based on those objects, or by creating an empty matrix and adding objects to it.

A matrix is not a model, but is associated with a specific group in the ARIS group hierarchy. When a matrix has been created for that group, the icon for the group in the *Explorer Module Tree View* (or the *Navigation Bar* in the *Matrix Editor*) changes to show a matrix symbol.

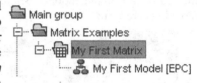

Expert Tip – a group can only have a single matrix associated with it, so if you wish to create several matrix views you will need to create a number of dummy groups for this purpose.

A word of explanation before we carry on looking at creating a matrix; the terms '*relationship*' and '*connection*' are often used interchangeably. Strictly speaking, the term *relationship* refers to any type of association created between two objects, irrespective of how it is created. In earlier versions of ARIS, the term *connection* specifically referred to *relationships* made by connecting objects graphically within a model. In *ARIS Business Architect*, the term *connection* is now extended to also refer to *relationships* made in the *Matrix Editor*.

4.2.1   Creating an Empty Matrix

To create a new, empty, matrix, first create a new group in the *Explorer Module* and then do either of:

- File > New > Matrix from the *Main Menu*,
- New > Matrix from the *Right-Click Menu*.

ARIS will now switch to the *Matrix Editor* and open a new matrix (see Section 4.5).

4.2.2   Creating a Matrix from Existing Objects

To create a new matrix based on some existing objects, select an existing group in the *Explorer Module Tree View* that doesn't already have a matrix associated with it (look for the normal group icon) and that also contains some or all of the objects you wish to work with. As before, do either of:

* File > New > Matrix from the *Main Menu*,
* New > Matrix from the *Right-Click Menu*.

Typically, this group will contain one or more models whose relationships you wish to build on. You don't need to worry whether all the objects you need are in the group where you create the Matrix because you can easily add additional objects later from within the *Matrix Editor* (Section 4.7.2).

4.2.3   Opening a Matrix

To open an existing matrix, select a group in the *Explorer Module* (or the *Navigation Bar* of the *Matrix Editor*) with a matrix icon associated with it and select either of:

* File > Open > Matrix from the *Main Menu*,
* Open matrix from the *Right-Click Menu*.

ARIS will switch to the *Matrix Editor* and open the matrix (see Section 4.5).

?   **Question** – I have selected a group in the *Explorer Module* with a matrix icon associated with it and switched to the *Matrix Editor*, but why do I not see a matrix display?
Answer – as well as selecting a group with a matrix icon, you also have to specifically open the matrix using File > Open > Matrix.

4.3   Saving a Matrix

ARIS does not automatically save any connection definitions made within the *Matrix Editor* so it is important to periodically save the matrix by either of:

* File > Save from the *Main Menu*,
* Click on the Save Button on the *Toolbar*.

You can close a matrix by:

- <u>F</u>ile > C<u>l</u>ose,
- <u>F</u>ile > Close a<u>ll</u>,
- Clicking the Close Button (**x**) on one of the *Matrix Tabs*.

If you try to close an unsaved matrix, ARIS will ask you if you want to save it before the window closes.

 Question – how do I save a copy of my matrix?
Answer – it is not possible to save a copy of a matrix. Copying a group with a matrix attached to it will create a new group and a new matrix, but the matrix will only contain connections made in the original matrix that are associated with the models and objects copied into the new group. Any connections made in the original matrix to objects from other groups (see Section 4.7.2) will not be added to the new matrix.

4.4 Deleting a Matrix

To delete an existing matrix, select a group with a matrix icon associated with it and:

- Delete mat<u>r</u>ix from the Right-Click Menu.

The matrix will be deleted and the group icon will return to the standard format. Any connections that have been created in the matrix and that do not appear in any other matrix or models will be deleted when the database is next reorganised.

 Question – I have deleted a matrix, but why does one of the connections created in the matrix still appear in another matrix?
Answer – if you make a connection visible in a matrix it becomes defined by that matrix in addition to any other matrix it may have been created or viewed in. The connection will only be deleted from the database if all the matrix containing it are deleted and the database is reorganised.

4.5 Matrix Window

The *Matrix Editor Window* has three main panes (Fig. 4.1):

- *Navigation Bar*,
- *Matrix Tabs*,
- *Contents Bar*.

The *Matrix Tabs* have a tab for each matrix currently open. The *Navigation Bar* and *Contents Bar* can be toggled on and off with the *Navigation Checkbox* and *Contents Checkbox* at the top right of the *Matrix Editor Window.*

4.5.1   Navigation Bar

The left-hand pane of the *Matrix Editor Window,* the *Navigation Bar* (Fig. 4.1), has a hierarchical browser, or *Explorer Tree,* similar to that in the *Explorer Module.* It displays folders containing ARIS models, objects and associated matrix. The *Explorer Tree* normally displays the groups and the models in those groups. You can alter the display to also show the objects in the groups (or just the objects or neither) by selecting the Models Checkbox or Objects Checkbox in the *Filter Checkboxes* area at the top of the *Navigation Bar.*

If you select a group, model or object and choose an edit command from the *Main Menu,* or the *Right-Click Menu,* you can undertake various tasks such as Open matrix and Delete matrix.

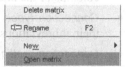

The *Explorer Tree* can be turned on and off by selecting the *Navigation Checkbox* at the top right-hand corner of the *Matrix Window* or from the View menu. If the *Explorer Tree* is turned off, the *Matrix Tabs* occupy the full width of the window area.

4.5.2   Matrix Tabs

Each open matrix has a *Matrix Tab* with a simple grid of rows and columns representing the objects selected for the matrix. The cell marking the intersection of a particular row and column represents the connection between the objects represented by the row and column. The connection type may or may not be valid depending on the ARIS Method and Method Filter in use. A tick in the cell shows that particular

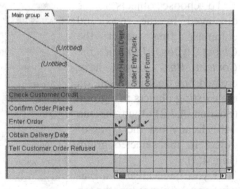

connection has been defined, either in the matrix or in another model. In general, ticks in white boxes can be changed, while those in 'greyed-out' boxes are fixed because they have been defined graphically in other models (it is actually not quite as simple as this as we shall see in Section 4.10).

The selection of which objects and connections appear in the matrix is made using the *Contents Bar* (Section 4.5.3), although some of these selections will have automatically been made when a matrix is created from existing objects (see Section 4.2.2).

The column and row title cells can have their text and properties changed by clicking on one of them and selecting appropriate options in the *Matrix properties Dialog Box* (see Section 4.10.6).

4.5.3 Contents Bar

The *Contents Bar* occupies the full width of the bottom of the *Matrix Editor Window*. Its size can be adjusted by dragging up and down the window resizing bar.

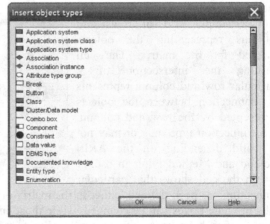

The *Contents Bar* has three tabs:

- *Object types* – used to select the types of objects that appear in the rows and columns of the *Matrix Tabs*,

- *Connection types* – used to select the types of connections (and optionally, their abbreviations) represented by the cells in the *Matrix Tabs*,

- *Connection settings* – used to control the display of the connections represented by the cells in the *Matrix Tabs*.

4.6 Selecting Object Types

The rows and columns in the matrix represent ARIS objects. When you create a new matrix the rows and columns will initially be empty.

To choose objects to be displayed in the rows and columns, first select the *Object types Tab* in the *Content Bar*. If you have created the matrix based on the existing objects in a group (Section 4.2.2), then the tab will already list the types of object in the selected group (Fig. 4.3).

If you have created a matrix in an empty group, the tab will be empty so click on the Insert Button at the bottom right-hand corner of the tab. This will display the *Insert Object types Dialog Box* (Fig. 4.2) from which you can select one or more object types (use Ctrl + click to select multiple entries).

Fig. 4.2 Insert Object Types Dialog Box

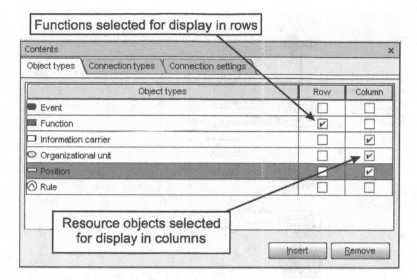

Fig. 4.3 Object Types Tab

Click OK and these object types will now appear listed in the *Object types Tab* along with a checkbox at the right-hand side (Fig. 4.3). You can also use the Insert Button when you have created a matrix based on the existing objects to add object types additional to those already present in the selected group.

Tick the checkboxes to select which object types you want to appear in the rows and columns. Rows and columns can have more than one type of object in them and an object type can appear in both rows and columns at the same time. Typically you might choose to have the columns associated with ARIS Function objects and the rows associated with resource objects, for instance *Application system type*, *Organizational unit type*, *Position* or *Technical terms*.

You can remove an object type from the list by selecting its entry in the tab and clicking the Remove Button at the far right of the *Object types Tab*. Deselecting the row and column checkboxes has the same effect on the *Matrix Tab* display, but the object type entry remains in the *Object types Tab* so you can easily turn it back on later if you wish.

The *Matrix Tab* rows and columns will now update to show the names of all the objects in the selected group that are of the types selected in *Object types Tab*.

Fig. 4.5 shows the *Matrix Tab* updated with the objects types chosen in Fig. 4.3 for the example ***My First Model*** shown in Fig. 4.4. If you have selected objects types for which there are no corresponding objects in the selected group, then no objects of that type will be shown. However, you can include objects in the matrix that are in groups other than the selected group, or create completely new objects, as we shall see in the next section.

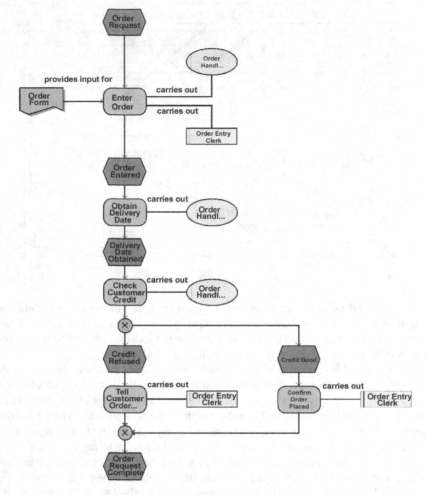

Fig. 4.4 My First Model (example EPC)

4.7   Inserting Objects into a Matrix

In addition to any objects already shown in the matrix, you can add more objects using any of:

- Select Edit > Insert object from the *Main Menu*,
- Select a row or column and select Insert new objects or Insert existing objects from the *Right-Click Menu*,
- Click on the Insert object Button on the *ARIS Toolbar*.

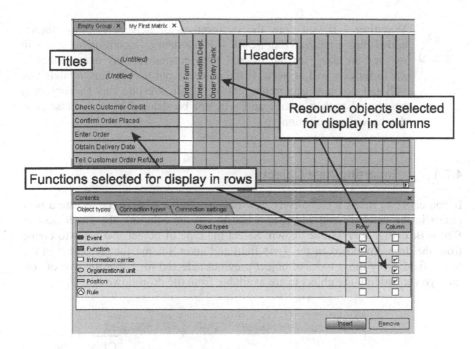

Fig. 4.5 Matrix Tab Showing Selected Objects

Selecting Edit > Insert object will display the *Insert object Dialog Box* (Fig. 4.6) which will allow you to select whether you want to insert the object into a row or column and also whether you want to create a new object or use an existing one. Alternatively, by selecting a row or column and using the *Right-Click Menu* you can go straight to the operation you want.

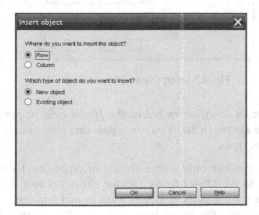

Fig. 4.6 Insert Object Dialog Box

Warning – if you view the occurrences of new or existing objects added into a matrix (Right-Click > Properties / Occurrences) you will not see an entry for the matrix, only entries for any occurrences in ARIS models will be seen. If the object is not used in any models you will not see any occurrence entries at all. Despite this the object is associated with a matrix and will not be deleted by any subsequent database reorganisation.

4.7.1   Inserting New Objects

If you chose to insert a completely new object into the Matrix (i.e. create a new object in the database and add it to a matrix row or column), the *Insert objects Dialog Box* (Fig. 4.7) will be shown. Select the type of object you want to create from the drop-down box in the *Type* field and enter a name for the object in the *Name* field. Only those types of object previous selected for either the row or column you are adding the object to are available from the drop-down list.

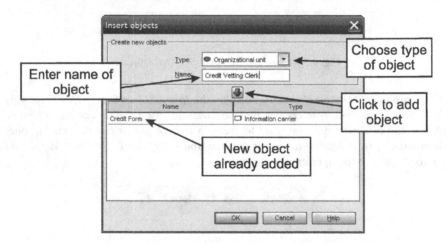

Fig. 4.7 Insert (New) Objects Dialog Box

Click on the small down arrow below the *Name* field or press Enter and the new object will be shown in list. You can repeat this operation to create a range of objects of different types.

 Hint – you can only create objects of types that have previously been chosen in the *Object types Tab* for either the row or column to which you are adding objects. If you want to add additional types of objects, then first use the Insert Button in the *Object types Tab* to add those object type (Section 4.6).

Once you have created all the objects you want, click OK. The new objects will now be shown in the chosen row or column.

 Hint – to find out the type of an object shown in a row or column, hover your mouse over the entry and a tooltip will display the object name and type. If the tooltip is not visible, then make sure the *Show tooltips* checkbox is ticked in the *View > Options [Models / General / Objects] Dialog Box.*

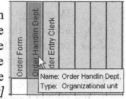

You can use the new object entry straightaway and allocate connections from it to other objects. However, its object definition will not appear in the group associated with the matrix until the matrix is saved (File > Save from the *Main Menu*).

 Expert Tip – to find out in which group the object definition for an object shown in a matrix is located, right-click on the object name and select Go to > Occurrence in Explorer. The *Navigation Bar* will open in the appropriate group and display the object definition.

A new object created using the *Matrix Editor* will be stored in the group associated with the matrix. Once an object has been created in the *Matrix Editor* you cannot delete its definition from within the editor. If you wish to delete it, go to the *Navigation Bar* and delete it from there (select the object and Right-Click > Delete). The row or column in the *Matrix Editor* containing the object will still be visible until you refresh the display (View > Refresh or press F5).

If you don't wish to see the object row or column, but still want to retain the object and any relationship defined for it, you can hide it by selecting the row or column and Right-Click > Hide rows or Right-Click > Hide columns (see Section 4.10.4). The important thing to note is that if a

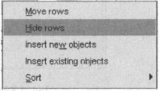

relationship was defined in the matrix, then it still exists even though it can't currently be seen in the matrix. If you insert the object back into a row or column so the cell representing the relationship is displayed again, you will see a tick in the cell showing the relationship still exists.

4.7.2 Inserting Existing Objects

If you chose to insert an existing object, a different version of the *Insert objects Dialog Box* (Fig. 4.8) will appear. You can also quickly insert an existing object by double-clicking on a row or column header.

The left-hand pane of the dialog box shows a *Tree View* showing the database group structure and existing objects. Choose one or more objects and press the right arrow button or press Enter and the list in the right-hand pane will show the objects chosen. You can also double-click on the objects in the left-hand pane to quickly move them to the right-hand pane. Once you have selected all the objects you require click OK and the *Matrix Tab* will be updated.

 Warning – a limitation with ARIS 7.02 is that once an object has been added to the right-hand pane of the *Insert objects Dialog Box* you cannot remove it. If you add an object by mistake, click Cancel to abandon all additions or delete the object once it has been added to the *Matrix Tab*.

Once again you can only insert objects of types that have previously been chosen in the *Object types Tab* and hence the *Insert objects Dialog Box* will only display objects of the chosen type (or an error message if no types have been selected). If you want to add additional types of objects, then first use the Insert Button in the *Object types Tab* to add the required object type (Section 4.6).

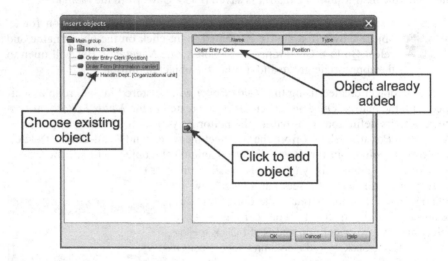

Fig. 4.8 Insert (Existing) Objects Dialog Box

4.8   Selecting Connection Types

Once we have chosen the objects we wish to display in the matrix rows and columns, we can then choose which connections we want to display or edit. Select the *Connection types Tab* in the *Contents Bar*. The list will display all of the connection types relevant to the objects selected for the rows and columns (Fig. 4.9).

 Warning – the list of connections shown in the *Connection types Tab* contains all the valid connection types defined by the ARIS Method. It is not limited by the Method Filter in use so you may see connection types you are not necessarily familiar with.

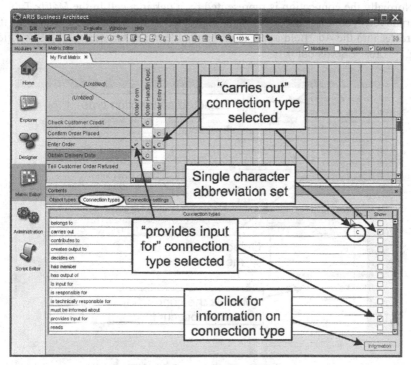

Fig. 4.9 Connection Types Tab

If you want to know more about a particular connection and the object types for which it is valid, select the connection and click the Information Button at the bottom right of the tab. The *Information on connection type Dialog Box* (Fig. 4.10) will show between which object types the connection is valid and in which models a connection representing that connection can be made.

 Warning – some apparently different object types are actually based on the same underlying type of object (e.g. a *Value-added chain* object in a *Value-added chain diagram* and an *Activity* in a *UML Activity diagram* are both based on a Function object). The *Matrix Editor* shows all the connection types valid for an object type in all its forms so you may see more connection types in the *Connection types Tab* than you might initially expect.

Select the connections you wish to display by ticking the checkbox associated with each connection. The cells in *Matrix Tab* will update to show connections for the previously selected object (Fig. 4.9).

Normally the connection is represented by a tick in a cell in the *Matrix Tab*, but alternatively you can choose a single character to be displayed by entering the character into the *Ab..* field at the right-hand side of the tab next to the *Show* field (e.g. "C" for "*Carries out*").

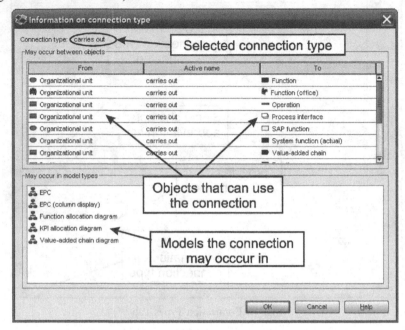

Fig. 4.10 Information on Connection Type Dialog Box

4.9   Selecting Connection Settings

There are many different connection types we can select for display and editing in the matrix and, because it is also possible to have more than one type of connection type between some pairs of objects, it is useful to have some additional control over the connection types visible in the *Matrix Tabs*. The *Connection settings Tab* provides this extra control.

The *Connection type* drop-down box in the *Connection settings Tab* (Fig. 4.11) allows you to choose the type of connection you are interested in from the list of those enabled in the *Connection types Tab* (Fig. 4.9). The *Connection direction* field in the *Connection settings Tab* provides a visual indication of the direction of the chosen connection (i.e. from column to row or vice versa).

Any cell in the *Matrix Tab* which represents a valid connection of the type selected in the *Connection settings Tab* will be activated. If new connections of the chosen type are allowed, the cell will have a white background and any new connections you now create (see Section 4.11.1) will be of the chosen type. Similarly you can only delete existing connections of that type (see Section 4.11.2 for more on deleting connections).

The fact that a cell has a white background and a tick or single letter in it does not necessarily mean it represents a relationship of the chosen type. The objects represented by the rows and columns may have more than one valid type of connection between them and the *Matrix Tabs* will still display all the other types of connections (where they exist) that have been selected in the *Connection types Tab*. If you want to view just one specific connection type, go to the *Connection settings Tab,* make the appropriate selection from the *Connection type* drop-down box and, in addition, tick the *Display connections of the same type only* checkbox. The *Matrix Tabs* will now only display connections of the selected type.

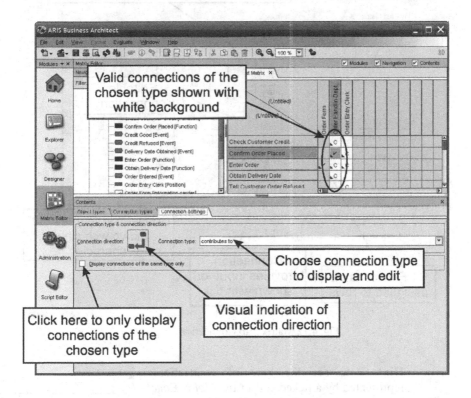

Fig. 4.11 The Connection Settings Tab

4.10   Viewing Connections

4.10.1   Connection Display

Now we have chosen the objects and connection types we wish to display, as described in the previous sections, we can see connections that already exist by looking for tick marks (or single character abbreviations) in the corresponding matrix cells (see Fig. 4.12).

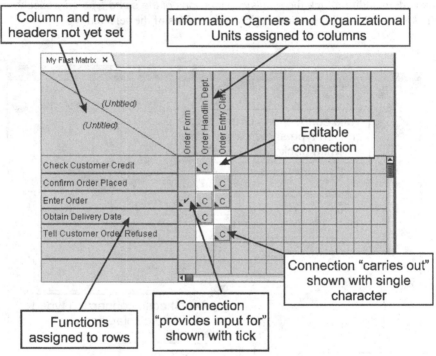

Fig. 4.12 Matrix Tab Connection Display

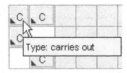

Hint – to see the type of connection(s) represented by a ticked cell in the *Matrix Editor*, hover your mouse over the cell and a tooltip will appear showing one or more connection types.

Where multiple connections exist between objects, a combination of ticks and letters can be used to represent the various connections. Where it is not possible to distinguish between different connections, because they are both represented by a tick or by the same letter, then these multiple relationships are represented by a single star (*).

Thus a cell may have combinations of ticks, letters and stars depending on the relationships created and the chosen display settings (see Table 4.1). Where these characters cannot all fit in cell width, the display will be truncated using three dots (…). You can expand the width of a cell to display all connections types by dragging the boundary of the column label.

Table 4.1 Representation of Multiple Connections in a Single Cell

Display	Header
A	Single connection type represented by a letter.
AB	Two connection types represented by letters.
A…	Two or more connection types represented by letters but truncated due to column width.
√	Single connection type represented by a tick.
√*	Two or more connection types represented by ticks.
√A	Two connection types, one represented by a tick and one represented by a letter.
√*A	Three or more connection types, two or more represented by ticks and one represented by a letter.
A*B	Three or more connection types, two or more represented by the letter "A" and one represented by the letter "B".
√…	Two or more connection types, at least one represented by a tick, but truncated due to column width.

As we saw in the previous section, if you want to view just one specific connection type, go to the *Connection settings Tab,* make the appropriate selection from the *Connection type* drop-down box and tick the *Display connections of the same type only* checkbox. The *Matrix Tabs* will now only display connections of the selected type.

4.10.2   Connection Properties, Attributes and Occurrences

As with any ARIS item, you can view the properties or attributes of an object or connection visible in the *Matrix Editor* by selecting a row or column header label (for an object) or a ticked cell (for a connection) and using:

- Right-Click > Attributes,
- Right-Click > Properties.

The familiar *Attributes Window* and *Properties Dialog Box* will be displayed. You can view the occurrences of an object or connection using the *Properties / Occurrences Dialog Box*; however it will not show the use of an object in a matrix as being an occurrence. As a result, if an object or connection is not used in any

ARIS models you will not see any occurrence entries at all. Despite this the object is associated with a matrix and will not be deleted by any subsequent database reorganisation.

Connections created in the *Matrix Editor* will be displayed in the *Properties / Relationships Dialog Box* although they look indistinguishable from connections made in models.

4.10.3   Changing the Display Order

The order in which the entries in a row or column are displayed is initially determined by how you added the objects to the matrix. You can alter the order by moving individual entries or by sorting the list.

Sorting

To sort the order of the entries in a row or column, select an object in either the row or column and:

*   Right-click > Sort.

    From the right-click menu choose:

*   Ascending (A-Z),

*   Descending (Z-A),

*   By type.

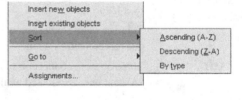

The *By type* option sorts the list in alphabetical order by the name of the type of the object (e.g. an *Application system type* object would be near the start of the list). You can see the type of an object in a matrix row or column by hovering your mouse over a cell and looking at the tooltip.

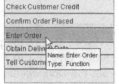

Moving Rows and Columns

You can move a single row or column, or a contiguous block of rows or columns (click and drag the mouse to select more than one row or column) by selecting them and:

*   Right-click > Move rows or Move columns.

The cursor will now change to a four-way arrow. Click a single row or column (or a previously selected block of rows or columns) and hold down the mouse key. If you now drag the mouse to a new position, an arrow will appear at the right-hand edge of the selected row header, or the bottom of column header, showing where the entries will be moved to. Release the mouse key and the rows or columns will move to their new position (see Fig. 4.13).

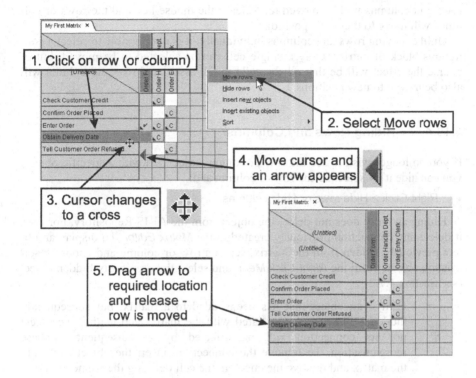

Fig. 4.13 Moving Rows and Columns

 Hint – to move a single row or column entry you can right-click (with your mouse over any row or column) and choose the Move rows or Move columns command and then select the entry you wish to move. If you wish to move a contiguous block of entries, you must first select them (click and drag the mouse to select more than one row or column), then choose the command and then click and drag the previously selected block of cells.

Moving Cells

In addition to moving a row or column, you can also select and move a cell which has the effect of moving both the row and column associated with cell at the same time. To move a cell, hover your mouse over the cell area and:

- Right-click > Move cells.

Now click on the required cell, hold down the mouse key and drag the mouse to a new position. You will see arrows will now appear at both the right-hand edge of the selected row header and the bottom of the column header showing where the rows and columns will be moved to. Release the mouse key and the rows or columns will move to their new position.

Unlike moving rows and columns individually, it is not possible to select a contiguous block of entries. Only a single cell can be selected to be moved, but of course the effect will be that all the cells in the associated row and column will also be moved to new positions.

4.10.4   Hiding Rows and Columns

If you no longer wish to see the row or column associated with a specific object, you can hide it by selecting the row or column and:

* Right-Click > Hide rows or Hide columns.

Hiding an entry does not delete the object from the ARIS Repository, nor does it delete any connection previously created in the *Matrix Editor*. To display an object previously hidden from the matrix, select a row or column and choose Insert existing objects from the *Right-Click Menu* and select the previously hidden object (see Section 4.7.2).

Hint – an object that has been added to a matrix, but subsequently hidden, still remains associated with the matrix and neither the object nor its connection will be affected by a subsequent database reorganisation. To remove the connection, insert the object back into the matrix and remove the check in the cell defining the connection (see Section 4.11.2). To remove the object, delete it in the *Explorer Module*.

Hint – you can't hide or delete a blank column; to remove it, move it to the right-hand side of the matrix (see Section 4.10.3). Similarly move a blank row to the bottom of the matrix.

4.10.5   Zoom

You can change the size of the matrix grid visible in the *Matrix Tabs* by dragging on the window borders at the bottom and left-hand side. You can alter the scaling of the matrix display within the *Matrix Tab* by using any of the following:

* *Zoom in* and *Zoom out* icons on the *ARIS Toolbar*,
* View > Zoom in or View > Zoom out from the *Main Menu*,

* Changing the % value in the *Size of appearance* box on the *ARIS Toolbar*,

* View > original size from the *Main Menu*,
* View > fit to window from the *Main Menu*.

4.10.6   Row and Column Titles

The text used for the row or column title can be set by double-clicking on the title cell. The *Matrix properties Dialog Box* (Fig. 4.14) opens at the appropriate *Column header* or *Row header* tab. You can enter a value for the other title cell by clicking on the other tab.

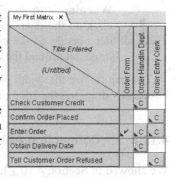

Type a text entry into the *Title* box and click the Preview Button to see how it will actually appear in the title cell. Click OK to make the change or Cancel to abandon the change.

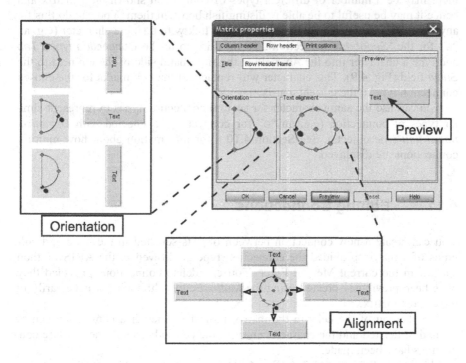

Fig. 4.14 Matrix Properties Dialog Box

You can change the orientation of the row or column headers (horizontal, vertical text up, vertical text down) by clicking on dots on the semicircle graphic in the *Orientation* area. The *Preview* area of the dialog box will change to show style of text orientation (using the word "text"). You can see what the header actually looks like by clicking the Preview Button which will change the actual title. In a similar manner you can alter the header cell text alignment (top, bottom, right, left, etc) by clicking on dots on the circle graphic in the *Text alignment* area.

Warning – in the *Orientation* and *Text alignment* boxes you have to click on the dots that lie on the circle to make the selection. The large dot outside of the circle indicates the selection. You cannot drag the large dot around the circle as you might perhaps expect.

You can re-size the width of row headers or height of column headers by dragging the edge of the header cell.

4.10.7   Connection Abbreviations

We showed in Section 4.10.1 how connections are marked with a tick. Of course, there may be a number of different types of connection shown on a matrix and hence it may be useful to be able to distinguish between them. You can do this for any specific connection type by replacing the tick with a single character (e.g. an "s" for the '*Supports*' connection). To do this, go to the *Connection types Tab* and type a character into the *Ab.* field at the right-hand side of the tab next to the *Show* field (Fig. 4.9). This character will replace all the tick marks for the chosen connection type in the current matrix.

You can use the same character for several connection types to represent similar types of connection (e.g. an "o" for connections connected with *Organizational unit type* objects). See Section 4.10.1 for information about how multiple connections are displayed.

4.11   Editing Connections

You can create a new connection between objects selected in the rows and columns of a matrix provided the connection type is allowed in the ARIS Method and set in the current Method Filter. You can delete connections provided they have been previously created using the *Matrix Editor*, although not necessarily in the current matrix.

The shading of the cells in the matrix indicates whether a connection can be created or deleted and the character entry in the cell indicates if one or more connections have been made.

The *Connection settings Tab* (Fig. 4.11) is important in setting the type of connection that can be edited. When a selection is made, all the cells with that type of connection associated with them will be activated. Empty white cells are always active and a connection of the type set in the *Connection settings Tab* can be made.

Activated cells with content appear raised. White cells with content can be edited to delete the connection if it is of the type set in the *Connection settings Tab* or to add a new connection of that type if one does not already exist.

Activated grey cells with content indicate a connection exists, but cannot be edited in the *Matrix Editor* because the connection was made in a model.

Table 4.2 provides a summary of the different appearance of cells and their edit status. The following two sections describe the procedure for creating and deleting connections.

4.11.1   Creating a Connection

To create a new connection:

1. Ensure the two objects between which you want to create the connection are visible in a matrix row and column (see Section 4.6).

2. Select the *Connection settings Tab* and make sure the required *Connection type* is selected (see Section 4.9), if necessary enable it first in the *Connection types Tab*. It is useful to also set the *Display connections of the same type only* checkbox so as to hide any other types of connections.

3. Look for the cell that is the intersection between the row and column containing the two objects. The cell should be white to indicate the connection can be made. If there is already a tick or character in the cell, hover your mouse over the cell to check if this is already the connection type you want or a different one. If it is a different one you can carry on and make the additional new connection. **Note:** a different connection type will only appear if you have <u>not</u> checked the *Display connections of the same type only* in the previous step.

4. Double-click in the cell and a tick will appear (or a single character abbreviation if this has been set in the *Connection types Tab*, see Section 4.8).

 Warning – there can be more than one connection type valid between the two chosen objects and you cannot immediately tell which type will be created when you double-click in the cell. To create the correct connection, make sure the correct *Connection type* is selected in the *Connection settings Tab*.

 Expert Tip – if you frequently work with multiple connections between objects, it is worth setting different single-character abbreviations for the connections that will be shown in the matrix cell instead of the default tick. You can configure the abbreviation in the *Connection types Tab* (Section 4.8).

Table 4.2 Matrix Edit Cell Representation

Cell Display	Create Action	Delete Action
Empty grey.	A connection cannot be created because a connection of this type is not set in the *Connection settings Tab* or is not valid for the object types related to this cell.	No connection to delete.
Empty white.	Double-click to create a connection of the type currently enabled in the *Connection settings Tab*.	No connection to delete.
Deactivated grey with tick or character.	A new connection cannot be created because a connection of this type is not valid or set in the *Connection settings Tab*.	A connection exists, but it is not of the type set in the *Connection settings Tab* so it cannot be deleted.
Activated grey with tick or character.	A connection of the type enabled in the *Connection settings Tab* already exists. A new connection of this type cannot be created.	A connection exists, but cannot be deleted in the *Matrix Editor* because it was created in an ARIS model.
Deactivated white cell with a single tick or character.	The connection shown is not of the type set in the *Connection settings Tab*, but a new connection of the selected type can be created in addition to the one shown.	A connection exists, but it is not of the type set in the *Connection settings Tab* so it cannot be deleted. To delete it, change the *Connection type* in the *Connection settings Tab* and double-click to delete.
Activated white cell with a single tick or character.	A connection of the type set in the *Connection settings Tab* already exists. A new connection of this type cannot be created.	A connection exists and can be deleted – double-click to delete.
Activated white cell with multiple ticks, characters, or stars.	One of the connections shown is of the type set in the *Connection settings Tab*. A new connection of this type cannot be created.	One of connections can be deleted – to delete, ensure the required connection is set in the *Connection settings Tab* and double-click.

4.11.2   Deleting a Connection

To delete a connection previously created in the *Matrix Editor*:

1. Ensure the two objects whose connection you wish to delete are visible in a matrix row and column (see Section 4.6).

2. Select the *Connection settings Tab* and make sure the required *Connection type* is selected (see Section 4.9), if necessary enable it first in the *Connection types Tab*. It is useful to also set the *Display connections of the same type only* checkbox so as to hide any other types of connections.

3. Look for the cell that is the intersection between the row and column containing the two objects. The cell should have a tick or single character in an activated white cell to indicate the connection has been previously made in the *Matrix Editor* and can be deleted (but see discussion below). If the cell is greyed out or not activated, you have either not set the correct *Connection type* (go back to step 2) or the connection was made in a model and cannot be deleted from the *Matrix Editor*. If there are multiple entries in the cell (ticks, stars or abbreviation characters), then there is more than one valid connection type in existence between the two objects. Go back to the *Connection settings Tab* (step 2) and make sure only the connection type you wish to delete is enabled.

4. Double-click in the cell and the tick (or a single-character abbreviation if this has been set in the *Connection types Tab*, see Section 4.8) will be removed.

    Warning – if you double-click to delete a connection in a cell that has multiple entries (ticks, stars or abbreviation characters) you cannot immediately tell which of the valid connections in existence will be deleted. To make sure you delete the correct connection, make sure the correct *Connection type* is selected in the *Connection settings Tab* and the *Display connections of the same type only* checkbox is set.

4.11.3   Interpreting Cell Displays

The display of the cells in the *Matrix Editor* can be rather confusing as you need to look at the background colour of the cell, whether it is activated or not and the number and type of characters in the cell. Where there are multiple characters displayed, interpreting which character the background colour refers to can be tricky (see Table 4.2).

The moral of this story is to always make sure the required connection type is enabled in the *Connection settings Tab* and the *Display connections of the same type only* checkbox is set (see Section 4.9).

You can also use connection abbreviations (Section 4.8) to distinguish more easily between different connection types.

4.12   Exporting to Excel

You can export the contents of a matrix to Microsoft Excel by using an *ARIS Report*:

1. In the *Explorer Module* (or the *Navigation Bar* of the *Matrix Editor*) select the group associated with the matrix you want to export (make sure you save the matrix if it is currently open),

2. Right-Click > Ev<u>a</u>luate > Sta<u>r</u>t report,

3. In the *Select report Dialog Box* of the *Report Wizard*, select *Administration* from the C<u>a</u>tegory drop-down box,

4. Select the *Export relationship matrix* report from the <u>R</u>eport list,

5. Click <u>N</u>ext,

6. Selected *Microsoft Excel (*.XLS)* in the O<u>u</u>tput format box and Click <u>F</u>inish.

The report will run and create and open the output in Microsoft Excel (Fig. 4.15).

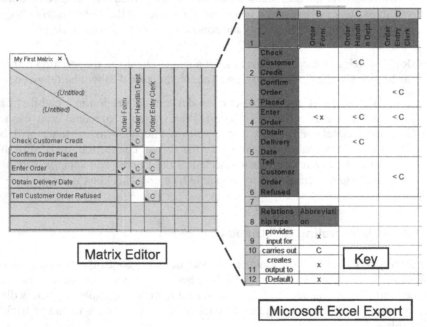

Fig. 4.15 Microsoft Excel Report Format

The format will replicate that of the *Matrix Tabs* using a cross (x) instead of a tick. If abbreviations have been defined in the *Connection types Tab* these characters will be used in the Excel cell and a key showing the meaning of the abbreviations will be shown under the connection cells.

The Excel format does not show the background cell colours shown in the *Matrix Tabs* as these are only relevant in the context of the selection made in the *Connection settings Tab*; all cells are white.

4.13   Printing a Matrix

To print a matrix:

1. Open the matrix in the *Matrix Editor*,
2. If required, adjust page margins using File > Page setup from the *Main Menu*,
3. If required, adjust *Print scale, Orientation* (*Portrait* or *Landscape*) and *Black and white* from the *Print options Tab* in *Matrix properties* (click on the row or column title cell to display *Matrix properties*),
4. Preview the print settings using File > Print preview from the *Main Menu* or <CTRL + F2>. The *Print preview Dialog Box* also allows the settings shown in step 3 to be adjusted as well as allowing the print format to be previewed,
5. Select File > Print from the *Main Menu*, click the Print Button on the *ARIS Toolbar* or type <CTRL + P>.

The matrix will now be printed using your default printer as set up in Microsoft Windows.

4.14   Matrix Editor 7.1

The *Matrix Editor* has been considerably updated for release 7.1 of ARIS due in 2008. Some of the new features include:

*   A matrix is now a model type like any other and can be located in any group,
*   You can drag and drop objects from the *Explorer Module Tree View* into the *Matrix Tab* rows and columns,
*   You can display an object symbol against the row and column entries,
*   You can create a hierarchy of objects by using a new hierarchy relationship only available in the *Matrix Editor*,
*   The *Matrix* model now appears in the Method Filter and the object and relationship types available in the Matrix model can be configured,
*   Derived *Matrix* models can be defined in by configuring the ARIS Method (see Chapter 12),
*   Rows and columns can be shaded in different colours.

Chapter 5   Find and Query

This chapter describes how to use the Find command to search for groups, models and objects in an ARIS database. It also looks at how to create pre-defined Queries which can extend the Find command to allow more complex searches.

5.1   Introduction to Find and Queries

The Find and Find objects with identical names commands familiar from *ARIS Toolset* both now appear in the new and extended F̲ind command in *ARIS Business Architect*. Also, in addition to the standard F̲ind command where users can enter the criteria on which to base the search, it is now possible to create and save search criteria as *Queries* which users can run to execute pre-defined searches. Multiple Queries can be combined to build up complex searches that previously could only be performed with an ARIS Report.

 Question – is there an equivalent of the *ARIS Toolset* Find in active model command?
Answer – this command is not available in *ARIS Business Architect*, but you can quickly locate objects in the *Designer Module* by looking in the *Occurrences Tab* of the *Navigation Bar*. You can order the list alphabetically by name or type and clicking on an object will highlight and locate it in the *Modelling Window*.

5.2   Standard Find

5.2.1   Opening the Find Dialog Box

To open the *Find Dialog Box*, select a database or group in which to search and do any of the following:

- File > F̲ind from the *Main Menu*,
- Right-Click > F̲ind,
- <CTRL + F>,
- Press the Find Button on the *ARIS Toolbar*.

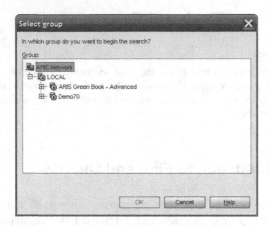

Fig. 5.1 Select Group Dialog Box

If you did not select a database or group before executing <u>F</u>ind, the *Select group Dialog Box* (Fig. 5.1) will open so you can choose where to base your search.

 Question – when I open the *Find Dialog Box* why does it default to the *Query Tab*?

Answer – if you have selected a model or object before issuing the <u>F</u>ind command, ARIS assumes that you actually want to run a Query (Section 5.4) and opens the *Query Tab*. To run a standard <u>F</u>ind, click on the *Standard Tab* (Fig. 5.2).

The *Find Dialog Box* is shown in Fig. 5.2. At the top of the dialog box the greyed-out *Look in* field shows the database and group in which the search will be performed. This has been set by default based on the previously selected group. You can change it by clicking on the browse button (the three dots) on the right-hand side and using the *Select group Dialog Box* (Fig. 5.1) to select a new database and group.

The *Find Dialog Box* opens in a separate window from the main ARIS window so you can leave it open while you work in other ARIS modules and return to the same search later. You can also open several *Find Dialog Boxes* so you can set up a number of different searches.

5.2.2   Selecting the Item Type

The Find <u>w</u>hat field allows you to select what type of item you wish to search for:

- *Groups*,
- *Models*,
- *Objects*,
- *Objects with identical names* (see Section 5.3).

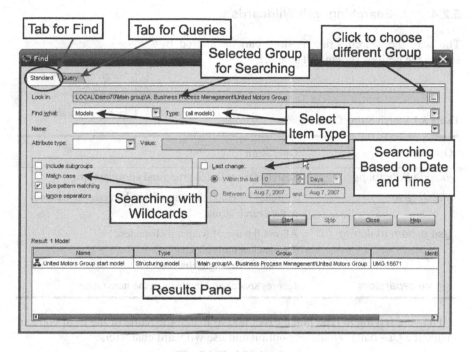

Fig. 5.2 Find Dialog Box

This normally defaults to *Models*, but you can change it to any of the other item types. If you select *Models* or *Objects* you can select the type of model or object from the drop-down list in the *Type* field or just leave it set to *(all models)* or *(all objects)*. The types shown in the list will be limited by the currently selected Method Filter.

5.2.3   Search Based on Item Name

Now we have chosen the type of item we are searching for we can either search for it based on its name or based on the value of one of its attributes (Section 5.2.6). To search based on name, enter a text string into the *Name* field. Press the Start button. The search will begin and if any results are found they will be displayed in the *Result* table at the bottom of the dialog box (Fig. 5.2). If nothing is found an appropriate message will be displayed and the *Result* table will not be visible.

The default setup for standard find is to search in the currently selected group for the item selected whose name exactly matches the search string entered, without any case-sensitivity.

5.2.4   Searching with Wildcards

The way the search string is used can be altered by
setting the options shown in Table 5.1.

☐	Include subgroups
☐	Match case
☑	Use pattern matching
☐	Ignore separators

Table 5.1 Search String Options

Option	Operation
Include Subgroups	Searches the selected group and all subgroups.
Match case	Searches based on the case of the characters as entered in the search string.
Use pattern matching	Allows the use of wildcard characters: * – matches multiple characters, ? – matches a single character.
Ignore separators	Ignores spaces and hyphens in the item name.

To avoid having to type in the exact text to match the name of the item you can
enable the *Use pattern matching* option and use wildcard characters:

- ? – replaces a single unknown character,

- * – replaces one or more unknown characters.

Wildcard characters can be used at any position in the search text string. If you
leave the *Name* field completely blank, the search will match any item of the selected type. For example, any of the following can be used to match to a model
called "my process model":

- `my process*`,

- `*process model`,

- `my*model`,

- `?y process model`,

- `my ?rocess model`,

- [an empty field].

Warning – when using the "*" wildcard character in a search string, be
careful not to accidentally add spaces before or after the "*" (e.g. "
process"). The spaces will be included in the search string and may
not give the results you expect.

5.2.5   Search with Time and Date Qualifier

When running searches based on models or objects you can qualify the search to only return items that have been changed:

- *Within the last* x *days or months,*

- *Between* firstdate *and* seconddate.

Tick the *Last change* checkbox and select the appropriate option and value.

5.2.6   Search Based on Attribute Value

For models and objects you can also search for items whose text-based attributes match the search string entered in the *Value* field or the value selected from the drop-down list for those attributes that have a fixed list of values. You can either choose to search *All text attributes* or a specific attribute by selecting the appropriate item from the *Attribute type* drop-down box.

After pressing the Start Button, the *Result* table will update to show all the matching items and the right-hand columns of the table will show the attribute field that matches the search string (Fig. 5.3). There may be multiple attribute columns if the *All text attributes* option was selected and the search text is matched in several different attribute types. If the *Value* field is left blank, then all items in the selected database and group will be selected.

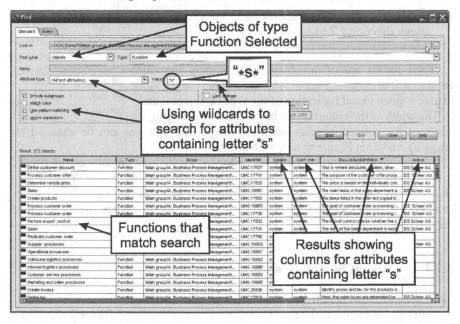

Fig. 5.3 Results of Search Based on Attribute Values

You can also use the *Use pattern matching* option and wildcard characters described in Section 5.2.4 in the *Value* field.

Searching on the *Name* and *Last change* attributes is specifically catered for by entering values into the *Name* field in the *Find Dialog Box* (Section 5.2.3) or ticking the *Last change* checkbox and entering values into the *Within the last* or *Between* fields (Section 5.2.5).

5.2.7   Viewing Search Results

If the search matches any items, a *Result* table will appear at the bottom of the dialog box (see Fig. 5.3) and a caption above the box will show how many items have been matched (e.g. "Result: 24 Objects"). If no items are matched, the table will not appear, but the caption will display a message (e.g. "No Objects found"). If the search returns a large number of objects, it may take some time for the results to be displayed. The search can be aborted by pressing the Stop Button.

The results table (Fig. 5.3) has columns for:

- *Name* – the value of the *Name* attribute of the item,
- *Type* – the type of model or object,
- *Group* – the location of the item in the group structure,
- *Identifier* – the value of the *Identifier* attribute of the item,
- [attribute] – one or more attributes that are the result of an attribute-based search (Section 5.2.6).

If the results are of an object-based search, the name column will also show a small symbol icon next to the name to give a quick visual indication of the type of object found.

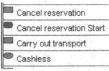

The width of the columns can be changed by dragging the edges of the column headers and the order of the columns can be changed by dragging a column header to a new position.

You can sort the order of the results table list by clicking on any column header to sort alphabetically. A small arrow next to the column header shows which column is being used for sorting and whether the order is ascending or descending. Click on the header again to change the direction of the sort order.

5.2.8   Using Search Results

Once a list of items results has been returned, you can select one or more using a combination of mouse and keys (Table 5.2) and use the *Right-Click Menu* to execute any of the commands appropriate to the type of item found.

Table 5.2 Selection Options

Select Required	Operation
Single item	Left mouse click.
Block of contiguous items	Left mouse click at start of the block, shift-left mouse click at end of the block.
Multiple non-contiguous items	Left mouse click on the first item, ctrl-left mouse click subsequent items.
All items	Left mouse click on any item, then <CTRL-A>.

Some of the more useful commands that can be executed on a set of items found as a result of using the Find command are:

- Attributes,
- Properties,
- Goto > Assigned model (objects) or Occurrence in Explorer,
- Goto > Superior model,
- Evaluate > Start report,
- Consolidate (objects) (see Chapter 10),
- Format > Apply template (models),
- Generate model,
- Find.

You can execute another search based on the items returned from the initial Find command to build up more complex searches. The results of the initial Find are used to build a Query and the *Find Dialog Box* will open on the *Query Tab*. We will see how to use Queries in Section 5.4.

5.3 Find Objects with Identical Names

A common problem experienced when modelling with large databases, and with many users, is the creation of duplicate objects with the same name. This is particularly problematic with resource objects (e.g. *Application system type, Organizational unit type*, etc) where people tend to keep creating new objects to represent what is in fact the same IT system or department.

It is important to manage your objects and remove duplicates using the Consolidate command (see Chapter 10). In *ARIS Toolset* there was a separate command to find objects with identical names, but in *Business Architect* this facility has been incorporated into the Find command and *Objects with identical names* is one of the options in the *Find what* field.

Objects with identical names ▼

To find objects with identical names in your database or in a group in the database:

1. Select the database or group in which to search,
2. File > Find from the *Main Menu*,
3. Select *Objects with identical names* in the *Find what* field,
4. Press Start.

You can select the *Include Subgroups* option to control whether the command searches the subgroups; the *Use pattern matching* option is automatically enabled, but *Last change* has no effect.

> **Hint** – when using Find *Objects with identical names*, its is recommended that you select Ignore separators and don't select *Match case* so that you find the widest range of objects with similar names (e.g. "Enter Order", "enter order" or "Enter-order").

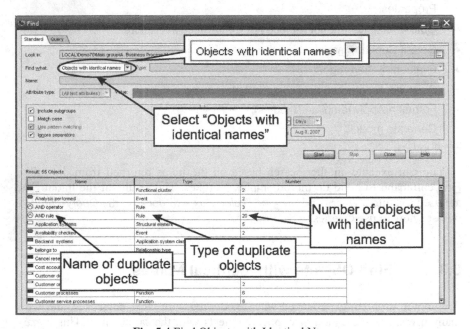

Fig. 5.4 Find Objects with Identical Names

The result of a find objects with identical names search is shown in Fig. 5.4. The *Name* and *Type* fields are similar to the normal search result display, but a new column, *Number*, displays the number of objects of the same type with the same name.

The power of the find *Objects with identical names* search is to identify objects for consolidation. You can select any line in the result list and Right-Click > Consolidate to consolidate all the objects with the same name (see Chapter 10). When viewing the results list using the *Objects with identical names* option,

Consolidate is the only command available from the *Right-Click Menu* and it is only possible to select one entry at a time.

> **Question** – I have noticed that I have an *Organizational unit type* object with the same name as a Function object; why does the find *Objects with identical names* not display these objects?
> **Answer** – find *Objects with identical names* only finds objects of the same type which have identical names. It may be valid to have objects of a different type with the same name.

5.4   Creating Queries

5.4.1   Introduction to Queries

In *ARIS Toolset* it is possible to create complex search criteria for searches based on attribute values. However, to undertake significantly more complex searches (e.g. show me all the Functions in an *EPC* executed by a specific *Organizational unit type*) it was necessary to create an ARIS Report using the *Script Wizard* or *Script Editor*. Reports normally only produce output in document format (e.g. Word or Excel) and don't provide access to the actual ARIS items for further processing in the way that the Find command does.

In *ARIS Business Architect* it is now possible to create complex searches without using ARIS Reports, but by using *Queries*. Queries can be created by anyone using *Business Architect* and made available to other users of *Business Designer* or *Business Architect*. These Queries are executed from *Queries Tab* of the *Find Dialog Box* (see Fig. 5.2) and display results in the same format as the standard Find command. Items can be selected from the list and further operations carried out on them as described in Section 5.2.8.

Queries are initially created using the *Query Wizard* in the *Administration Module* and require the use of *Business Architect*. To create Queries on an ARIS server so they are available to other users, server administration rights are needed.

5.4.2   Opening the Query Wizard

To open the *Query Wizard*:

1. Select the *Administration Module*,
2. Select the **Queries** folder in **LOCAL** or on an ARIS Server,
3. File > New > Query or Right-Click > New > Query or click the New Button on the *Query Toolbar*.

The *Query Wizard* will open. It has seven dialog boxes which are summarised in Table 5.3 (the exact dialog boxes that appear vary depending on what types of items are selected). The following sections describe the dialog boxes in detail and in Section 5.4.13 we will look at some specific examples.

Table 5.3 Query Wizard Tabs

Dialog Box	Options
Select creation mode	• Create a single Query or a Nested Query, • Choose the item from which to start the Query (groups, models or objects).
Create query	• Choose language, • Enter Name and Description, • Choose Filter to apply during Query creation.
Restrict input types	• If models or objects have been chosen as starting point, restrict the types of model and objects to be searched (e.g. only look in *EPCs*).
Restrict result types	• Restrict the types of models or objects that can be returned by the Query.
Select relationship	• Choose whether relationships, and what type of relationships (e.g., connection types, assignments, superior model) are to be used to determine results.
Select attributes	• Select attributes whose values can be searched to return results (only attribute names are selected here, the actual values for searching are entered when the Query is run).
Confirm input	• Optional confirmation of settings entered in previous pages.

Question – why don't I see a command to create a Query when I have selected a group in the *Explorer Module*?
Answer – you can only create new Queries in the **Queries** folder in the *Administration Module*.

5.4.3   Select Creation Mode

The first page of the *Query Wizard* is the *Select creation mode Dialog Box* (Fig. 5.5). Here you can choose whether to create a single Query or a Nested Query. We will look at Nested Queries in Section 5.5, but for now select *Create query*.

You can now choose whether you wish the Query to start based on a *Group*, *Model* or *Object*. For instance you may wish to start with a group and run a Query to find all the models in that group that were created by a particular author or you may want to start with a set of models and look for all the objects that have occurrences in those models. Choose the item and press Next.

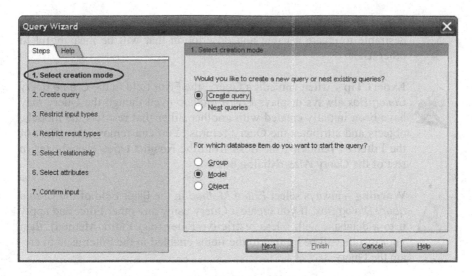

Fig. 5.5 Select Creation Mode Dialog Box

5.4.4   Create Query

In the *Create query Dialog Box* (Fig. 5.6), you can choose the *Language* you want to use, enter a *Name* for the Query and a textual *Description* of what it does. You can also choose a Method Filter to apply during the creation of the Query.

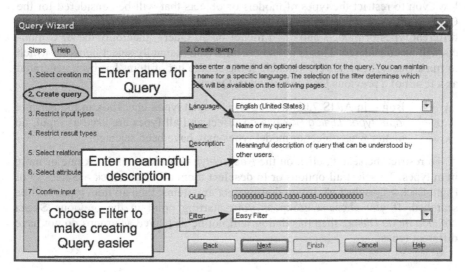

Fig. 5.6 Create Query Dialog Box

Hint – if you are going to make your Queries available to others it is desirable to create a name and description that will be meaningful to other users.

 Expert Tip – when you edit a Query, the *F*ilter field in the *Create query Dialog Box* always displays *Entire Method* even though the Query may have been initially created with another Filter that restricts the models, objects and attributes the Query returns. You can remove the effect of the Filter by removing the ticks from the Res*t*rict types checkboxes in rest of the *Query Wizard* dialog boxes.

 Warning – always select *Entire Method* in the *F*ilter field of the *Create query Dialog Box*. If you create a Query using any other Filter and apply it to a database with a less restrictive Filter (e.g. Entire Method), then your results will be limited to the items enabled in the Filter used to create the Query.

If a group was selected as a starting point in the previous *Select creation mode Dialog Box,* pressing *N*ext takes you to the *Restrict result types Dialog Box* (Section 5.4.6), otherwise you go to the *Restrict input types Dialog Box* (Section 5.4.5).

5.4.5   Restrict Input Types

If you select a model or an object as the starting point for the Query in the *Select creation mode Dialog Box,* then the *Restrict input types Dialog Box* (Fig. 5.7) allows you to restrict the types of models or objects that will be considered for the Query. For instance, if you set the model type to *EPC* and select a whole range of different types of models and run a model-based Query, then only the *EPC* models will be considered. This is not so useful if you manually select items on which to run a Query, but it is very valuable if the source list of items has been generated as a result of a previous *F*ind command or Query.

 Bug – in ARIS 7.02, ticking the Res*t*rict types checkbox in the *Restrict input types Dialog Box* has no effect and all types are used as input, no matter what object or model types may have been selected.

To restrict the search, click on the *Res*t*rict type* checkbox and tick one or more item types. To select all options or to deselect them all, Right-Click > Select *a*ll or Right-Click > *D*eselect *a*ll. If you don't select any items, then all item types will be searched. If you chose a group as your starting point in the previous *Select creation mode Dialog,* then this dialog will not be displayed as groups do not have different types.

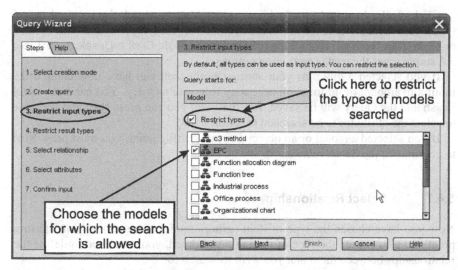

Fig. 5.7 Restrict Input Types Dialog Box

5.4.6 Restrict Result Types

The *Restrict result types Dialog Box* (Fig. 5.8) enables you to choose which type of models or objects will be returned in the list of search results.

If you chose a group or object as your starting point, then you can choose to restrict the type of models or objects to be returned. So for instance you can just display the *EPCs* from a set of returned models.

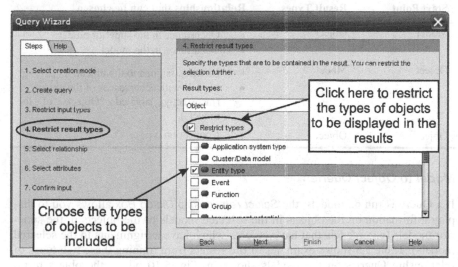

Fig. 5.8 Restrict Result Types Dialog Box

Click on the *Restrict type* checkbox, select *Model* and tick the required model types, then select *Object* and select the required object types. To select all options or to deselect them all, Right-Click > Select all or Right-Click > Deselect all. Table 5.4 summarises the results restriction options.

If you selected a group as your starting point then you have now entered the minimum amount of information necessary to create a Query. You can now select Finish and the Query will be saved. Alternatively you can press Next and continue to select the attributes to be searched (Section 5.4.8).

If you selected a model or an object as your starting point, you must press Next to continue to the *Select relationship Dialog Box*.

5.4.7   Select Relationship

Now you have chosen the type of item (group, model or object) as your starting point and also chosen the type of item to be returned, you now need to define the relationships between them that you wish to search for.

If you have chosen a group as the starting point, the relationship is the models or objects contained in that group and no relationship dialog box will be displayed.

If you have selected a model or an object as your starting point, then there are a number of different possible relationships and the *Select relationship Dialog Box* (Fig. 5.9) allows you to choose the one you want. The type of relationship that can be chosen depends on the combination of models or objects selected so far in the *Query Wizard* as shown in Table 5.4.

Table 5.4 Relationship Selections

Start Point	Result Types	Relationships that can be chosen
Model	Object	• Occurrence in the superior model, • Occurrence in the model.
Object	Model	• Models assigned to the object, • Models with occurrences of the object (incorrectly labelled "Objects of the model").
Object	Object	• Connection types.

Model to Object Queries

If a Query is run on models, the *Select relationship Dialog Box* allows you to display information on the objects in the selected models or the objects in the superior models (e.g. models that have objects which have assignments to the selected models). Table 5.5 shows examples of the results from running these two types of relationship Queries on the models shown in Fig. 5.10 where the object result types are restricted to Functions.

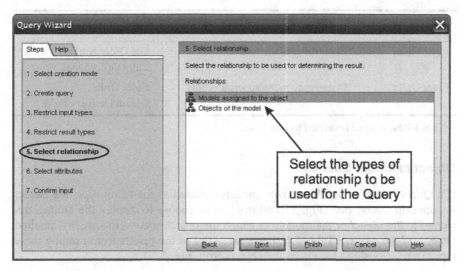

Fig. 5.9 Select Relationship Dialog Box (model results).

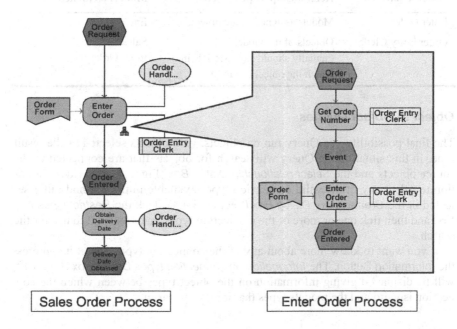

Fig. 5.10 Example of Model-Based Relationship Queries

Table 5.5 Example of Model-Based Relationship Queries

Model Selected	Relationship Type Selected	Objects Returned [Note 1]
Enter Order	Occurrence in the model.	Get Order Number, Enter Order Lines.
Enter Order	Occurrence in the superior model.	Enter Order, Obtain Delivery Date.

Note 1 Results type restricted to Functions.

Object to Model Queries

If a Query is run on an object, with models selected as the result type, the *Select relationship Dialog Box* (Fig. 5.9) allows you to choose to display the *Models assigned to the object* or the models in which the object occurs (incorrectly labelled *Objects of the model*). Table 5.6 shows examples of the results from running these types of relationship Queries on the objects from Fig. 5.10.

Table 5.6 Example of Object Based Relationship Queries

Objects Selected	Relationship Type Selected	Models Returned
Enter Order	Models assigned to the object.	Enter Order
Order Entry Clerk	Objects of the model (actually should say "Models in which the object occurs").	Sales Order, Enter Order

Object to Object Queries

The final possibility is a Query run on objects, with objects selected as the result type. In this situation the Query will search for objects that are connected to the source objects and the *Select relationship Dialog Box* (Fig. 5.11) provides the option to select any of the valid connection types available in the Method Filter selected in the *Create query Dialog Box* (Section 5.4.4). Tick the *Restrict types* box first and then tick one or more of the connection types that you want to use for the search.

If you want to know more about any of the connection types, select it and press the Information Button. The *Information on connection types Dialog Box* (Fig. 5.12) will be displayed giving information on the object types between which the connection is valid and the models types that it may appear in.

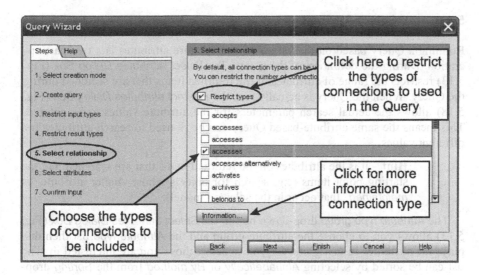

Fig. 5.11 Select Relationship Dialog Box (object results).

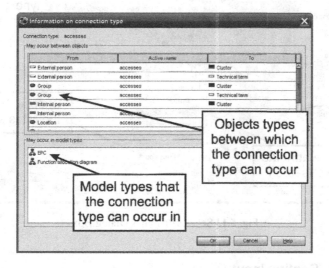

Fig. 5.12 Information on Connection Types Dialog Box

5.4.8   Select Attributes

Running a Query based on the values of one or more attributes is a two-part operation. During the definition of the Query, the *Select attributes Dialog Box* (Fig. 5.13) restricts the range of attributes of the returned items that are searched during the Query. When the Query is actually run, the *Restrict attributes Dialog Box* (Fig. 5.18) allows the actual search parameters for the attribute values to be entered. This means the same attribute-based Query can be re-used to search attributes for different values.

 Hint – it is the attributes on the returned items that are searched, not the starting point items (e.g. search for objects whose *Author* attribute "*is maintained*" that occur in the selected model).

The *Attribute type group* drop-down box in the *Select attributes Dialog Box* (Fig. 5.13) allows you to choose the attribute group and the *Attribute type* list then displays the attributes in that group for you to select those you are interested in. The list can be sorted by selecting *Alphabetically* or *By method* from the *Sorting* drop-down box. Only those attributes enabled in the Method Filter selected in the *Create query Dialog Box* will be shown.

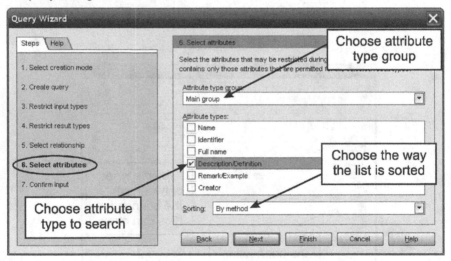

Fig. 5.13 Select Attributes Dialog Box

5.4.9   Confirm Input

You have now completed entering all the information required to define the Query. Pressing F̲inish in the *Select attributes Dialog Box* will save the Query or pressing N̲ext will move to the *Confirm input Dialog Box* (Fig. 5.14) to display a summary of the Query definition. If this is correct you can press F̲inish to save the Query, Cancel to abandon the Query or B̲ack to return and change previous selections.

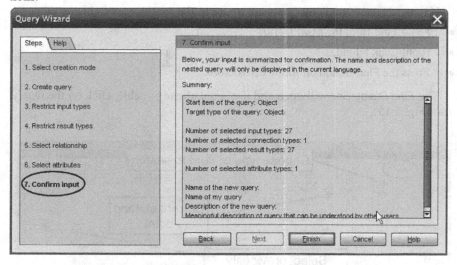

Fig. 5.14 Confirm Input Dialog Box

5.4.10   Editing Queries

You can edit an existing Query by selecting it from the **Queries** folder in the *Administration Module* and doing any of :

- Right-Click > Edit,
- Edit > Query from the *Main Menu*,
- Click the Edit Button on the *Query Toolbar*,
- Double-click on the Query name.

You can step through each dialog box in the *Query Wizard* and press Finish to save any changes. You can copy a Query by selecting the source Query and Right-Click > Duplicate. A copy of the Query will be made with the same name appended by a sequence number (e.g. "*myquery(1)*").

5.4.11   Running a Query

You can run a Query from scratch or on previously selected groups, models or objects. You can select a group, model or object in the *Explorer Module* or a model or object in the *Designer Module.* You can also run a Query based on the results of a previous Find command by selecting items from the results list. You can run a Query based on the results of a previous Query by creating a *Nested Query* (Section 5.5).

Having selected any items you want to use as the starting point, do any of:

- File > Find from the *Main Menu*,
- Right-Click > Find,
- Press the Find Button on the *ARIS Toolbar*.

The *Find Dialog Box* will open and if it's not already visible, click on the *Query Tab* (Fig. 5.15).

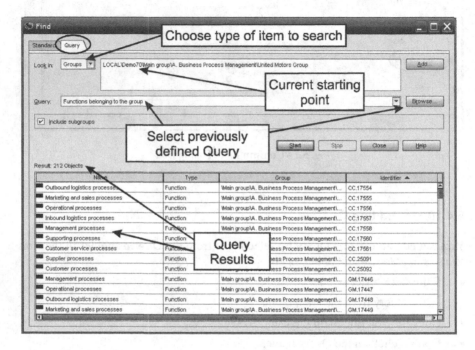

Fig. 5.15 Query Tab

The *Look in* drop-down box allows you to select the type of item (*Group, Model, Object*) you want to use as the starting point for your Query. If you previously selected a group, model or object before running the command, this will have already been set, but you can change it if you wish.

The large white box next to the *Look in* box displays any specific previously selected starting points. You can press the Add Button to the add one or more new items of the type selected in the *Look in* box (see Fig. 5.16 for a models example).

The power of Queries is that you can use the results of a Find command as the starting point of a new Query and run successive Queries to refine the results. You must always ensure that one or more starting points have been defined.

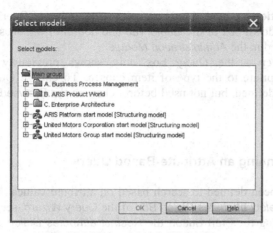

Fig. 5.16 Select Models Dialog Box

Question – how do I remove starting point entries added to the *Look in* box?

Answer – you can delete one or more entries by selecting them and Right-Click > Delete selected items (the option Remove selection undoes all selections).

The *Query* drop-down box allows you to choose a predefined Query. The box only shows previously used Queries that have been defined with the type of item set in the *Look in* box as their starting point (see Section 5.4.3). To choose Queries not used before, click on the Browse Button and select a Query from the *Select search query Dialog Box* (Fig. 5.17).

Press Start and any results will be displayed in the *Result* list in the same way as describe for the Find command in Section 5.2.7.

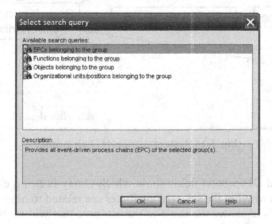

Fig. 5.17 Select Search Query Dialog Box

Question – why do I only see a limited number of Queries in the *Query* drop-down box of the *Query Tab* and not all of the ones that have been defined in the *Administration Module*?

Answer – the *Query* box only shows previously used Queries appropriate to the type of item chosen. To choose Queries that have been defined, but not used before, click on the B̲rowse Button (see Fig. 5.15).

5.4.12   Running an Attribute-Based Query

If a Query has been defined to search based on attribute values (by selecting attributes in the *Select attributes Dialog Box* of the *Query Wizard*, see Section 5.4.8), then after pressing the S̲tart Button the *Restrict attributes Dialog Box* (Fig. 5.18) will be displayed to allow search parameters to be entered.

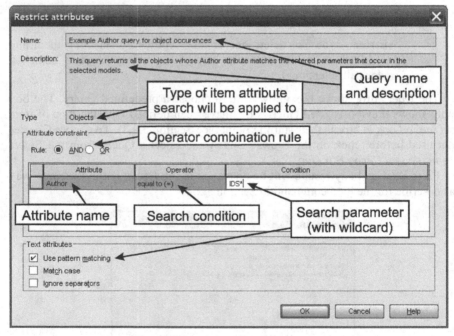

Fig. 5.18 Restrict Attributes Dialog Box

The *Name* and *Description* fields show which Query is being executed and the *Type* field shows whether the selected attributes are related to objects or models.

The *Attribute* field shows the name of the attribute that will be searched and the *Operator* field shows the logical operator that will be used to test the attribute or compare the attribute's value with the entry in the *Condition* field.

Initially the *Operator* is set to *"is maintained"*, but clicking on the entry for any of the listed attributes will reveal a drop-down box with different options depending on the type of attribute (see Table 5.7).

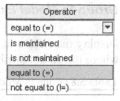

Table 5.7 Attribute Comparison Operators

Operator	Attribute Type
is maintained	Boolean, Date, Duration, Float, Integer, Text, Values
is not maintained	Boolean, Date, Duration, Float, Integer, Text, Values
is true	Boolean
is false	Boolean
equal to (=)	Date, Duration, Float, Integer, Text, Values
not equal to (!=)	Date, Duration, Float, Integer, Text, Values
less than (<)	Date, Duration, Float, Integer
less than or equal to(<=)	Date, Duration, Float, Integer
greater than (>)	Date, Duration, Float, Integer
greater than or equal to(>=)	Date, Duration, Float, Integer

If any of the comparison operators are selected (e.g. *"equal to (=)"*, or *"less than or equal to(<=)"*, etc), you can enter alphanumeric values into the *Condition* field. You can use the <u>U</u>se pattern matching, Match <u>c</u>ase and I<u>g</u>nore separators options as described in Section 5.2.4.

When you have finished setting the attribute search parameters, press OK and the Query will run and any results will be displayed in the *Result* list.

If multiple attributes were selected in the *Select attributes Dialog Box* (Fig. 5.3) when the Query was being defined, then each selected attribute appears in the *Attribute constraint* list linked either by an <u>A</u>ND rule or an <u>O</u>R rule depending on the state of the *Rule* checkboxes.

Attribute	Operator	Condition	
Name	is maintained		AND
Author	is maintained		AND
Description/Definition	is maintained		AND
Identifier	is maintained		

You can change the *Rule* so all the attributes are linked either by an <u>O</u>R or by an <u>A</u>ND, but it is not possible to mix the <u>O</u>R and <u>A</u>ND rules.

5.4.13   Example Queries

The following tables show examples of the settings required in the *Query Wizard* dialog tabs to perform the searches described.

Group to Model Example

Display the *EPC* and *Value-added chain diagram* models in the selected groups, where the author attribute of the models contains the string "IDS Scheer".

Table 5.8 Group to Model Example

Dialog Box	Settings
Select creation mode	• Tick *Create Query*, • Tick *Group*.
Create query	• Enter *Name*, • Enter *Description*.
Restrict result types	• *Result types* = *Model*, • Tick *Restrict types* checkbox, • Tick *EPC and Value-added chain diagram* boxes.
Select attributes	• Tick *Author* checkbox.

Note 1 The *Restrict input type* and *Select relationship* dialog boxes are not used in this scenario.

Note 2 When running the Query, in the *Restrict attributes Dialog Box* set the *Operator* field to "*equal to (=)*" and enter "IDS Scheer*" into the *Condition* field.

Model to Object Example

Display all the Function and *Organisational unit type* objects in the *EPC* and *Value-added chain diagram* models in the selected list of models, where the author attribute of the objects contains the string "IDS Scheer".

Table 5.9 Model to Object Example

Dialog Box	Settings
Select creation mode	• Tick *Create Query*, • Tick *Model*.
Create query	• Enter *Name*, • Enter *Description*.
Restrict input types	• Tick *Restrict types* checkbox, • Tick *EPC* and *Value-added chain diagram* boxes.
Restrict result types	• *Result types* = *Object*, • Tick *Restrict types* checkbox, • Tick Function and *Organisational unit* boxes.
Select relationship	• Select *Occurrence in the model*.
Select attributes	• Tick *Author* checkbox.

Note When running the Query, in the *Restrict attributes Dialog Box* set the *Operator* field to "*equal to (=)*" and enter "IDS Scheer*" into the *Condition* field.

Object to Model Example

Display all the models assigned to the *Organisational unit* objects in the selected list of objects.

Table 5.10 Object to Model Example

Dialog Box	Settings
Select creation mode	• Tick *Create Query*, • Tick *Object*.
Create query	• Enter *Name*, • Enter *Description*.
Restrict input types	• Tick *Restrict types* checkbox, • Tick *Organisational unit* box.
Restrict result types	• Result types = Model, • Do not tick *Restrict types* checkbox.
Select relationship	• Select *Models assigned to the object*.
Select attributes	• Do not tick any boxes.

Note   The results from this Query will not distinguish between models assigned to different *Organisation unit* objects and multiple models assigned to the same object.

Object to Object Example

Display all the *Organisational unit* objects connected to Function objects in the selected list of objects that have the *carries out* or *contributes to* relationship.

Table 5.11 Object to Model Example

Dialog Box	Settings
Select creation mode	• Tick *Create Query*, • Tick *Object*.
Create query	• Enter *Name*, • Enter *Description*.
Restrict input types	• Tick *Restrict types* checkbox, • Tick Function box.
Restrict result types	• Result types = Object, • Tick *Restrict types* checkbox, • Tick *Organisational unit* box.
Select relationship	• Tick *Restrict types* checkbox, • Tick *carries out* box, • Tick *contributes to* box.
Select attributes	• Do not tick any boxes.

5.5   Nesting Queries

We can do a lot with the simple Queries described above, but we can get more value when we *nest* Queries so the output of one Query provides the starting point for the next Query. This is possible provided, we make sure the input type of the following Query is the same as that returned by the first Query. Table 5.12 shows the possible types of output from Queries based on different types of input.

Table 5.12 Query Starting Points and Outputs

Starting Point	Query Output Type
Group	• Models in group, • Objects in group.
Model	• Objects in model, • Objects in superior model.
Object	• Models assigned to object, • Model with occurrences of object, • Objects connected to object.

Based on the starting points and outputs shown in Table 5.12 we can see that we can nest two Queries together with inputs and outputs linked in the following way:

- Group = Model > Model = Object,
- Group = Object > Object = Model,
- Group = Object > Object = Object,
- Model = Object > Object = Model,
- Model = Object > Object = Object,
- Object = Object > Object = Object,
- Object = Object > Object = Model,
- Object = Model > Model = Object.

We can also nest combinations of Nested and simple Queries to build up even more complex sequences of Queries provide we again ensure that the input of the next Query is the same type as the out of the previous Query. Possible complex Query sequences include:

- Group > Model > Object,
- Group > Model > Object > Object,
- Group > Model > Object > Model,
- Group > Model > Object > Model > Object.

Although the Nested Query facility cannot create the diversity of complex Reports that are possible when using ARIS Reports, combining these complex sequences with attribute-based Queries does allow a wide range of practical Queries to be carried out.

The big advantage of Nested Queries is that they produce lists of models and objects on which further commands can be executed.

 Expert Tip – ARIS Help suggests that Queries with attribute restrictions cannot be used in Nested Queries, but in fact this works as you would expect.

5.5.1   Creating Nested Queries

To create a Nested Query we first need to create two single Queries that, when run in sequence, will produce the required output. We then create a new Query as described in Section 5.4.2, but in the *Select creation mode Dialog Box* (Fig. 5.5) we select Nest queries.

Complete the *Create query Dialog Box* (Fig. 5.6) as before, but this time when we click Next we see the *Select first query Dialog Box* (Fig. 5.19).

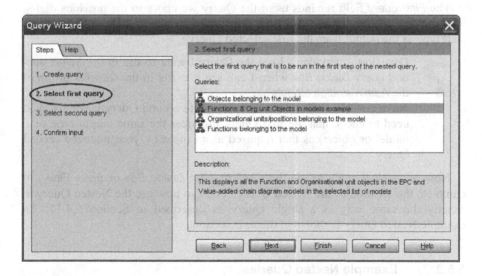

Fig. 5.19 Select First Query Dialog Box

The *Queries* list shows all the previously created Queries with the same start type as we selected in the *Select creation mode Dialog Box*. Select the Query you wish to use and press Next. We now see the *Select second query Dialog Box* (Fig. 5.20).

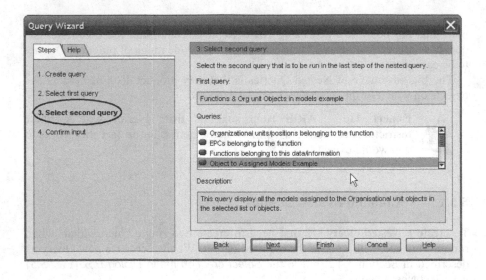

Fig. 5.20 Select Second Query Dialog Box

The *First query* field reminds us of the Query we chose in the previous dialog box and the *Queries* list shows all the previously created Queries with the same start type as the output from the first selected Query.

 Question – why don't I see the Query I want to use in the *Select second query Dialog Box* when I can see it exists in the **Queries** group of the *Administration Module*?

Answer – if you don't see an appropriate second Query in the list, you need to check that the first Query produces the same output type (e.g. model or object) as that required as an input by your intended second Query.

Now press <u>N</u>ext again to see the *Confirm input Dialog Box* or press <u>F</u>inish to complete the creation of the Nested Query. You can now use the Nested Query in exactly the same way as a single Query as described in Section 5.4.11. An example Nested Query is shown in the next section.

5.5.2   Example Nested Queries

Suppose we wish to display all the models assigned to the *Organisational unit* objects in the *EPC* and *Value-added chain diagram* models in a selected list of models, where the author attribute of the *Organisational unit* objects contains the string "IDS Scheer".

The input to this Query is a set of models and the output is a set of models linked via an assignment relationship with the objects in the input set of models. If we look again at Table 5.12, we can see there is no single Query with the correct input and output types and relationships. We therefore need two Queries.

From Table 5.12, we can see that to get an output of the "models assigned to object" we need a Query that starts with a list of objects. To get that list of objects we can also see that we can use a Query that starts with a list of models and uses the "objects in model relationship." This is summarised in Table 5.13.

Table 5.13 Nested Query Example

Query	Starting Point	Relationship	Output Type
First	List of models	Objects in model	List of objects
Second	List of objects	Models assigned to object	List of models

The "*Functions & org units in models example*" summarised in Table 5.9 will provide us with the first Query, listing all the Function and *Organisational unit* objects in the *EPC* and *Value-added chain diagram* models in the selected list of models, where the *author* attribute contains a search string which will be entered when the Query is run.

The "*Objects assigned to models example*" summarised in Table 5.10 will provide us with the second Query, taking the list of Function and *Organisational unit* objects from the first and displaying all the models assigned to the *Organisational unit* objects in the list.

We can therefore use the settings shown in Table 5.14 to produce a Nested Query that will produce the required search. When we run the Query the *Restrict attributes Dialog Box* (Fig. 5.18) will ask us to enter a search string condition for the *author* attribute (e.g. "IDS Scheer").

Table 5.14 Example Nested Query

Dialog Box	Settings
Select creation mode	• Tick *Nest Queries*, • Tick *Model*.
Create query	• Enter *Name*, • Enter *Description*.
Select first query	• Select **Functions & org units in models example**.
Select second query	• Select **Objects assigned to models example**.

5.6   Distributing Queries

5.6.1   Export

Once you have created a Query you can export it and send it to other users or import it onto a shared ARIS Business Server.

To export a Query:

1.   Select the Query in the **Queries** folder of the *Administration Module*,

2.   Right-Click > E<u>x</u>port,

3.   In the *Export query Dialog Box*, enter a name and location on your PC hard drive to save the file.

The Query file will be saved in ".aqu" format.

    Expert Tip – if you export a Nested Query, the individual Queries will automatically be exported as well; you don't have to separately export them.

5.6.2   Import

To import a Query into a **LOCAL** database or onto a shared ARIS Business Server:

1.   Select the **Queries** folder of the *Administration Module*,

2.   Right-Click > <u>I</u>mport,

3.   Browse to the location of an ".aqu" format file on your PC hard disk,

4.   Choose if you want *Overwrite <u>q</u>uery* if a Query of that name already exists,

5.   Press OK.

The Query will now be saved in the **Queries** folder of the *Administration Module*.

Chapter 6   Model Generation

This chapter describes Model Generation and shows how it can be used to create end-to-end process models directly from a set of horizontally linked models and how to generate hierarchical models from sets of assigned models.

6.1   Introducing Model Generation

An ARIS model is not just a drawing, but a representation of the information contained in the underlying ARIS Repository (database). Each time we place an object in a model, a definition of the object is made in the database along with a reference to its occurrence in the model. If we include the same object in other models, the definition is not copied, but the occurrence list is updated to show the additional use of the object. The same is true for the connections between objects; a definition is made in the database with pointers to the occurrences of the connection.

It is this concept that enables the concept of Model Generation to work. This allows us to choose one or more ARIS models and, using the objects in those models, generate a completely new model. The source models can be of the same type, or a mixture of types. The type of the target model is chosen from a list defined by the ARIS Method and depends on the type of source models chosen. For instance we can generate an *EPC* that represents an end-to-end process from a set of horizontal *EPC* sub-process models or we can generate a *Function tree* from a set of hierarchically assigned *EPCs*.

Executing the Generate model command causes ARIS to look at each object occurrence in the source models. Provided the ARIS Method allows the object type in the target model, one occurrence of the object is placed in the target model. ARIS then looks up the definitions of the target model objects in the database and identifies all the relationships defined between each target model object and all the other target model objects. These may be connections defined in models or they may be other sorts of relationships, for instance, *assignment relationships* or *implicit relationships*.

Provided these relationships can be shown using connection types allowed in the target model, ARIS creates occurrences of those connections in the model. Finally, the new model is automatically arranged in accordance with the layout algorithm defined for that model type.

Model generation therefore creates a new view of information already held in the ARIS repository. No new information (e.g. new objects or connections) is created; the new model just reflects a view of all information contained in the database for the objects present in the chosen source models and the relationships previously defined between them. However, the view is constrained by the representation of the information allowed in the target model type.

As well as generating a model from a set of chosen source models, we can also generate a model from a set of objects selected in the *Explorer Module*. The principle is the same with an occurrence of each of the source objects being placed in the target model.

We can also choose to only include relationships (connections) in the generated model that are present in the source models rather than all relationships defined in the entire database. This is often more appropriate, especially in large databases where there may be multiple versions of models with different connections.

6.2   Using Model Generation

6.2.1   Generating Models from Other Models

Although model generation sounds complicated, it is actually quite easy to use:

1.   In the right-hand pane of the *Explorer Module* select some or all of the required source models,
2.   Right-Click > Generate model.

The *Model Generation Wizard* will now appear. The *Select source models Dialog Box* (Fig. 6.1) allows you to confirm the source models you have chosen. You may remove a selected model by clicking the Remove button to delete it from the list, or you can choose additional models for inclusion by clicking the Add. button and choosing models from the *Add items Dialog Box*.

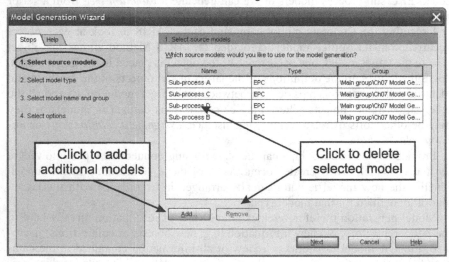

Fig. 6.1 The Model Generation Wizard

When you are satisfied you have the correct set of source models, click Next. The *Select model type dialog box* (Fig. 6.2) will allow you to select the target model type using the familiar ARIS House model chooser.

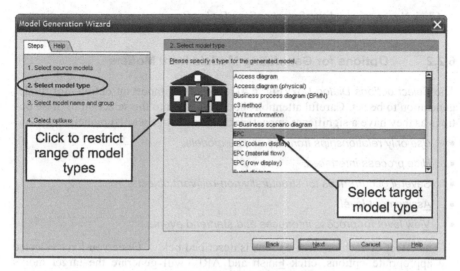

Fig. 6.2 Select Model Type Dialog Box

Click Next again and in the *Select model name and group Dialog Box* (Fig. 6.3) enter a name for your model and select the group in which you wish to save it.

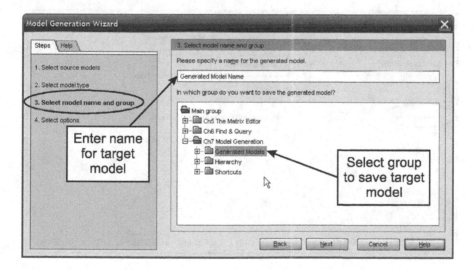

Fig. 6.3 Select Model Name and Group Dialog Box

Hint – it is recommend you name the generated model so it is clear that it is a generated model and maybe also save it in a specific directory for generated models.

Click <u>N</u>ext again and the *Select options Dialog Box* appears (see next section).

6.2.2   Options for Generating Models from Models

The *Select options Dialog Box* (Fig. 6.4) allows five important options for model generation to be set. Careful attention should be given to the selection of these options as they have a significant impact on the resultant generated model:

- *<u>U</u>se only relationships from the source models,*
- *Hi<u>d</u>e process interfaces,*
- *Several <u>o</u>ccurrences for structurally non-relevant objects,*
- *<u>A</u>ssignment level,*
- *<u>V</u>iew level for process interfaces and start/end events.*

The effect of each of these options is described below. Once you have selected the appropriate options, click <u>F</u>inish and ARIS will generate the target model based on the selected source models. The amount of time taken to do this will vary considerably depending on the number of source models chosen and the complexity of their object relationships. Very large and complex generations may take as long as an hour.

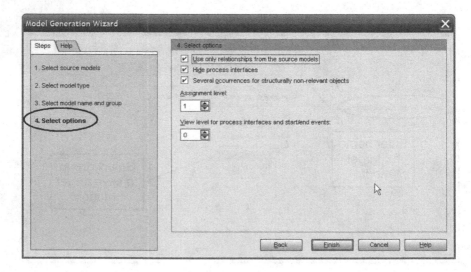

Fig. 6.4 Select Options Dialog Box

Use Only Relationships from the Source Models

When a model is generated from a set of source models, ticking the *Use only rela-tionships from the source models* option allows only the relationships defined in the source models to be used in the target model, rather than all relationships de-fined in the database. This is a very useful option because it allows you to control exactly what relationships you will see in the target model. If you don't set this option, then any relationship between the chosen objects defined anywhere in the database may be used. Often you may have different versions or releases of mod-els; you may have models used for testing, *'what-if?'* analysis models, or many other models that are not really part of your core set of models. Without the *Use only* option set, you may inadvertently include many undesirable relationships from these other models.

Hint – select the *Use only relationships from the source models* option to limit generated relationships to just those from the source models.

Warning – generated models are models in their own right. If you generate a model and then make changes to the source models, the original objects and connections are still present in the generated model. Delete generated models no longer required and select the *Use only relationships from the source models* to ensure only the correct objects and relationship appear in any new generated models.

Hide Process Interfaces

If you have chosen to use *Process interface* objects (in addition to Events) to link between horizontally related *EPCs* (see Section 6.5.2), then these will be included in an *EPC* generated from them and shown attached to the side of the appropriate Events. Fig. 6.5 shows an example model generated from four sub-process models (A, B, C and D). If you don't want to see *Process interface* objects, then tick the *Hide process interfaces* box.

Hint – when first generating an end-to-end process model from a set of sub-processes, uncheck the *Hide process interfaces* option so that you can see the *Process interface* objects and use them to show the bounda-ries between the assembled processes. Once you are happy the models are correctly linking together, set the *Hide process interfaces* option so the *Process interfaces* will no longer be shown.

Warning – the *Hide process interfaces* option only works for *Process interface* objects that are occurrences of Functions that were created in a *Superior model* and that had the sub-process models assigned to them (see Section 6.5.2). If you create new *Process interfaces* in the sub-process models, and assign the adjacent model in the chain to them, then the *Hide process interfaces* option has no effect.

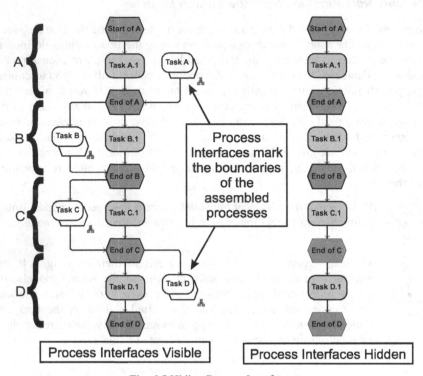

Fig. 6.5 Hiding Process Interfaces

Several Occurrences for Structurally Non-relevant Objects

This option is used to control how *structurally non-relevant* objects (e.g. *Organizational unit type*, *Technical term*, etc) appear in the generated model. Unlike Functions and Events, there maybe multiple occurrences of these objects in the source models. For instance, it is usual to associate an *Organizational unit type* object representing a 'department' to each of the Functions it applies to, rather than to have one object and have multiple links to all the Functions.

Normally, the Generate model command places a single occurrence of each object found in the sources model into the target model and then connects them up with the appropriate relationships. This would produce a single object for the 'department' and multiple connections leading to a model that is difficult to understand (Fig. 6.6a).

Setting the *Several occurrences for structurally non-relevant objects* option ensures separate occurrences of objects such as *Organizational unit types* are used wherever they are needed (Fig. 6.6b).

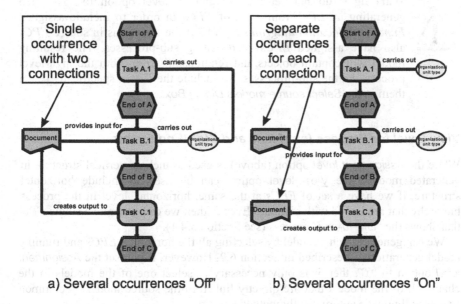

a) Several occurrences "Off"   b) Several occurrences "On"

Fig. 6.6 Several Occurrences for Structurally Non-relevant Objects

Assignment Level

This option allows objects from models assigned to objects in the source models to be included in the generated target model. The default option of "0" only includes the selected source models, but setting the option to "1" includes all models assigned to objects in the source models and so on up to a maximum of five levels of assignment.

The use of the Assignment level option is typically used to generate models that show vertical, hierarchical structure from a set of models linked through assignment relationships. For instance generating a *Function tree* from a set of hierarchically linked *EPCs* (see Section 6.3.2), an *Application system type diagram* from other linked *Application system type diagrams* and similarly for *Organizational charts*.

Generating an *EPC* from a set of existing *EPCs* that also have assigned *EPC* sub-process models and with the *Assignment level* option set to anything other than "0" will not produce sensible results. The generated model will have all the objects and relationships from the top-level process as well as those from the sub-process models. Generating an *EPC* from other *EPCs* only makes sense with the *Assignment level* set to "0" and when the source *EPCs* are a set of horizontally linked models at the same level of the process hierarchy (see Section 6.4.1).

Warning – do not set the *Assignment level* option to "1" when generating an *EPC* from a set of *EPCs* in order to include assigned *Function allocation diagrams* (*FADs*) if the Functions in source *EPCs* also have assigned *EPCs* representing sub-processes. The resulting model will contain objects and relationships from both the high-level process and the sub-processes. To include the *FADs*, specifically select them in the *Select source models Dialog Box*.

View Level for Process Interfaces and Start/End Events

While the *Assignment level* option (above) is used to include vertical structure in generated models, the <u>V</u>iew level option can be used to include horizontal structure. If we have a set of *EPCs* at the same, horizontal, level in the process hierarchy that are linked with common Events, then we can generate a single *EPC* that shows the "*end-to-end*" process (see Section 6.4.1).

We can generate such a model by selecting all the horizontal *EPCs* and running model generation as described in Section 6.2. However, if you set the *Assignment level* option to "1", then it is only necessary to select one of the models in the chain. All of the models that are directly linked to the source model by common Events will now be automatically included.

Hint – you may be tempted to think that setting the *Assignment level* option to"1" would only include objects from adjacent models and that to include other models in the chain you would need to progressively increase the value. However, setting the value to "1" is sufficient to include all linked models. The purpose of setting the *Assignment level* option to a value greater than "1" is unclear.

Warning – if any of the Functions in a chain of linked *EPCs* models has a sub-process model assigned to it, and if that model has included Events from the superior model (the correct way of modelling), then do not use the *Assignment level* option = "1" to generate an end-to-end *EPC*. If you do, you will find that the model will also include the sub-process models as the Generate <u>m</u>odel command will assume they should be included because they share common Events. Instead, select all the of the required *EPC* source models in the *Select source models Dialog Box*.

6.2.3   Generating Models from Objects

Generating a model from selected objects proceeds in similar way to that described in the previous section, but the starting point is a set of objects, selected in the *Explorer Module*. This time a *Select source objects Dialog Box* (Fig. 6.7) allows you to confirm and select the set of source objects.

Expert Tip – it is not possible to select a mixture of models and objects as the source for the Generate model command, but you can accomplish this by creating a dummy model containing the chosen objects and including this as one of the source models.

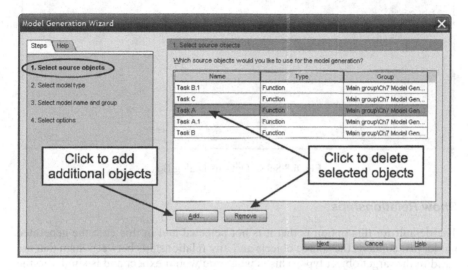

Fig. 6.7 Select Source Objects Dialog Box

After selecting the appropriate objects, click Next and proceed to the *Select model type Dialog Box* and *Select model name and group Dialog Box* as described above. A different set of options for model generation are used when objects are the source as described in the next section.

6.2.4 Options for Generating Models from Objects

The *Select options Dialog Box* (Fig. 6.8) show three options for generating models from objects:

- *Show relationships,*
- *Several occurrences for structurally non-relevant objects,*
- *Display level.*

The *Several occurrences for structurally non-relevant objects* option is the same as that described in Section 6.2.2 for generating from models, but the other two options are specific to model generation from objects.

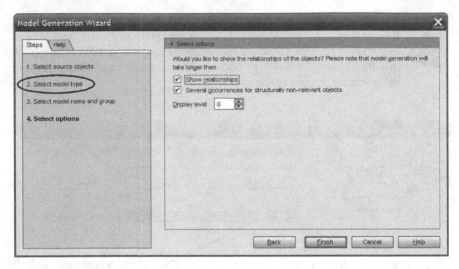

Fig. 6.8 Select Options Dialog Box

Show Relationships

The default for this option is that it is not selected and in this case the generated model just contains the source objects and any relationships between them that are valid in the target object type. This is what you would expect and is similar to the *Use only relationships from the source models* when generating from models.

When the *Show relationships option* is selected, ARIS looks for any additional relationships between the source objects and other objects in the database and includes occurrences of these additional objects and their relationships in the target model.

 Warning – the *Show relationships option* has no effect unless the *Display level* (see next section) is set to a value greater that zero.

Display Level

This option controls how many levels of indirection the *Show relationships* option uses to display connected objects. It only becomes active when the *Show relationships* option is selected and the default value of "0" is equivalent to deselecting the *Show relationships* checkbox (see Fig. 6.10a for an example *Function allocation diagram* generated from the object **Task B.1** in Fig. 6.9 with *Display level* = "0").

Setting the level to "1" displays the source objects and their connections, plus any additional objects in the database that are connected to the source objects and their additional connections (see Fig. 6.10b). This is provided the objects and connections are valid in the chosen target model type.

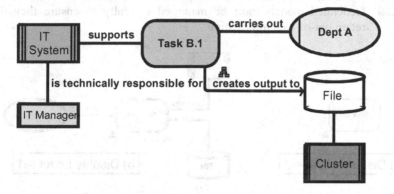

Fig. 6.9 Example Function Allocation Diagram

Setting the level to "2" checks the additional objects for other objects in the database that are connected to them and also includes these further objects and their relationships (see Fig. 6.10c). You can increase the level up to "5" to 'walk through' the database finding further objects and their connections.

The effect of running this type of model generation becomes very dependent on the relationship types allowed in the target model.

 Expert Tip – when generating models using the _Display level_ option set to values greater than zero, it is usually best to remove the tick in the _Several occurrences for structurally non-relevant objects_ checkbox. This may need some experimentation to get the best results.

6.2.5   Managing Generated Models

Although generated models create alternative views of existing database contents, they are also valid models in their own right. All the objects and connections shown in the generated model will already have occurrences in other models, but now additional occurrences will be created in the generated model. If the objects and connections in the source models are changed, the original object and connection definitions will remain in the database by virtue of their existence in the generated model. Reorganisation of the database will not delete them so to remove out-of-date objects and relationships the generated model must be deleted. If required, a new model can be generated to reflect the changes made in the source models.

Having many models defining the same information is always dangerous from a change management point of view, so generated models should be used with caution.

Warning – generated models are complete models in their own right. By their very nature they duplicate information in other models. Generated models must be managed carefully to ensure they don't retain out-of-date information.

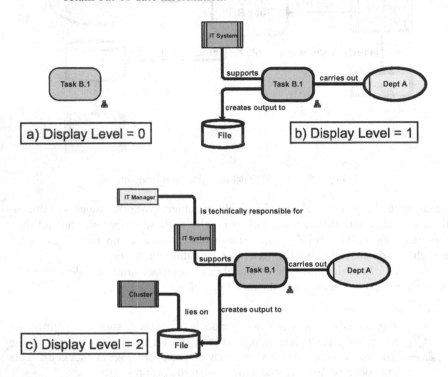

Fig. 6.10 Display Level Setting Example

The Generate model command should be used sparingly, for very specific purposes and only when you are clear how the generated models will be managed as part of your overall database structure.

6.2.6   Model Generation from Shortcuts

The set of source models used with the Generate model command can initially be selected in the *Explorer Module*. The selection can be optionally extended or reduced using the *Select Source Models Dialog Box* (Fig. 6.1) in the *Model Generation Wizard*. However, each time you execute the command you have to go through the same selection process which, if you have many source models or they are widely distributed across the group structure, can be tedious and repetitive.

Hint – to create a repeatable definition of source models for use with the Generate model command, create a new group and in it place shortcuts to all the required models.

ARIS shortcuts are pointers to models located anywhere in the group structure. If you create shortcuts in the same group for all the models from which you want to generate a model they can be easily used to refer to the source models. You simply select all the models in the group and Right-Click > Generate model. You can create different shortcut groups for different Generate model command definitions.

To create a shortcut:

1. Create a new group in the *Explorer Module*,

2. Select one or more existing models from other groups in the *Explorer Module*,

3. Select Right-Click > Copy,

4. Return to the shortcut group,

5. Select Right-Click > Paste as,

6. Select Shortcuts.

A set of shortcuts will be created in the new group pointing to the chosen models.

Expert Tip – as well as the models pointed to in the shortcut group, you can also add additional objects to the source for the Generate model command by creating a model containing the chosen objects and including this in the shortcut group.

6.3 Generating Vertical Views of the Hierarchy

Although we can navigate a hierarchy of models both horizontally and vertically, it takes considerable mental effort to try and visualise the structure of a complex set of hierarchical models. Instead, we can use different ARIS model types to view various horizontal and vertical slices through the hierarchy. We may produce some of these models manually, as part of the modelling process, but the real value of ARIS becomes apparent when we use the Generate model command to generate new views from the existing structure.

6.3.1 The Function Hierarchy and the Function Tree

The assignment of an *EPC* to a Function in a high-level model automatically creates a "*process-oriented superior*" relationship between the high-level Function and all the Functions in the sub-process. This type of relationship is an *assignment relationship*. If you create multiple levels of model assignments, a hierarchy of these relationships will be created. We can model and view these relationships using the *Function tree* model.

The *Function tree* shows a static view of the Function hierarchy, as opposed to the hierarchy of assigned *EPCs* that shows a dynamic view. That is to say, it just shows how a Function is broken down into sub-tasks without any consideration of process flow.

Fig. 6.11 shows an example of a *Function tree* with four levels of hierarchy. At the point where the **Level 3 B** Function decomposes to three **Level 4** Functions, the model automatically changes from a horizontal layout to a vertical layout. This option helps produce easy-to-read diagrams.

 Expert Tip – the level at which the layout orientation changes can be set by the *Change to vertical layout* field in the *Layout Wizard*. The default for this setting can be set in View > Options [Model / For new models / Layout]. In the *Layout Procedure* drop-down box, select **Hierarchy** and change the value in the *Change to vertical layout* box (the default is 2).

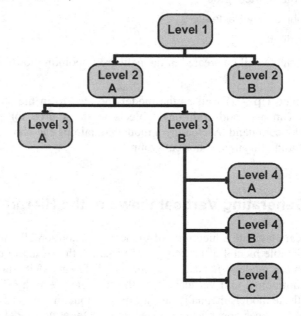

Fig. 6.11 The Function Tree Model

When you connect Functions together in the *Function tree* you will be given a choice of one of three relationship types:

- *is process-oriented superior,*
- *is execution-oriented superior,*
- *is object-oriented superior.*

Process-oriented means the Functions are all associated with the same process, albeit at different levels of detail. *Execution-oriented* means the Functions all do the same type of task, for instance 'planning' or 'data entry'. *Object-oriented* means all the Functions are associated with processing the same thing (typically a data object).

The relationship "*is process-oriented superior*" is created automatically between Functions in a hierarchy of assigned *EPCs*. Section 6.3.2 shows how to automatically generate a *Function tree* showing these relationships.

6.3.2   Generating a Function Hierarchy

Now we have learnt how to use the Generate model command, we can use it to generate a *Function tree* from a hierarchy of assigned *EPCs* such as that shown in Fig. 6.12. This shows a high-level process and four sub-processes. Let us also assume that the high-level process is itself assigned to a Function in a top-level model; for instance in a *Value-added chain diagram* (*VACD*). This gives us a three-level hierarchy. There are now several different ways we can generate the *Function tree*.

Generate From All Models

The standard way (and safest way) is to:

1.   Select the *VACD*, the high-level *EPC* and the four sub-process *EPCs* in the Explorer Module,
2.   Right-Click > Generate model,
3.   Select *Function tree* as the target model type.

The generated model with have all the Functions from the *VACD* and the hierarchy of Functions below it.

Generate Based on Assignment Hierarchy

We can simplify the generation by just selecting the top-level *VACD* and setting the Assignment level so that the lower-level models are automatically included:

1.   Select just the *VACD*,
2.   Right-Click > Generate model,
3.   Select *Function tree* as the target model type,
4.   Set the Assignment level = "2".

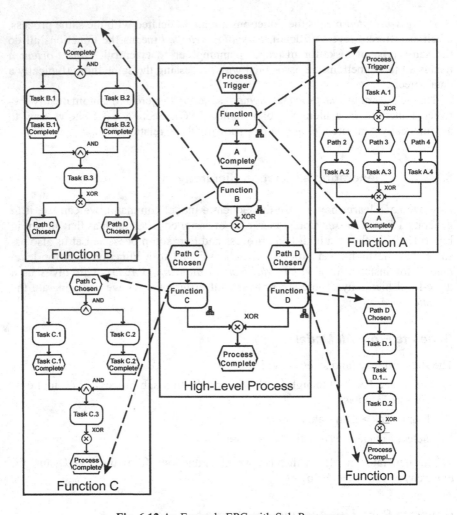

Fig. 6.12 An Example EPC with Sub-Processes

Generate Based on Object Hierarchy

We can also generate a *Function tree* based on objects using the *Display level* option to include the object hierarchy:

1.   Select the **High-Level Process** object in the *Explorer Module*,
2.   Right-Click > Generate model,
3.   Select *Function tree* as the target model type,
4.   Tick *Show relationships*,
5.   Set *Display level* = "2".

The Generated Function Tree

Whichever approach you choose. the Generate model command will now create a *Function tree* looking like that shown in Fig. 6.13. At the top of the model we see the **High-level Process** Function and beneath it we see the Functions from the high-level process model (**Function A, Function B**, etc.). Beneath those we see the Functions from the sub-processes. Using either of the first two methods for generating the model described above would also include any other Functions present in the *VACD*.

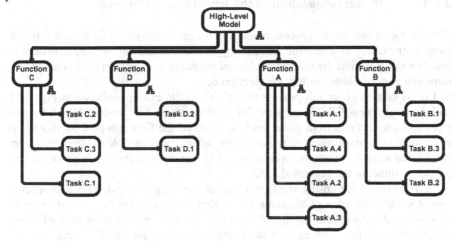

Fig. 6.13 Generated Function Tree Example

 Warning – the order that the Generate model command lays out objects (horizontally or vertically) is determined by the layout algorithm and internal settings such as the order in which you created the objects. It is not necessarily the order that you might choose yourself (e.g. in alpha-numerical sequence).

If the models shown were part of a more complex database of interlinked models, then using the *Assignment level* and *Show relationships* options of the Generate model command might introduce other objects and relationship that you didn't intend. In which case using the first method is the safest.

 Hint – the safest way to ensure your generated model only contains the objects and relationships that you want is to directly select all the models or objects that you wish to include, select the *Use only relationships from the source models* option and don't use the *Assignment level* and *Show relationships* options.

I hope you can see that being able to generate such a model automatically from a previously created hierarchical structure is extremely useful. It acts both as a check that you have created the hierarchy correctly and, more importantly, as a way of viewing the functional breakdown of the processes. You don't have to generate the model for the entire hierarchy; by choosing a more limited set of source models you can generate *Function trees* for just some levels.

6.4   Horizontal Views of the Hierarchy

6.4.1   Model Generation of the End-to-End Process

Generating an end-to-end process model from a set of linked *EPCs* is probably the most valuable use to which the Generate model command can be put. In order for this to work it is vital the models are linked correctly using common Events. For a reminder about linking models, see Section 6.5.

Let us take the four sub-process models from the example shown in Fig. 6.12 and generate a new *EPC* from them. This will create an *EPC* containing all the objects and connections from those models. Each of the four sub-process models is consistent in its own right, so provided we select the *Use only relationships from the source models* option, we would expect to see each of those sub-processes reproduced intact in the generated *EPC*.

In addition, if we ensure the Event that is the trigger Event for a sub-process model is an occurrence of the same Event that is the outcome of one of the sub-process models to which it is linked, then the Generate model command will only place one occurrence of each *structurally relevant* object in the target model. Functions, Events and Rules are structurally relevant, so only one occurrence of each Event will be placed in the target model. Because the linking Events have occurrences and connections in the two adjacent sub-processes, both sub-processes will be seamlessly connected together through the common Event. If we have built our segmented models correctly, then all the sub-processes will connect together into one, seamless, end-to-end process.

Fig. 6.14 shows all of the four sub-process models generated into a complete end-to-end process. If there are *Function allocation diagrams* assigned to the Functions in the sub-processes, then the objects and relationships from these can also be included in the generated end-to-end process by including them as source models.

 Warning – do not set the *Assignment level* option to "1" when generating an *EPC* from a set of *EPCs* in order to include assigned *Function allocation diagrams* (*FADs*) if the Functions in source *EPCs* also have assigned *EPCs* that represent sub-processes. The resulting model will contain objects and relationships from both the high-level process and the sub-processes. To include the *FADs*, specifically select them in the *Select source models Dialog Box*.

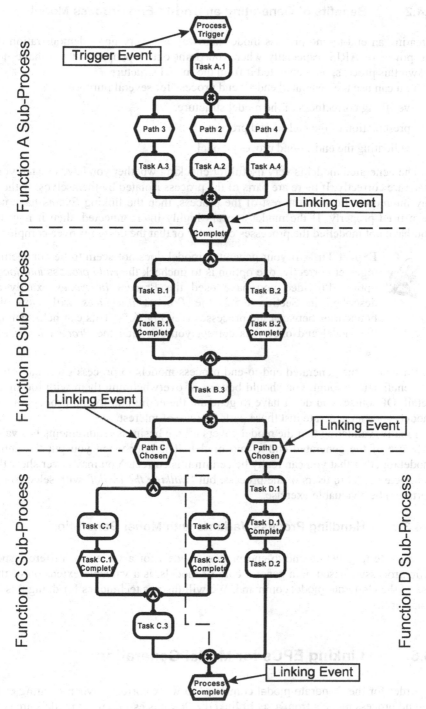

Fig. 6.14 A Generated End-to-End Process

6.4.2   Benefits of Generating an End-to-End Process Model

Creating an end-to-end process model this way is a very good demonstration of the power of ARIS, especially when you point out to people that you have not drawn this process, but generated it from the model structure.

You can use the generated end-to-end process for several purposes:

- verifying correctness of the model structure,
- presentation of the end-to-end process,
- validating the end-to-end process model.

The generated model is very useful for checking whether you have created your structure correctly. If there are parts of the process isolated by themselves, without any interconnections to the rest of the process, then the linking Events have not been used properly. If the model appears highly interconnected, then it may be you have not modelled the processes correctly or that the design is over-complex.

Expert Tip – if your generated model does not seem to be connecting together correctly, one option is to uncheck the *Hide process interfaces* option. Provided you have used the *Process interfaces* exactly as described in Section 6.5.2, the *Process interfaces* will show the boundaries between the processes (see Fig. 6.5). This can help 'debug' the model and once it is correct you can hide the *Process interfaces* again.

Presenting the generated end-to-end process models to process users can often be beneficial, although you should beware of overwhelming them with too much detail. Of course, you don't have to generate the entire end-to-end process in one model; you can generate just those parts that are of interest.

Finally, validating that the model covers all the business requirements is a valuable use of the generated end-to-end model. It is only when you put the entire model together that you can really be certain it is correct. You may never show the complete model to users of the process, but '*walking the model*' with selected experts can be a valuable exercise.

6.4.3   Handling Process Variants with Model Generation

Being able to generate end-to-end process models for a variety of different specific processes, based on a generic core of models, is a valuable extension of the use of the Generate model command. We will discuss techniques for doing this in Chapter 8.

6.5   Linking EPCs for Model Generation

In order for the Generate model command to work correctly when creating end-to-end process models from a set of linked *EPCs* it is essential the models are correctly linked. Models are linked using common Events and, optionally, *Process interface* objects.

6.5.1   Linking Models Using Events

When creating models of complex and large processes it makes sense to split the model into a number of smaller models that are easy to manage and understand. However, we still want to indicate that the component models form part of an overall end-to-end process and that they are directly linked to one another. The way we do this is to use a common Event that represents the outcome of one process and the trigger for the next.

In the example shown in Fig. 6.12, we can see the last Event in the sub-process for **Function A** is **A Complete**. We can also see the start Event for the **Function B** sub-process is also **A Complete**. Similarly, the **Function B** sub-process has two end Events (**Path C Chosen** and **Path D Chosen**) that link to the **Function C** and **Function D** sub-processes and we can see these Events also appear at the start of the appropriate sub-processes.

By using these common Events we can generate an end-to-end process model as described in Section 6.4.1 and shown in Fig. 6.14. It is important to use an *occurrence copy* of the same object in the connecting models. If you use two different objects, but with the same name, there is no link between the models and the Generate model command will not link the models together.

 Warning – do not be tempted to copy an Event occurring in the middle of a process flow in one model and re-use it in another model. If you do, you are effectively linking the two models together in an incorrect way. Instead use different Events and give them slightly different names.

If you look again at the high-level model in Fig. 6.12 you will notice there is an **XOR** Rule, after **Function C** and **Function D** before the final **Process Complete** Event. If you look in the **Function C** and **Function D** sub-process models you will also see the same Rule, but with only one connection. This may look strange a first sight and seem to go against normal modelling conventions, however it is necessary in order for model generation to work correctly.

If we were to just connect **Task C.3** to the **Process Complete** Event in the **Function C** model, and connect **Task D.3** to the **Process Complete** Event in the **Function D** model, then the generated model would show the two Functions directly connected to the end Event without any Rule. Remember, the objects in the generated model are only those from the source, sub-process models. In order for the Rule to appear, and be connected correctly, it must be placed in both sub-processes as shown. It is essential the corresponding Rules in the sub-process models are *occurrence copies* of each other. It does not matter if they are *occurrence copies* of those in the high-level model, but it is probable easier if they are.

6.5.2   Linking Using the Process Interface Object

Readers who have used other modelling or drawing tools will be familiar with the concept of an 'off-page connector'. The connector is a symbol indicating the drawing of the process model continues on a separate sheet.

There is an equivalent symbol available in ARIS called the '*Process interface*'. However, in ARIS we create more than just drawings, and we can use the *Process interface* object to represent the process the common Event links to as shown in Fig. 6.15. This gives a more visual indication of the connecting models in the horizontal structure and avoids the need to look at the occurrences of the linking Event.

Expert Tip – if you use the *Process interface* to connect models, your models will fail the `StructureRules.sem` *Semantic Check* if the "*Each path must begin and end with an event*" rule is chosen. Instead choose the "*Each path must start and end with an event or a process interface*" rule.

There are two different ways you can use *Process interface* objects to link models. These are described below. The *Process interface* does not play any direct part in the creation of an end-to-end model using the Generate model command, but it does affect how the model appears.

Process interface

Process Interface as Functions from Superior Models

IDS Scheer recommend the approach shown in Fig. 6.15. The superior or top-level model has Functions (**Function A**, **Function B**, etc) which have the sub-process models assigned to them. The *Process interface* objects in the sub-process models are *occurrence copies* of the Functions from the top-level model with their symbols changed from Functions to *Process interfaces*.

Hint – to change the symbol of a Function to a *Process interface*, select the object and Right-Click > Properties [Format / Object appearance]. Select the *Process interface* symbol from the *Symbol* drop-down box.

Because the *Process interface* objects are *occurrence copies* of the Functions they retain their assignments to the appropriate sub-process models. You can therefore navigate from one sub-process to the adjacent one by double-clicking the assignment icon on the *Process interface*.

If you generate an end-to-end *EPC* using models linked in this way you can control whether the *Process interfaces* appear in the generated model (Fig. 6.5) by using the *Hide process interfaces* option in the *Select options Dialog Box* (Fig. 6.4) as described in Section 6.2.2.

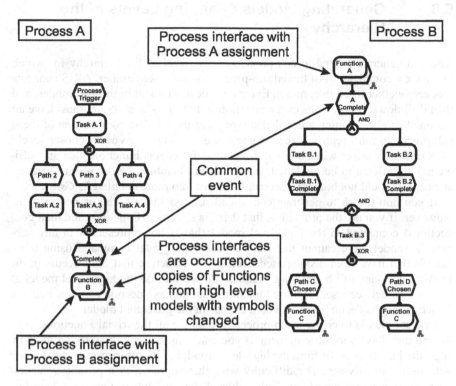

Fig. 6.15 Linking Using the Process Interface

Separate Process Interface Objects in Source and Target Models

An alternative way of using *Process interface* objects to that described above, is to not to re-use Functions from the superior model, but create new *Process interface* objects whenever you need them. Using this approach you will have to manually assign the appropriate sub-process model to the *Process interface*, but the advantage is that you can give the *Process interface* more meaningful names (e.g. "TO: Manufacturing Process" or "FROM: Order Handling Process"). This can be very useful in large complex models with many interconnections between processes.

If you generate an end-to-end *EPC* using models linked in this way, the *Hide process interfaces* option will not work and the *Process interfaces* will always be shown in the generated model. However, you can manually delete them if you wish.

6.6　　Generating Models Spanning Levels of the Hierarchy

You can generate an end-to-end process at any level of the hierarchy for which you have a complete set of linked sub-process models. Remember, ARIS connects models together through common Events; it doesn't look at high-level models and then drill down. This means every Function in the high-level model must have an assigned *EPC* containing a detailed sub-process model. The combination of these sub-processes must represent the complete end-to-end process at the chosen level.

A difficulty arises when the high-level model contains Functions that are sufficiently significant to be modelled, but trivial in operation. Under normal circumstance, we would not bother to decompose them into more detailed *EPCs*.

If you don't wish to generate end-to-end process models, this is not an issue. However, if you do, the problem is that there is structure (Functions and their connections) contained in the high-level model that is not represented in any sub-process models. We cannot just run the Generate model command using those models that have been decomposed because the structure that only occurs in the high-level model will be missing. Neither can we include the high-level model as a source model because, for those Functions that do have decompositions, both the Function and its decomposition would appear in the generated model.

One solution is to create a sub-process model for all the trivial Functions, even though they have very little in them. If you can't think of anything to put in them, copy the Function down from the high-level model to its sub-process model along with its linking Events. The difficulty with this approach is it produces decomposed models which are of very little value. If there are lots of these, and very few detailed models, then it becomes tedious to find out which sub-process models are worth looking at.

6.6.1　　The Linking Diagram

A solution to the problem of generating models where some of the detail has not been modelled at the chosen layer of the hierarchy is to create what I call a '*linking diagram*'. This model contains the missing structure and is included as one of the set of source models for the Generate model command.

The linking diagram is simply a copy of the high-level model with those Functions that have decomposed sub-process models deleted. When it is included as a source model it provides the detail and connections for those Functions that don't have sub-process models. It doesn't need to include those Functions that have been decomposed because their sub-process models will be included as source models. They will be correctly linked into the 'linking diagram' through the 'linking' Events. To make this work it is essential to ensure the linking Events and any associated Rules in the sub-process models are *occurrence copies* of those in the high-level model.

To demonstrate this, consider the high-level model and its associated decomposed models shown in Fig. 6.12. Let us assume that, instead of having all four high-level Functions decomposed, we only have decomposed models for **Function A** and **Function D**. To create a linking diagram, we take an *occurrence copy* of the high-level model (Fig. 6.16a) and delete **Function A** and **Function D**. The result is shown in Fig. 6.16b. It looks rather strange, but this is not important because we will only use it with the Generate model command.

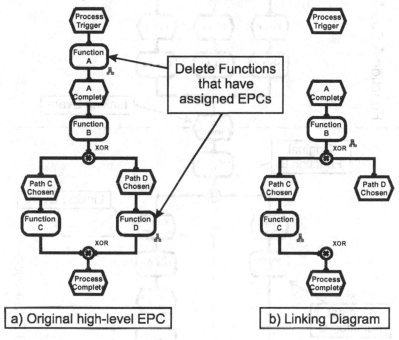

a) Original high-level EPC   b) Linking Diagram

Fig. 6.16 Creating a Linking Diagram

We now run the Generate model command with the linking diagram and the **Function A** and **Function D** sub-process models as source models. The result is shown in Fig. 6.17. We can see that it is the high-level model with **Function A** and **Function D** replaced with the detail from their sub-process models. You may wish to compare this with the complete end-to-end process generated from all four sub-process models shown in Fig. 6.14.

What we have effectively done by using the linking diagram is to generate a model that spans (and mixes) more than one level of the hierarchy. This can be a useful technique when you want to show a model with just a few elements of it expanded into more detail. However, do remember that the linking diagram is a copy of part of the original high-level model and hence duplicates some of it. Treat it like you would a generated model. Clearly label it and delete it when it is no longer required. If the high-level model changes and you wish to generate a new model, then first you will need to make a new linking diagram from a copy of the new high-level model.

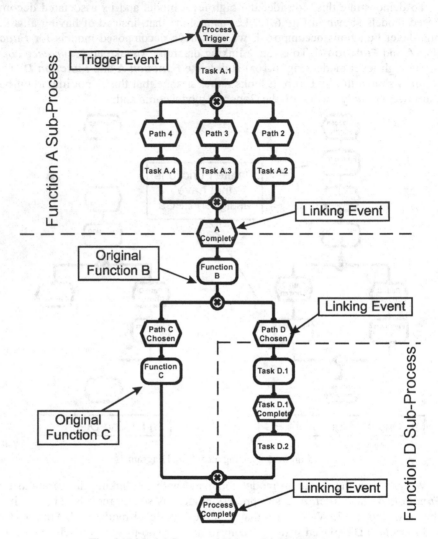

Fig. 6.17 Model Generated Using a Linking Diagram

Chapter 7   Modelling in Rows and Columns

This chapter introduces the concept of modelling using swim-lane models and describes the row and column EPCs. It discusses the benefits and trade-offs with this approach, and looks at how to use Model Generation to transfer models back and forwards to standard EPCs. A brief introduction is given to the Process Chain Diagram and the e-Business Scenario Diagram.

7.1   Row and Column Models

7.1.1   Modelling in Swim-lanes

A process modelled in rows or columns is often known as a 'swim-lane model', so called because it resembles a bird's eye view of a swimming pool divided into different lanes (see Fig. 7.1).

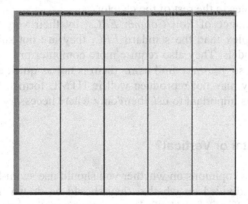

Fig. 7.1 A Swim-lane Model

The model is divided into rows and columns where each row or column represents a different *Organizational unit type* or a different *Application system type* (or maybe both). The model is drawn so the parts of the process executed by each organisation or system are confined to the appropriate row or column. In this way it is easy to see how different organisations execute the process and, more importantly, where the process is handed from one organisation to another. Many complex processes are inefficient due to the large number of organisation hand-offs, each of which adds delay, cost, and provides opportunity for error to creep in. Modelling in this way enables the hand-offs to be quickly visualised and the process optimised to reduce them. The relationships these rows or columns represent can be selected by the user (see Section 7.2.6).

7.1.2   When to Use a Swim-lane Model

Opinions tend to be divided over the use of swim-lane models. Some people want to use them for everything while other people never use them at all. In practice, the swim-lane is a specialised model and should only be used for specific purposes to which it is suited. By default, you should normally use the standard *EPC* for process modelling, but consider using a swim-lane model:

- to show high-level process execution,
- to model organisation hand-offs,
- to perform '*what-if?*' analysis on organisational structure,
- to understand the IT systems supporting processes,
- to model the interface between processes.

There are two main swim-lane models in ARIS:

- *EPC (column display)* – vertical swim-lane model,
- *EPC (row display)* – horizontal swim-lane model.

The operation and use of these two model types is exactly the same and will be referred to as *Row/Column EPCs*. For convenience I shall use the *EPC (column display)* for the examples in the rest of the chapter.

Because the appearance of *Row/Column EPCs*, by their very nature, makes them look more complex than the standard *EPC*, they are not suitable for very large and complex models. They also require more computer processing power to draw and manipulate, so you may find using them is not as quick as the standard *EPC*. In addition, they may not reproduce well in HTML format. So, while they can be very useful, it is important to use them only where necessary.

7.1.3   Horizontal or Vertical?

Just as there are divided opinions on whether you should use swim-lane models at all, opinions are also divided on whether they should be drawn horizontally or vertically. Experience has shown that when creating complex process models a vertical layout is easier to understand and manipulate, and the same recommendation applies for swim-lane models. However, many people like to draw a high-level swim-lane model horizontally so it represents the business process flowing from left to right. For instance, customer orders arrive at the left-hand side and deliveries are shown on the right-hand side. Used in this way, the high-level swim-lane model is used in a similar way to the *Value-added chain diagram* and can be used as the top-level model in a process hierarchy. This is fine provided the model is high-level and is relatively simple. As soon as it becomes more complex it is better to use the vertical approach. In addition, horizontal swim-lane models tend to produce short and wide models, which are difficult to print and do not reproduce well in HTML format.

7.1.4   Row/Column EPCs in a Model Hierarchy

It is possible to create a hierarchy of *Row/Column EPCs* by assigning them to Functions in exactly the same way as you would for standard *EPCs*. You can also assign a standard *EPC* to a Function in a *Row/Column EPCs*, and vice versa. In this way, you can swap between the swim-lane approach and a standard approach at any level. Used well, swim-lane models can add clarity and show detail not readily visible in other models. However, by their very nature, they quickly become more complex than standard models, so they should be used sparingly. Remember a key principle:

"Keep it simple – clever models often confuse."

7.2   The Row and Column EPC

7.2.1   The Layout of a Row/Column EPC

Fig. 7.2 shows an example of an *EPC (column display)*. The *EPC (row display)* is exactly the same, but is laid out horizontally rather than vertically. Throughout this chapter we will look at the *EPC (column display)*, but everything is equally applicable to the *EPC (row display)*, you just need to transpose all the concepts from vertical to horizontal.

At the top of each column is a *header cell*. In the header cell are one or more organisation or system resource objects (e.g. *Organizational unit type* or *Application system type*). The label for the row in which the header cell sits shows which objects may be put in the header cell. It is difficult to read in Fig. 7.2, but it says: *Organizational elements & Application system*. Each column has a label showing the relationship type that the object in the header cell has with the objects in the main part of the column. In the example we can see the first two columns are labelled *Carries out & Supports*, and the third is labelled *Decides on*. We can select the relationship we want to use when we add new columns (see Section 7.2.6). In the main part of each column are fragments of the process model.

The meaning of this display is quite straightforward:

- **Function A**, in the first column, *"is carried out by"* **Organization A**,
- **Function B**, in the second column, *"is carried out by"* **Organization B** and *"supported by"* the **Application System Type**,
- **Function C**, in the third column, *"is decided on"* by **Organization B**.

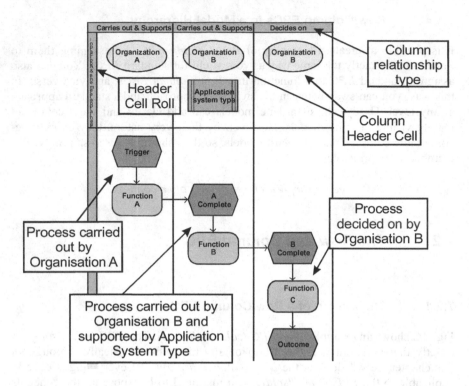

Fig. 7.2 A Column EPC

So, by placing part of the process in a particular column, a relationship is automatically made between the objects in the header cell and the Functions in that column. The effect is the same as connecting the objects in the header cell to each one of the Functions in that column. Therefore, when a large number of Functions need to have the same relationship with the same resource object, using a *Row/Column EPC* is much quicker than connecting them all manually in a standard *EPC*.

There is no relationship between the object in the header cell and the Events or Rules in the column; only with the Functions. Typically, the trigger Event for a Function is located in the same column as the Function. When a *Row/Column EPC* is generated from a standard *EPC*, this is the style of layout that will be used. However, you can manually drag an Event into a different column, if you wish, and the automatic layout algorithm will keep it associated with that column.

You can adjust the width of the columns or the depth of the header cell row; hover your mouse over the border between the labels of the columns or rows. When the *Drag Icon* appears, Left-Click and drag the border to the required location.

7.2.2   The Implicit Relationship

The relationship made between the object in the header cell and the Functions in the column is slightly different from the relationship made by connecting the object directly to the Function in a standard *EPC*; it is an *implicit relationship*. All this means is that it is made *implicitly*, by virtue of being in the same column, rather than by being made by a direct connection. It makes little difference to the way the relationship is viewed or used. If we select **Function B** and look at the *Relationships Tab* in the *Properties Bar*, we will see the display shown in Fig. 7.3.

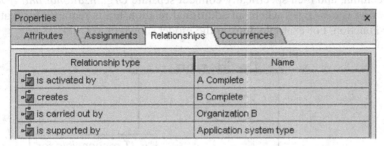

Fig. 7.3 Column EPC Relationships

This is exactly what we would expect to see; **Function B** has relationships to the Events connected to either side of it and to **Organization B** and to the **Application System Type**.

The type of implicit relationship made between the object in the header cell and the Function in the column depends on the type of object and the relationship type operating for that column. Column 2 is labelled *Carries out & Supports*. So if we put an *Organisational unit type* in the header cell, it will have a *"carries out"* relationship with the Function. If we put an *Application system Type* object in the header cell, it will have a *"supports"* relationship with the Function. Column three is labelled *Decides on*. So if we put an *Organisational unit type* in the header column, it will have a *"decides on"* relationship with the Function. However, if we put an *Application system type* in the header cell, no relationship will be made to the Function, because no relationship for that object type has been selected for that column.

7.2.3   Multiple Relationships in Row/Column EPCs

By placing a resource object in the header cell we automatically create a relationship between that object and every Function in the column using the relationship defined for that column. However, we may also want to establish additional relationships between other resource objects and specific Functions. We can easily do this by placing the resource object in the main area of the column and specifically connecting it the Function. Because the object is not in the header cell, it will have no implicit relationship defined and hence it can be connected in just the same way as you would using a standard *EPC*.

ARIS 7 – in earlier releases of ARIS it was not possible to create multiple relationships to individual Functions in a *Row/Column EPC*. Any resource object placed in a column would automatically have a relationship with every Function, irrespective of whether the object was in the header cell or not. In ARIS 7, only objects in the header cell have implicit relationships, thus allowing multiple relationships to be established to resource objects placed in the main area of the column.

So we can use the column to define relationships that apply to all the Functions in the column, and then specifically connect separate *Organizational unit types* or *Application system types* where an additional relationship is required for that particular Function. For example, look at the model shown in Fig. 7.4.

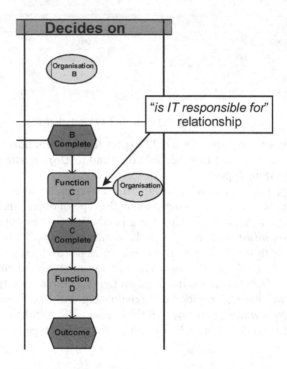

Fig. 7.4 Multiple Relationships in Column EPCs

There is now an additional Function (**Function D**) in the *Decides on* column and a new *Organisational unit type* object, **Organization C**, connected to **Function C** with the "*IT responsible for*" relationship. This now defines that **Function C** and **Function D** are both "*decided on*" by **Organization B**, but in addition, **Organization C** is also "*IT responsible for*" **Function C**. We can confirm these relationships have been created by looking at the *Relationships Tab* in Fig. 7.5.

Properties	✕
Attributes \ Assignments \ **Relationships** \ Occurrences	

Relationship type	Name ▼
is activated by	B Complete
creates	C Complete
is under IT responsibility of	Organization C
is decided by	Organization B

(a) Function C

Properties	✕
Attributes \ Assignments \ **Relationships** \ Occurrences	

Relationship type	Name ▼
is activated by	C Complete
creates	Outcome
is decided by	Organization B

(b) Function D

Fig. 7.5 Displaying Multiple Relationships in Column EPCs

7.2.4   Modelling Multiple Systems

You may wonder why the standard relationship for a column is labelled *Carries out & Supports*. This is useful when you want to show, at the same time, both the system (e.g. *Application system type*) and the organisation (e.g. *Organizational unit type*) associated with the same part of the process. You can place objects of both types in the header cell (see Fig. 7.2) and, at the same time, automatically establish implicit relationships to the Functions in the column (see Fig. 7.6).

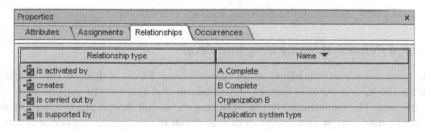

Properties	✕
Attributes \ Assignments \ **Relationships** \ Occurrences	

Relationship type	Name ▼
is activated by	A Complete
creates	B Complete
is carried out by	Organization B
is supported by	Application system type

Fig. 7.6 System and Organisation Relationships

If you want to add relationships to show particular Functions are supported by additional *Application system types*, place the objects in the main body of the column and connect them directly to the Function as we saw in the previous section.

 ARIS 7.1 – in the next release of ARIS separate columns will be available for the "*carries out*" and for the "*supports*" relationships.
ARIS 7.1

7.2.5   Modelling Other Resources in Row/Column EPCs

You can place any resource objects in the main part of a *Row/Column EPC* and connect them to Functions in the usual way. Thus you can model data, documented knowledge, risks, etc, as you would normally. However, in general, you should be wary of using these objects in *Row/Column EPCs*. The swim-lane format is intended to show the relationship of the process to organisation and systems, and these additional relationships are best put in a *FAD* in the normal way.

 Question – why is an implicit relationship not established between the Functions in a *Row/Column EPC* and the *Documented knowledge* object I have put in the header cell?
Answer – rows and columns can only be added with implicit relationship types valid for system (e.g. *Application system type*) and organisation (e.g. *Organizational unit type*) objects. Other objects placed in the header cell will not define any implicit relationships.

7.2.6   Changing Implicit Relationships

We can change the implicit relationship between a Function and the resource objects in the header cells in several ways:

- Drag the process fragment into another column,
- Put different resource objects in the header cell,
- Add a new column with a different implicit relationship.

Change Relationships by Drag and Drop

The main benefit of modelling using *Row/Column EPCs* is that we can quickly change the allocation of resources (organisation and systems) to various parts of the process. This is particularly useful during the initial design phase where these decisions may change frequently, or during 'what if?' analysis. To change the implicit relationship of part of the process, select the appropriate objects (e.g. the Functions with their associated Rules and Events) and drag them into the column representing the relationship you want. You can drag and drop objects from single or from multiple columns.

Hint – if you select multiple objects and drag them into a narrow column, you may find ARIS re-sizes all the objects to make the arrangement fit into the column. To avoid this, make the target column much wider than the width of the group of selected objects so they will fit without re-scaling.

If you view the relationships for the Functions you have moved you will see they now have the implicit relationships represented by the new column.

Warning – once you save a *Row/Column EPC* the implicit relationships will be saved in the database. If you then move a Function from one column to another, save the model and then look at the *Relationships Tab* you will see the implicit relationships from the old column will be visible as well as those from the new column. The old relationships will not disappear until the database is reorganised.

Changing the Object in the Header Cell

If we want to change the resource relationship for the complete process fragment modelled in an entire column, we can simply delete the current object from the header cell and replace it with a new one. This is a very quick way to make organisation changes. You can also place additional resource objects into the header cell to define multiple relationships to all Functions in the column.

Adding Rows and Columns with Different Implicit Relationships

When a new *Row/Column EPC* is created, it will automatically contain rows or columns labelled *Carries out & Supports*. Once a row or column exists, its implicit relationship type cannot be changed. If you require a different relationship you must create, a new row or column with the required relationship. For instance, to add a new column with a different relationship:

1. Right-Click on the column label,
2. Select Add column/row from the pop-up menu,
3. Select the relationship type from the *Select Column* dialog box (Fig. 7.7),
4. Click OK.

A new column with the chosen relationship type will be inserted to the right of the column you initially selected.

You can also add a new row into an *EPC (column display)* using a similar procedure, this time right-clicking on the row label. You will only be offered one type of row to create: *OrgElements/Application System*. This effectively adds another row of header cells and you may find this useful if you need to have multiple objects in your header cells. The same principle applies for adding a new column to an *EPC (row display)*.

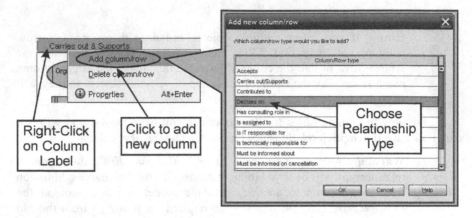

Fig. 7.7 Add New Column

Deleting Rows and Columns

To delete a row or column:

1.   Right-Click on the header label,
2.   Select Delete column/row from the pop-up menu.

If the row or column is empty it will be deleted straight away. If it contains objects you will first be given a warning message and asked to confirm that you wish to delete the objects. Click Yes and the objects will be deleted and then the row or column will be deleted.

7.2.7   Row and Column Properties

Rows and columns have properties which you can view by selecting the row or column header label and Right-Click > Properties. The *Row/Column properties Dialog Box* allows you to select the *Colour* of the dividing line (the 'lane' of the 'swim lane') and its line *Style* (e.g. *solid*, *dotted*, *dashed*). You can view the effect using the Preview button or save it by clicking OK.

 Hint – changing the *Colour* or line *Style* in the *Row/Column properties Dialog Box* affects the dividing line at the bottom of a row or the right-hand side of a column.

 Bug – the effect of selecting multiple rows and columns and changing the *Colour* or line *Style* in the *Row/Column properties Dialog Box* seems to be unpredictable.

7.2.8   Automatic Layout of Row and Column EPCs

The automatic layout facility is available for *Row/Column EPCs,* but it is constrained by the definition of the rows and columns. To layout a *Row/Column EPC* do either of:

1.   Arrange > Layout from the *Main Menu,*
2.   Right-Click > Arrange > Layout.

The *Layout procedure* field in *the Layout Dialog Box* (Fig. 7.8) shows that the *Models as column/row display* algorithm will be used for layout. You can change the normal *Minimum object spacing* settings as well as selecting the *Minimize connection anchor points* and *Insert space using part layout* options.

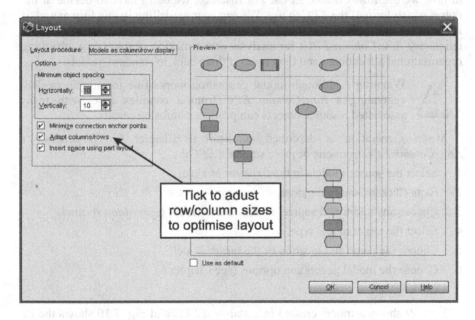

Fig. 7.8 The Layout Dialog Box

In addition, the algorithm has an *Adapt columns/rows* option. If the *Adapt columns/rows* option is not selected, the layout algorithm will fit the layout into the column widths currently set. If the box is selected, the layout algorithm will expand or contract the width of the columns to optimise the layout.

 Bug – if you connect resource objects (e.g. *Application system type* or *Organizational unit type*) directly to Functions and use the automatic layout facility, you will find the resource objects will all be collected to the top of the column underneath the header cell.

Because of the nature of *Row/Column EPCs*, the layout of complex models can become very confusing and highly interconnected. *Row/Column EPCs* work best when a single system or organisation handles several consecutive steps in a process. If a different unit does every step, and each unit does many steps widely distributed throughout the process, then the display will be very confused. Such processes are better modelled in a standard *EPC*.

7.2.9   Model Generation and Row/Column EPCs

We can automatically generate *Row/Column EPCs* from standard *EPCs*, or a row *EPC* from a column *EPC* and vice versa. This gives us a great deal of flexibility in how we use *Row/Column EPCs*. For instance, we don't have to decide at the outset which form of the *EPC* to use. We can start modelling in one format and, if it doesn't seem appropriate, transfer to a different format. We can also generate temporary *Row/Column EPCs* for analysis or for making changes (e.g. changing organisational allocations) and then convert them back to standard models.

Warning – although model generation works fine for simple models, generating a *Row/Column EPC* from a complex *EPC* with many associated resource objects can produce confusing results.

Model Generation is described in detail in Chapter 6. To generate a *Row/Column EPC* from one or more standard *EPCs*:

1. Select the source models in the *Explorer Module*,
2. Right-Click > Generate model,
3. Choose any additional source models in the *Model Generation Wizard*,
4. Select the target model type,
5. Choose the name and location of the target model,
6. Choose the model generation options (see Chapter 6),
7. Click Finish.

Fig. 7.9 shows a model created in a standard *EPC* and Fig. 7.10 shows the result of using the Model Generator to convert it to a *EPC (column display)* (the layout has been adjusted very slightly to allow the figure to fit on the page). Converting the *EPC (column display)* back into a standard *EPC* creates exactly the same model as originally shown in Fig. 7.9.

You will notice the Model Generator seems quite sensible in the way it uses both columns and direct connections. Of course, with very complex models, the results may not be as neat.

Hint – if you generate a *Row/Column EPC* from a standard *EPC* with assigned *FADs*, but don't include the *FADs* as source files, the relationships in the *FAD* will not be taken into account and all of the model will be placed into a single column.

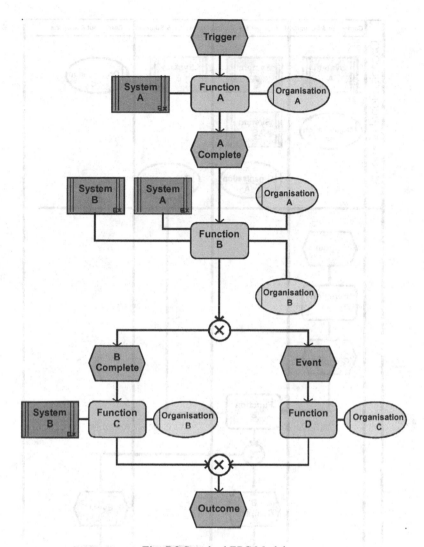

Fig. 7.9 Standard EPC Model

It is recommended you do not manually create models in row or column format. Always create a standard *EPC* and, when needed, use the Model Generator to create a *Row/Column EPC* as needed. That way you will:

- benefit from the rigour of modelling using standard *EPCs* and *FADs*,
- not be tempted into poor quality modelling in swim-lane format,
- have the flexibility to generate other model types as needed.

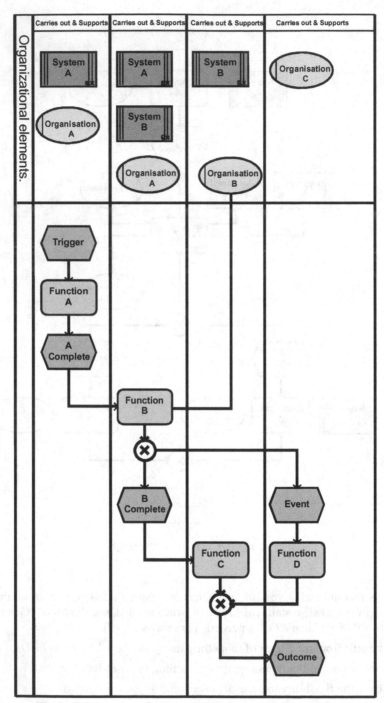

Fig. 7.10 Generation of a Column EPC from a Standard EPC

Expert Tip – when generating a *Row/Column EPC* from a standard *EPC* with a large range of resource objects, take a copy of the original model and delete any types of resource object you don't absolutely need in the *Row/Column EPC*. This way the generated model will not be over-complicated.

7.3   Specialised Row/Column Models

Many of the more specialised models in ARIS also use the row/column format. Below is a brief introduction to two of them: the *Process chain diagram* and the *e-Business scenario diagram*. It is also possible to use the standard *Row/Column EPC* in other ways, and in Section the *EPC (column display)* is used to model systems interfaces.

7.3.1   The Process Chain Diagram

The *Process chain diagram (PCD)* is a form of *EPC (column display)*. However, instead of the columns just representing different organisations or system allocations, they contain the different object types that appear in the model. Fig. 7.11 shows an example of a *PCD* generated from the standard *EPC* shown in Fig. 7.9. The first column contains all the Events, the second column contains Functions, the third *Application system types* and the fourth *Organizational unit types*. The exact allocation of columns will depend on the objects present in the model. The model is also divided into rows representing the parts of the process carried out by the *Organizational unit type* whose object is shown in the organisation column.

The *PCD* can provide a very useful way of visualising a process and the resources needed to deliver it. It works well with straightforward, linear models, but becomes too confusing with very complex models. However, because it can be generated from other *EPC* models, it is easy to generate a *PCD* to see if it adds any value.

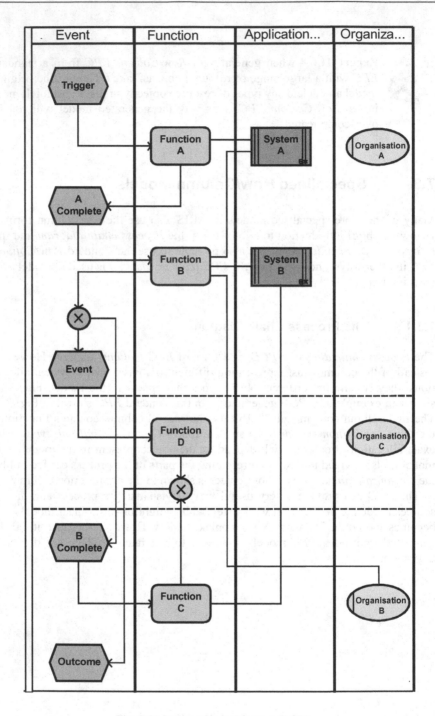

Fig. 7.11 Process Chain Diagram (PCD)

7.3.2   E-Business Scenario Diagram

The *e-Business scenario diagram* is a model introduced as part of the development of ARIS to support the creation of e-Business applications, but it may have other uses. The model allows the interfaces to be defined between different businesses collaborating in an end-to-end e-Business solution. However, it can be used to model the interfaces between any collaborating organisational entities, whether e-Business or not.

Fig. 7.12 shows a *"Vehicle Sales and Distribution"* e-Business scenario diagram. Each column in the model represents a different business unit participating in the process, indicated by the *Organisation unit type* object in the header cell. The main objects in the model (green in ARIS itself) represent the key business processes (they are in fact Functions). The round business document objects (red in ARIS) represent the interfaces between the key business processes in the different organisation.

Attached to the business process objects are employee role (*Person type*) objects representing people who play a key role in the business interface.

Information carrier objects are also available to represent the media by which the business documents are passed from one organisation to another. Data models can be assigned to the business document objects to provide a precise and detailed definition of the information that passes between the businesses.

7.3.3   Column EPC for Modelling Systems Interfaces

We can use the *EPC (column display)* for other purposes. A frequent requirement is the need to model the interfaces between co-operating IT systems. People often talk about "systems interfaces" and "systems talking to one another". Of course, in reality, the IT systems merely implement processes (albeit in software) and it is those processes that interact with one another.

Fig. 7.13 shows an *EPC (column display)* used to model the interaction between three different IT systems. Each system runs its own process and the processes interact via data messages passed between the systems using an electronic message format.

A column has been created for the process running on each system (**System A, System B** and **System C**). In between are columns representing the interfaces between **System A** and **System B**, and **System B** and **System C**. The data transferred between the systems is represented by *Entity type* objects (**A-B Data Flow**, etc). These are attached to *File Information* carriers (**A-B Message**, etc) which represented the actual message format.

In the top part of the model, the process running on **System A** passes a message to **System B**, which translates it and passes it on to **System C**. Now **System C** processes the message and, if successful, sends a message back to **System B** which passes it on to **System A**. If the process on **System C** fails, then a failure-handling mechanism is initiated on **System C**, and in the original full model, failure messages were sent back to **System A**.

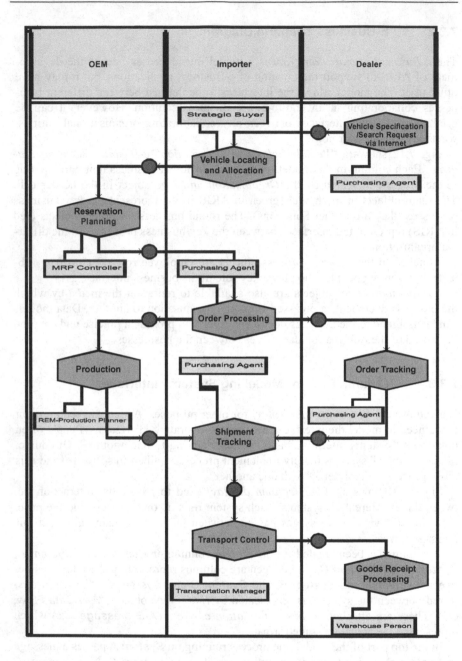

Fig. 7.12 e-Business Scenario Diagram

In the real application from which this example was taken, the electronic message mechanism had a set of standard formats that were re-used for different data messages. An *eERM attribute allocation diagram* was assigned to each *Entity type* to represent the data passed from one system to another. Another data model, the *Relations diagram*, was assigned to the *File Information carrier* to show how the data passed over the interface was actually mapped into the specific fields in the standard electronic message format.

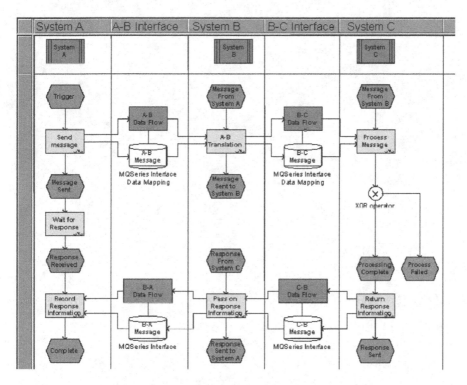

Fig. 7.13 Modelling Systems Interfaces in a Column EPC

Modelling the systems interface in this way had several benefits. The nature of the data interface between the processes could be modelled in detail. The way the processes interact as a result of the data interchange could be directly seen, along with the failure modes. Also the Functions in the message-passing processes (e.g. **A-B Translation** on **System B**) could be decomposed further to show the exact nature of the data translation taking place.

By using some imagination, the power and variety of ARIS models can be harnessed to model situations for which there are no specific ARIS models provided.

Chapter 8   Modelling Process Variants

This chapter looks at how to avoid creating 'stovepipe' processes and how to take account of variety within processes using variants. It describes how to use Model Generation to generate a complete end-to-end process for any set of process variants.

8.1   Avoiding Stovepipes

In most practical situations we don't have a single process to model, but a whole variety of different processes and different versions of those processes. In order to create the most efficient and cost-effective business we want to use a common approach wherever possible; only creating different specific processes when absolutely necessary. However, in practice this is hard to achieve. For instance, what often happens is that different teams are given responsibility for designing processes for different products. Because it takes extra effort for them to talk to their colleagues, find common ways of working and share 'best practice', they create a completely new design from scratch. These new designs are often called 'stovepipes', because instead of the processes fitting within an existing process hierarchy each product has its own, narrowly focused and distinct process hierarchy or stack. These vertical *stovepipe* process stacks resemble the tall thin smokestacks of old-fashioned wood burning stoves.

If every process team creates stovepipe processes, the business is prevented from achieving the economies of scale that result from sharing common processes and having flexible staff deployment. Moreover, customers do not see a single seamless organisation, but get a different experience depending on which part of the business they contact.

Instead of creating stovepipe solutions, we want to create a process hierarchy that promotes reuse, allows flexibility, but manages and contains that flexibility. We can do this in ARIS by using a number of techniques including *variants*.

8.2   Modelling Variety

Let us imagine we have a high-level process for selling, manufacturing, delivering and invoicing vehicle products, as shown in Fig. 8.1. We have four types of product (Car, Van, Bus and Truck) and let us assume they are reasonably complex, but are based on a set of common underlying components.

Ideally, we would like each of the four sub-processes shown in the high-level model (**Sell Product, Manufacture Product,** etc) to be exactly the same for each of the four product types. To try and achieve this, we start by modelling a generic set of sub-processes and assigning them to the Functions shown in the example *EPC*. We make sure the generic processes link together using common start and end Events.

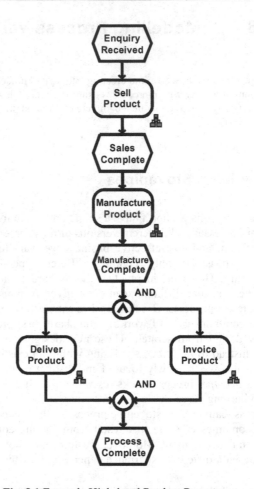

Fig. 8.1 Example High-level Product Process

Let us further imagine that, as the detailed design work progresses, we find the components for trucks are very specialised. We can't use the generic manufacturing process to produce them, but have to set up a separate unit with its own processes. We also find that each product has a totally different set of delivery requirements, so we need a different version of the delivery process for each product. To add to the complexity, buses are sold to a highly regulated industry. Therefore, we have to set up separate sales teams to follow the specific tendering and contract procedures defined by this industry.

Table 8.1 shows the variety of sub-processes we now require to implement this example situation. Our goal of having a completely generic approach and a common process structure is now beginning to look rather impractical. However, all is not lost; modelling in ARIS can help. Because we have modelled our processes in a hierarchical way, our high-level process model (Fig. 8.1) can remain generic. The variability occurs at the more detailed level in the assigned models. Therefore we can model each different version (or *variant*) of our sub-processes in a separate *EPC* and assign them to the high-level model.

Table 8.1 Sub-process Variants Example

	Car	Van	Bus	Truck
Sales	Generic	Generic	Bus-Specific	Generic
Manufacture	Generic	Generic	Generic	Truck-Specific
Delivery	Car-Specific	Van-Specific	Bus-Specific	Truck-Specific
Invoicing	Generic	Generic	Generic	Generic

However, what we might be tempted to do is create four process hierarchies; making a copy of the high-level model for each product and linking the required sub-processes for that particular product to the appropriate high-level Functions. This would work, but it is leading us towards a stovepipe approach and is unnecessary. In ARIS we can assign any number of *EPCs* to the same Function so using this capability we can keep one generic high-level model and to each of the high-level Functions we assign a generic version of the sub-process, plus all the varieties of the sub-process needed for the specific versions of the products.

8.3 Creating Multiple EPC Assignments

To create multiple assignments: select the Function in the high-level *EPC* and Right-Click > Assignments. In the *Assignments Tab* of the *Properties Dialog Box* click New and use the *Assignment Wizard* to assign a new *EPC* to the Function. This will create an *EPC* with the same name as the Function and place it in the chosen ARIS group. We can then repeat the action for as many assigned models as required. Subsequent assigned *EPCs* will have the same name as the Function, but with a sequence number appended (e.g. "Sell Product" and "Sell Product(1)"). Now we rename each of the assigned models representing the different sub-processes (Right-Click > Rename in the *Explorer Module*) to a name representing the particular variant (e.g. "Sell Product" becomes "Sell Bus").

It is also best to create new groups for each of the high-level operations (**Sell Product**, etc.) to hold the generic model and each of the product-specific variant models. You can create the groups beforehand, and then choose the appropriate group when creating and assigning the model, or create all the assigned models in the same group and move them afterwards. Moving assigned models has no effect on the assignment link; ARIS updates the link automatically to reflect the new location of the model. The group structure to support the process variants identified in Table 8.1 now looks like that shown in Fig. 8.2.

We must now populate each of the sub-process *EPCs* with the appropriate detailed model. Once you have created the generic model, the product-specific models will probably be very similar, so you can copy and paste the generic model into the product-specific sub-process *EPCs* and make the necessary changes. If you already have *EPCs* that represent some of the sub-processes then instead of creating them as new models when you make the assignments, you can assign the existing models to the appropriate Function.

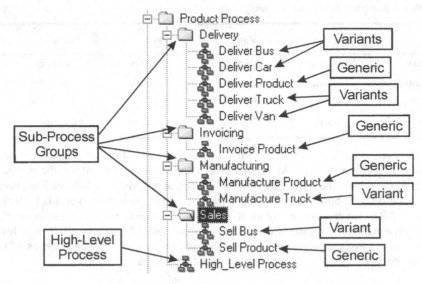

Fig. 8.2 Variant Hierarchy Group Structure

When you open the *Assignment Wizard*, tick the *Existing Model* box, and choose the appropriate existing model from the *Select model/group Dialog Box*.

Of course, whichever way you create your sub-process models, you must remember to make sure the trigger and outcome Events of all the sub-processes for the same Function use the same object occurrence. This will ensure that any of the alternative sub-process models for a particular Function will link correctly with the set of sub-process models of other Functions.

8.4   A Model Hierarchy with Variant Sub-Processes

The result of creating a hierarchy with these alternative sub-processes is shown in Fig. 8.3. We can see that by examining the model assignments for each Function, it immediately shows us how our process hierarchy supports each product. For instance, the **Sell Product** Function has an assigned generic **Sell Product** sub-process, plus a variant sub-process **Sell Bus**. This tells us that Cars, Vans and Trucks all use the generic sales process. For **Manufacture Product** we see that only Trucks need a specific process (**Manufacture Bus**), and for **Invoice Product** all the products use the generic process. Finally, for **Deliver Product**, although we have defined a generic sub-process, all the products need their own specific version of it.

This structure allows us to visualise and manage both the hierarchy and the variability. If we now wish to add a new product, our starting point is to use the generic sub-process for each high-level Function. If we find the generic is not suitable, then if an alternative sub-process already exists for another product we try to use it. If we can use an existing variant sub-process we then change its name to reflect that it now supports more than one product. If we can't use an existing variant then, and only as a last resort, we create another product-specific sub-process model.

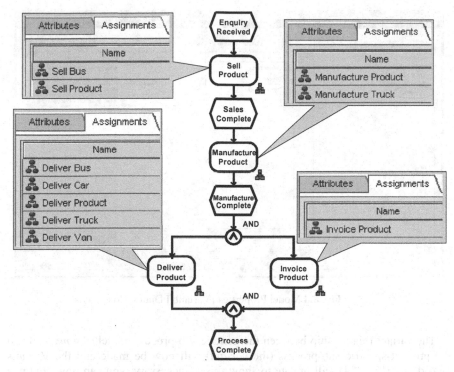

Fig. 8.3 Variant Sub-Process Hierarchy Assignments

8.4.1 Creating Variant Relationships Between Sub-Processes

By assigning a generic sub-process and several product-specific sub-process models
to the same Function, we have been implying that the product sub-processes are
'*variants*' of the generic model. However, apart from the fact the sub-processes are
assigned from the same Function, there is no other relationship between the processes. If we look at a sub-process in isolation, how do we know that it is related to a
generic process or to other variants? ARIS solves this problem by allowing us to
create special '*variant relationships*' between models (and also between objects).

To create a variant relationship between models:

1. Select the *master* model (e.g. the generic sub-process) in the *Explorer Module*,

2. Right-Click > Prop<u>e</u>rties,

3. Select the *Variants Dialog Box* (Fig. 8.4), click <u>N</u>ew,

4. Tick the <u>U</u>se existing Model box in the *Select creation mode Dialog box* of the
   Variant Wizard, click <u>N</u>ext,

5. In the *Select Models Dialog Box*, click <u>A</u>dd,

6. Locate the variant model in the *Select Model Dialog Box* (e.g. one of the
   product-specific sub-process models) and Click OK,

7. Click <u>F</u>inish.

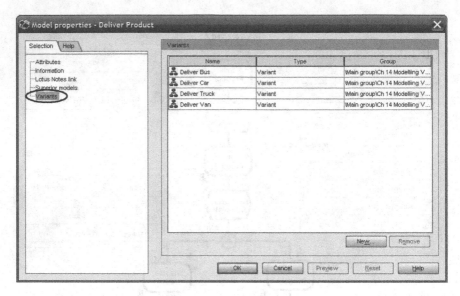

Fig. 8.4 Model Properties [Variants] Dialog Box

The variant relationship between the generic sub-process model (the *master*) and the product-specific sub-process (the *variant*) will now be made and the *Variants Dialog Box* (Fig. 8.4) will update to show this. If necessary, you can now continue and add addition variants for the same master model. For instance, the **Deliver Product** generic sub-process (the *master*) will require all four product-specific sub-processes assigning as *variants*.

The *variant relationship* created between the models is simply a link between the two models. The models have to be of the same type, but the relationship takes no account of the content of the models. Of course, we have an expectation that there is some similarity between the contents of the models, otherwise we wouldn't think of them as variants, but the variant relationship itself doesn't require this.

8.4.2   Creating Sub-Processes as Variant Copies

If we use the procedure described above, we will have created a variant relationship between the generic sub-process model and the product-specific variant sub-processes. When we look inside the models, many of the Functions will have copies in the other variant models. If we look at any one of those Functions in isolation, it will not be immediately obvious that copies of them exist. However, just as we established a variant relationship between models, we can also create a variant relationship between objects.

We could create the variant relationship between objects using the *Properties Dialog Box* in exactly the same way as we saw above for models. However, it would be very tedious to do this for every object. A better way is, rather than creating the product-specific sub-process models and then making the variant relationship, initially create the models as variant copies of the generic sub-process.

For more information on creating variant copies of models and objects see "*Chapter 15 - Definitions, Occurrences and Copies*" in Davis and Brabänder 2007. The procedure now becomes:

1. Make a *variant copy* of the generic sub-process model,

2. Assign it to the high-level Function,

3. Make appropriate changes to the product-specific sub-process model,

4. Replace the trigger and outcome Events of the variant model with occurrence copies of those from the generic process.

This approach has the significant advantage that, as well as the product-specific model having a variant relationship to the generic sub-process, all the objects in the product-specific sub-process models are variants of the objects in the generic sub-process model. We can now make changes to the product-specific sub-process to reflect its product-specific nature.

It is important to make sure that the trigger and outcome Events of all the variant sub-processes are the same as those in the generic sub-process. In that way, any one of the variant sub-processes will link with other sub-processes in exactly the same way as the generic sub-processes link together. By taking a variant copy of the generic sub-process we have made definition copies of all the objects. This means the trigger and outcome Events are not occurrence copies, so we must replace these Events with occurrence copies of the originals to make sure the linking still works. The easiest way to do this is to copy and paste them from the generic model into the variant model, and replace the existing objects with them.

8.4.3 Viewing Variant Relationships

Now we have created variant relationships between the generic sub-process and the product-specific sub-processes, we can view the relationships from the *Model Properties [Variants] Dialog Box*. For instance, if we select the **Deliver Product** generic model in the *Explorer Module*, and Right-Click > Properties and select the *Variants Dialog Box*, we will see the display shown above in Fig. 8.4. We selected the master object so the *Variants Dialog Box* lists all the variant sub-process models for all the products and it indicates they are variants by the **Variant** entry in the *Type* column.

If we now select one of the variant sub-process and view the *Variants Dialog Box* it will show the master process (**Deliver Product**) and the *Type* column will display **Master**.

8.4.4 Creating Variants of Variants

We can create a variant relationship to a model that is itself a variant of another model. Creating a variant of a variant might be useful, for instance if we suddenly find we have two types of a Bus (e.g. large and small), each with their own specific sales sub-process. We would create two variant copies of the **Sell Bus** sub-process and make the necessary changes to the specific models. We could then assign their sub-processes to the **Sell Product** Function. Now we would have a **Sell Product** generic process, a generic version of the *Sell Bus* product-specific process, and two sub-variants of it (e.g. *Sell Large Bus* and *Sell Small Bus*).

If we view the variant relationship for the *Sell Bus* model (Fig. 8.5), we will now see it has a master model (*Sell Product*) and two variant models (*Sell Large Bus* and *Sell Small Bus*).

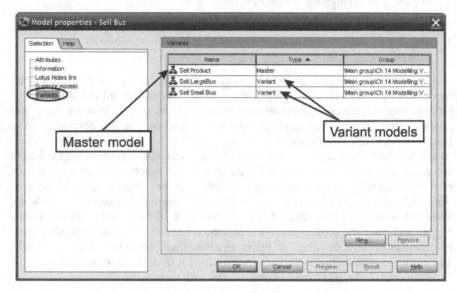

Fig. 8.5 Example Variants of Variants Relationship Display

8.4.5   Modelling the Product/Process Hierarchy

In addition to viewing the various sub-processes (generic and product-specific) that deliver the products using model assignments, we can also model this directly using a *Product/Service tree* model.

The *Product/Service tree* allows you to create a hierarchical definition of your product structure and also to associate a Function with the *Product* objects to represent the processes that create those products. We can assign the appropriate set of product-specific sub-processes to each of the Functions representing the end-to-end process for a specific product.

Fig. 8.6 shows a *Product/Service tree* for the example defined in Table 8.1. The symbol at the top of the model represents the product family (*Vehicles*). This is then decomposed into the five product types: *Generic*, plus *Car*, *Van*, *Bus* and *Truck*. The *Bus* category is further divided into *Large Bus* and *Small Bus*. At the bottom of the model we can see Functions representing the end-to-end processes. They are connected to the *Products* to show that the end-to-end processes "*produce*" the products.

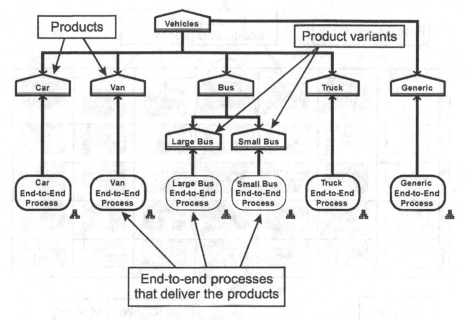

Fig. 8.6 Product/Service Tree for End-to-End Process Definitions

Each Function representing the end-to-end processes has the appropriate sub-process models assigned to it. If we select any of the Functions and Right-Click > Properties and select the *Assignments Tab* we will see the list of sub-processes that deliver the product (see Fig. 8.7 for an example of the sub-process for *Large Bus*).

Name	Type
Deliver Bus	EPC
Invoice Product	EPC
Manufacture Product	EPC
Sell LargeBus	EPC

Fig. 8.7 End-to-End Process Assignments in the Product/Service Tree

8.4.6   Modelling the Product/Process Matrix

An alternative to using the *Product/Service tree* for representing the sub-processes that deliver a particular product is to use a *Process selection diagram* (Fig. 8.8).

On the top row we have objects that represent the particular *Scenarios* we want to model. In this example they are the end-to-end processes for each of our products. In the left-hand column we have the *Main process* groupings which in this example represent our key sub-processes (*Sell*, *Manufacture*, *Deliver* and *Invoice*).

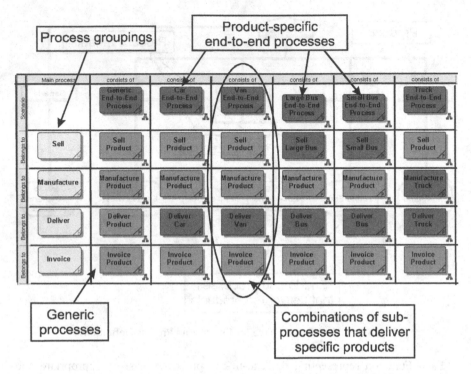

Fig. 8.8 Process Selection Diagram for End-to-End Process Definitions

Each of the main columns now represents the particular sub-processes that to-gether deliver the end-to-end process. The first column shows the sub-processes for the **Generic End-to-End Process**, the next column the set for the **Car End-to-End Process**, etc. The cell at the intersection of a row or column shows the specific sub-process in each of the main process groupings that contributes to the specific end-to-end process.

The *Process selection diagram* provides a very visual way of showing the variety of different processes that are required. It has the advantage that it can be expanded horizontally and vertically to cater for large product/process combinations which may be difficult to represent in a *Product/Service tree*. Another advantage over just looking at the model assignments to understand the structure is that *implicit relationships* (e.g. "*is component of*") are automatically established between the objects in the cells and those in the *Scenario* row and *Main process* column. If we select a specific sub-process and look at the *Relationships Tab* (see the example in Fig. 8.9 for **Sell Product**), we can quickly see all the end-to-end processes the sub-process is involved in.

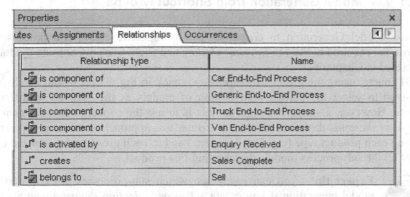

Fig. 8.9 Implicit Relationships in the Process Selection Diagram

8.5   Generating a Product-Specific End-to-End Process

The variant process hierarchy approach described above has the advantage that it manages the variability in the process hierarchy while preserving those parts of the process that can remain generic. Its disadvantage is that it can be difficult to visualise the complete process for any particular product. However, in Chapter 6 we saw how we could generate a complete end-to-end model from a set of linked sub-processes using *Model Generation*. Provided we take great care to make sure our variant sub-processes link with other sub-processes we can choose a particular combination of generic and product-specific sub-processes and use Model Generation to generate a product-specific end-to-end process.

For instance, to generate the end-to-end process for a Car we would choose the combination of:

- *Sell Product* (generic),
- *Manufacture Product* (generic),
- *Deliver Car* (product-specific),
- *Invoice Product* (generic).

To generate the end-to-end process for a Large Bus we would choose:

- *Sell Large Bus* (product-specific sub-variant),
- *Manufacture Product* (generic),
- *Deliver Bus* (product-specific),
- *Invoice Product* (generic).

8.5.1   Model Generation from Shortcut Groups

To use Model Generation to create the product-specific end-to-end process we choose the required models in *Explorer Module* and Right-Click > Generate model as described in Chapter 6.

Of course, using the group structure shown back in Fig. 8.2, it would be slightly involved to select the correct combination of models as they are all in different groups. However, a simple way around this is to use the concept of *model generation from shortcuts* described Chapter 6. To use this approach, create a group representing each product type (e.g. Car, Van, etc.) and in each group make shortcut copies of all the sub-process models representing that product.

 Expert tip – you can easily see which sub-processes are required for model generation if you create a *Process selection diagram* (see Section 8.4.6).

If there are no product-specific variants, then link to the generic sub-process for that operation. The result is a set of groups as shown in Fig. 8.10.

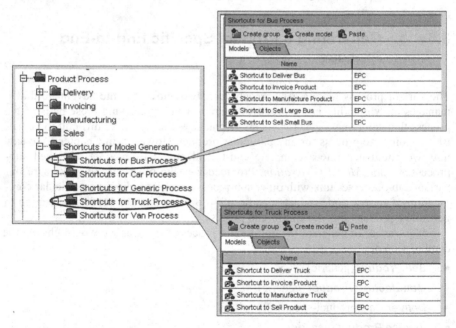

Fig. 8.10 Shortcut Groups Product-Specific Model Generation

In the left-hand pane of the *Explorer Module* we can see the shortcut groups for the generic process and each of the four specific products. In the right-hand pane you can see examples of the contents of the **Bus** and **Truck** shortcut groups.

To run Model Generation for Trucks all we need to do is select all the files in the group and select Right-Click > Generate model. In the **Bus** group, the shortcuts for both the **Sell Small Bus** and **Sell Large Bus** sub-processes have been included so we would need to select the correct alternative. We could, of course, have created individual sub-groups for both the Large Bus and Small Bus.

Once we have generated the end-to-end process it can be assigned to one of the Functions representing the end-to-end process in the *Product/Service tree* or *Process selection diagram*, along with the set of sub-process models.

8.6 Benefits of Modelling with a Variant Hierarchy

The approach described above gives us a direct way of modelling our product structure and the sub-processes that support various versions of those products. By fitting these sub-processes into the hierarchy it encourages us to re-use the generic sub-process or previously developed sub-process variants. By creating the variant relationships between the generic and its variants, we can always keep track of the parentage of the sub-process designs. Moreover, if the variant sub-processes are initially created by making variant copies we can make direct links between the generic and the variants. Finally, we can use the model structure itself as a clear, repeatable definition from which we can directly generate a product-specific end-to-end process. This end-to-end process shows the entirety of all the sub-processes needed to support the product, and how they connect together.

In order to achieve the full benefit of this approach it was necessary to introduce a number of complex ARIS techniques. Probably the most complicated part is understanding the need to use common Events to connect together sub-processes (see Chapter 6 for a detailed description). Understanding this is fundamental to ensuring that Model Generation operates correctly.

Although this approach seems complicated at first, once you have grasped the key concepts, it is relatively easy to implement (at least for straightforward models). Of course, this approach does rely on being able to sensibly segment your models, both horizontally and vertically. You will find some projects produce models that are far too complex and interconnected to attempt this approach. However, our goal must always be to produce process designs that are straightforward and have limited interactions. So this approach suits the processes we would like to have, even if it doesn't always suit the processes we actually have!

References
Davis R, Brabänder E (2007) ARIS design Platform: Getting Started with BPM, Springer-Verlag, London.

Chapter 9 ARIS Evaluations

This chapter looks at the types of ARIS Evaluations that can be performed on the contents of an ARIS database. Although it doesn't describe how to write Java based Evaluation Scripts, it does look at how to configure the settings of existing Reports, Semantic Checks, Macros and Transformations. It also describes how to trigger Macros and Transformations based on events occurring in ARIS.

9.1 Evaluations

9.1.1 Introduction

Once we have created a set of models in *ARIS Business Architect* we need to do something with them. We can print them out and physically show them one by one to the people in our organisation, but we can get more value by analysing them, creating reports, publishing them on the Intranet and using them as the basis for many of the more sophisticated ARIS Platform tools.

While some of these options require special tools, such as *ARIS Business Publisher,* in *ARIS Business Architect* there are a range of *Evaluations* that can be performed on databases, models, objects and other ARIS items. The key characteristic of an Evaluation is that it is based on an *Evaluation Script* (e.g. an *ARIS Report Script*) written with the *ARIS Script Editor* using *JavaScript* and the *ARIS Script* programming language.

ARIS 7 – prior to ARIS 7, Visual Basic was used to program *Evaluation Scripts,* but in ARIS 7 JavaScript is now used. VB based scripts can still be created using *ARIS Toolset* and can be run in *Toolset* or *Business Architect,* but only Java based scripts can be created in *Business Architect.* VB scripts can also be imported into *Business Architect* and converted to Java, but some manual editing may be required.

A number of Evaluation Scripts are provided with ARIS and users familiar with programming languages can write their own scripts. There are four categories of Evaluation Scripts:

- Reports,
- Semantic Checks,
- Macros,
- Transformations.

Typically, Evaluation Scripts will be provided on an ARIS Business Server so as to be available to all users modelling on the server. However, users can also use Evaluations stored on the **LOCAL** server on their own PC.

In the sections below we will look at how Evaluation Scripts are created, configured and used, although we will not be looking at how to program scripts as this would require a book in its own right!

9.1.2   Reports

ARIS Reports are primarily used to analyse and produce summaries of the contents, attributes and relationships of databases, models and objects in a variety formats (e.g. Microsoft Word, Excel, PDF, etc). Using Reports has the benefit that, not only can Reports formally document the information you can see in the *Attributes Window*, the *Assignments Dialog Box* or *Relationships Dialog Box*, but also they can produce analysis based on the contents of the entire database rather than just a single model.

By using advanced programming, you can identify and analyse complex secondary relationships between objects. For instance, you could report on all the *Application system types* used by particular *Organizational unit types* by looking at the relationship between *Application system types* and *Functions* and the same *Functions* and their connected *Organizational unit types*. The extent and complexity of the analysis you can perform is only limited by the skills of the Report Script programmer and the information actually in the database.

In addition to accessing the information in the ARIS database, the script language also allows access to the Microsoft application programming language so comprehensive formatting of documents can be programmed. This allows high quality formal process documents to be automatically generated directly from ARIS models (see Fig. 9.1).

 ARIS 7 – in release 7.1 of ARIS there will be a *WYSIWYG* ("what you see is what you get") *Report Wizard* which will enable users to create ARIS 7.1 their own reports without the need for programming.

As well as accessing ARIS database information, the ARIS Evaluation Script Language can also execute ARIS commands and perform modelling tasks. For instance, to add or delete an object, or to change the properties of an object. It is therefore possible to create Evaluation Scripts that manipulate database, models or objects rather than producing documented output. Some examples of such reports (e.g. *Consolidate objects*) are given in Chapter 16 which describes reports used to aid database administration.

Id	Name	Description	Accountability	Deliverables	Output to	Guidance notes
4.3.1	Schedule meeting to identify Architecturally significant Use Cases.	Schedule meeting to identify Architecturally significant Use Cases.	System Engineer	Meeting invitation	Stakeholders, Designer, Requirements Analyst, Chief Architect, Third Party Suppliers	
4.3.2	Chair the Process meeting	Chair the Process meeting	System Engineer			
4.3.3	Manage Process meeting.	Manage the Process meeting. Take minutes Identify and assign action items Document decisions made	System Engineer	Action items, Documented decisions , Meeting minutes		Reference # 12, Produce Interface Catalogue and Definitions WI
4.3.4	Review Use Case Catalogue	Review Use Case Catalogue and identify Architecturally significant Use Cases with the following attributes: - Involving Sub-system interaction - External System interaction - System performance - Other	System Engineer	List of Significant Use Cases		
4.3.5	Update Use Case Catalogue with Significant Use Cases	Update Use Case Catalogue with Significant Use Cases	Requirements Analyst	Use Case Catalogue		
4.3.6	Identify missing Use Cases or requirements	Identify any missing Use Cases or requirements associated with significant Use Cases	System Engineer	Supplementary Requirements	Requirements Analyst	
4.3.7	Produce Supplementary Requirements	Produce Supplementary Requirements to address missing Use Cases or requirements	System Engineer	Supplementary Requirements	Requirements Analyst	

Fig. 9.1 Example Document Generated from ARIS Report

ARIS 7 – prior to ARIS 7, Reports could be used to automate ARIS commands or modelling tasks in addition to producing documented output. In ARIS 7 we can now use Macros and Transformations for task automation and just use Reports when we need to produce documentation.

ARIS 7

9.1.3   Semantic Checks

Method Filters allow organisations to define their own standards for process modelling and to limit the range of models, objects, relationship and attributes available to users. Despite the use of Method Filters, there is still a great deal of flexibility in the way ARIS can be used. For instance, the standard approach to modelling with an *EPC* is to start and end each process flow with an Event. The Method Filter defines how Events are connected to other objects, but there is nothing in the Method Filter that can force users to always have an Event at the start and end of a process.

In addition to modelling standards that always should apply when using ARIS, organisations may also have their own modelling conventions. For instance, you might wish to define that all Functions in a *Value-added chain diagram* should have *EPCs* assigned to them, or all Functions in an *EPC* should have *Organizational unit types* connected to them.

To make sure these modelling conventions are being followed, it is necessary to evaluate each model against a set of rules. To make this task easier, ARIS Semantic Checks can be used to automatically evaluate models against a configurable set of rules provided with ARIS, or against rules programmed by using the *Script Editor*.

Different *Rule Types* can be grouped together into *Profiles* which define a set of checks be carried out for groups, models or objects. The Semantic Check can be instigated manually or automated using *Macros*.

9.1.4   Macros

ARIS Macros allow modelling tasks to be configured and run automatically. The functionality triggered by Macros can be programmed in a user-defined script or Macros can use pre-existing Reports or Semantic Checks.

Macros can be configured to be initiated manually, by including them as menu entries or toolbar buttons, or to run automatically when some ARIS event occurs (e.g. a new model is created or a model is saved, etc). Thus Macros can be used to enforce modelling conventions, for instance by triggering a Semantic Check each time a model is saved.

 Hint – when we refer to *events* triggering Macros, the events we are referring to are things that occur in ARIS (e.g. a new object being created or a model being saved, etc). There is no connection with *Event* objects.

 Warning – although the use of Macros to automatically trigger Semantic Checks seems quite appealing at first, the continued triggering of macros when models are saved can be very irritating to users and should be implemented sparingly.

9.1.5   Transformations

ARIS Transformations are another type of Evaluation Script, primarily designed for carrying out modelling tasks that perform conversions (e.g. creating new models or objects from existing ones). For instance, several of the transformations provided with ARIS create UML objects from existing ARIS objects (e.g. a *Use*

Case from a Function). Transformations cannot be triggered by Macros (see above), but they can themselves be configured to be triggered by ARIS events (e.g. saving a model) in the same way Macros can. Transformations cannot produce documented output.

9.2 Creating and Managing Evaluation Scripts

9.2.1 The Evaluation Folder

Evaluation Scripts are created and managed using the *Administration Module* and *Script Editor* in *ARIS Business Architect*. The **Evaluations** folder is visible in the folder structure of **LOCAL**, or an ARIS Business Server, using either of these modules (see Fig. 9.2). To create and manage Evaluation Scripts you will need to know the Scripts Administrator password.

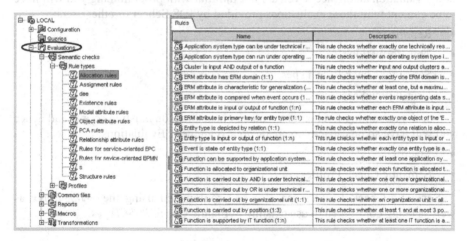

Fig. 9.2 The Evaluations Folder

The **Evaluations** folder contains sub-folders for:

- Common files,
- Reports,
- Macros,
- Transformations,
- Semantic Checks.

The **Common files** folder, as its name suggests, contains common items such as gif files for logos and some standard Java scripts used by all types of Evaluation Script.

Hint – if you are using a **LOCAL** server, the Scripts Administrator password will probably be set to the default "Semantic ChecksRIPTAD-MIN". If you are working on an ARIS Business Server the password will probably have been changed by the server administrator.

9.2.2   Creating New Evaluations

Creating new Evaluations is generally a two-stage process. The first stage invokes the *Script Wizard* which guides you through the process of defining the basic properties of the Evaluation; its name, description and context (e.g. does it run on groups, models, objects, etc) and any other specific configuration information. The second stage then requires you to use the *Script Editor* to actually program the content of the script associated with the Evaluation.

For the following Evaluations, you have to create a script in order to create the new Evaluation and hence if you are not familiar with programming you will have to be content with those evaluations provided by IDS Scheer or other users:

*   Reports,
*   Transformations,
*   Semantic Check Rule Types,
*   User-defined Macros.

For the remaining Evaluations, you can base them on existing scripts and hence you will have some capacity to create your own, new, Evaluations:

*   Macros,
*   Semantic Check Profiles.

Semantic Check *Profiles* can also be programmed using the *Script Editor* as well as being configured to use existing Semantic Check *Rule Types*.

9.2.3   Editing Evaluation Scripts

If you select any Evaluation Script in the *Administration Module* and Right-Click > Edit, click the Edit button on the *Evaluations Toolbar* or double-click the Evaluation name, ARIS will switch to the *Script Editor* and open the selected script for editing. Further discussion of the *Script Editor* is beyond the scope of this book.

You can delete and rename Evaluation Scripts using the familiar Right-Click > Delete and Right-Click > Rename commands or the buttons on the *Evaluations Toolbar*.

Question – why does the *Script Editor* appear when I try and Evaluate an ARIS model?

Answer – if you inadvertently open an Evaluation Script in the *Script Editor*, and switch to the *Explorer Module* or *Designer Module* to perform an Evaluation, then when the report runs, it will switch to the *Script Editor* so as to run the script in 'debug' mode. To stop this happing, close the Evaluation Script in the *Script Editor*.

9.2.4 Evaluation Properties

Selecting an Evaluation Script in the *Administration Module* and accessing its properties using Right-Click > Properties or clicking the Properties button on the *Evaluations Toolbar* will invoke the *Script Wizard*.

The *Script Wizard* will typically enable you to maintain the Name, Description and Language of script in the *General Dialog Box*, the database, group, model or object type for which the script will run in the *Context Dialog Box* and, where applicable, the output document format in the *Output Dialog Box*. Even for Evaluations where you cannot create your own new Evaluations without using the *Script Editor*, the *Script Wizard* will often be useful for modifying the configuration of the Evaluation.

For Macros and Semantic Check Profiles, the *Script Wizard* will enable you to configure the existing scripts used by the Evaluation (see more detailed information below).

Warning – double clicking on an Evaluation Script does not bring up the *Properties Window* as you might expect, but opens the script using the *Script Editor*. To display the script's properties, Right-Click > Properties or click the Properties button.

9.2.5 Exporting Scripts

You can export Evaluation Scripts in an appropriate file format so as to exchange Evaluations with other users or to load them onto an ARIS Business Server. To export an Evaluation Script:

1. Select the Evaluation Script in the *Administration Module*,

2. Right-Click > Export or click the Export button on the *Evaluations Toolbar*,

3. Save the file onto you hard disk.

Reports, Macros and Transformations will be saved as "*.arx" files. Semantic Check *Rule Types* are saved as "*.asx" files and Semantic Check Profiles as "*.apx" files.

9.2.6   Importing Scripts

You can import Evaluation Scripts created by others users. To import an Evaluation Script:

1.   Select the folder in the *Administration Module* where you want to import the script,

2.   Right-Click > Import or click the Import button on the *Evaluations Toolbar*,

3.   Locate the appropriate file type on your hard disk.

9.3   Reports

9.3.1   Creating Reports

To create a new Report:

1.   Select a category sub-folder in **Reports** folder in the *Administration Module* where you want to create the new Report,

2.   Right-Click > New or click the New button on the *Evaluations Toolbar*.

   The *Script Wizard* will now guide you through configuring a Report (we will look at the *Script Wizard* dialog boxes in the next section) and when you click Finish it will open a new, empty, script in the *Script Editor*. You will now need to create the program script for the report before it can be run.

   Hint – you cannot create a Report in the top level **Reports** folder, but only in a *category* sub-folder. To create a category folder, select the **Reports** folder, Right-Click > New > Category and enter a name in the Create category Dialog Box.

9.3.2   Modifying Report Settings

To configure the settings of an existing Report:

1.   Select the Report in the *Administration Module*,

2.   Right-Click > Properties or click the Properties button on the *Evaluations Toolbar*.

   The *Script Wizard* will now allow you to change the Report configuration (the dialog boxes are the same as those displayed when creating a new Report). Even if you have not created the Report yourself, and have no intention of using the *Script*

Editor, you can still make useful changes to Report configuration using the *Script Wizard*.

General Dialog Box

The *General Dialog Box* (Fig. 9.3) allows you to modify the content of, and choose the <u>L</u>anguage in which you want to maintain, various entries such as the <u>N</u>ame, <u>D</u>escription, A<u>u</u>thor, etc. You can maintain these settings in multiple languages.

 Hint – if you are creating a new Report to be used by other people, you should include a comprehensive description of the report's functionality so other users can clearly understand what it does.

The <u>V</u>ersion and <u>I</u>dentifier fields are maintained automatically by ARIS and will be populated once a new Report has been saved. The <u>V</u>ersion field shows in which version of ARIS the Report has been created.

 Hint – the <u>I</u>dentifier field shows the GUID of the Report. It is not the same as the *Identifier* attribute assigned to ARIS items such as models and objects, etc.

 Expert Tip – Evaluation Scripts are specific to the version of ARIS used to create them. To use existing scripts with a newer version of ARIS they must be first converted using the *ARIS Script Converter*.

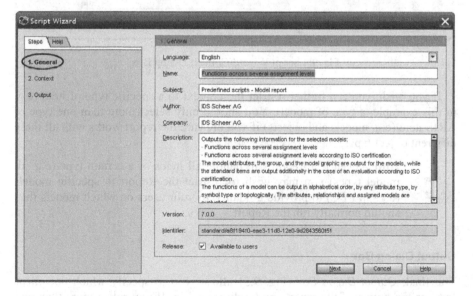

Fig. 9.3 Script Wizard General Dialog Box

Context Dialog Box

The *Context Dialog Box* (Fig. 9.4) allows you to select which ARIS Items (e.g. Method Filters, Database, groups, models or objects) the report can be run on. Normally Reports are programmed to start based on a particular type of item, for instance to display information on assignments in selected models. There would be little point in trying to run this report on a selected object, so by making the appropriate selections in the *Context Dialog Box* you can ensure the option to run this report is only provided when a model is selected.

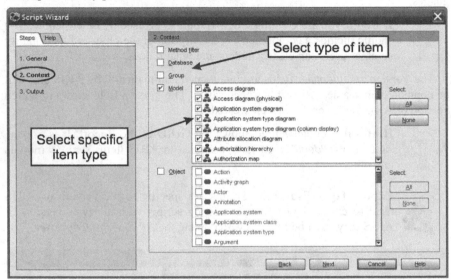

Fig. 9.4 Script Wizard Context Dialog Box

If you wish, you can further restrict the context to a specific type of item (e.g. in this example, a type of model). You should only select more than one type of ARIS item (e.g. models and objects) if you are sure the report works with all these different object types.

 Hint – even if a Report can handle all items of a certain type (e.g. all model types) you may wish to restrict the Report to specific models (e.g. an *EPC*) to provide guidance to your users on which models they should normally run the Report.

Output Dialog Box

The final, *Output Dialog Box* (Fig. 9.5) allows you to specify which document formats the output of the report can be displayed in. If you select more than one format, then when the user runs the report (see Section 9.3.3) they will be given the choice of which format they wish to use.

Some Reports may be suitable for display in any format while others (e.g. a script designed to produce Excel worksheets) may only work in a specific format. Some reports may not produce any output all, in which case the *Do not create output file* option can be selected. Click Finish and the Report will be saved.

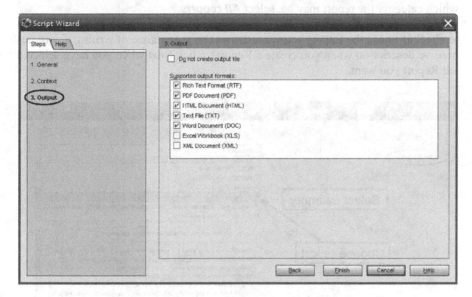

Fig. 9.5 Script Wizard Output Dialog Box

9.3.3   Running Reports

Reports can be run in the *Explorer Module* or *Designer Module*, depending on the ARIS item you wish to run it on. To run a Report, select an ARIS item (e.g. a group, model, object, etc) and do any of the following:

- Evaluate > Start report from the *Main Menu*,
- Right-Click > Evaluate > Start report,
- Click the Start report button on the *ARIS Toolbar*

The *Report Wizard* will guide you through running the Report (see below).

Expert Tip – if you frequently use the same reports, you can avoid the need to keep using the *Select report Dialog Box* and the *Select output settings Dialog Box* by creating a Macro (see Section 9.5) and assigning this to the *Main Menu* or to a button on the *ARIS Toolbar*.

Select Report

In the *Select report Dialog Box* (Fig. 9.6) first choose the <u>C</u>ategory of report you wish to run. The <u>C</u>ategory field corresponds to the name of the category sub-folder of the **Reports** folder in the *Administration Module*. If you are not sure in which category the report may be, select **All reports**.

Now select the Report from the <u>R</u>eport field. You can read the <u>D</u>escription field to check if this is the Report you want (hence the importance of writing a compre-hensive description when you create a Report). Click <u>N</u>ext when you have selected the Report you want.

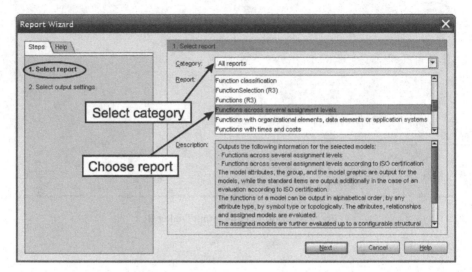

Fig. 9.6 Report Wizard Select Report Dialog Box

Select Output Settings

In the *Select output settings Dialog Box* (Fig. 9.7) you can first select the <u>Data-base Language</u> you want to use for any attributes that will be displayed by the re-port.

The <u>E</u>valuation filter field allows you to select a Filter that will restrict the out-put of the report. Typically Evaluation Filters are created to be much more restric-tive than a normal Method Filter. When used with a Report, they have the effect of removing many of the attributes (e.g. *Last user, Last change*, etc) you may wish to see when modelling, but would clutter up a report. Evaluation Filters are not lim-ited to restricting attributes and you can use them to restrict the range of models or objects considered by the Report.

The *Output format* field allows you to choose in which document format you wish to display the results. The available options in the list will have been set in the *Output Dialog Box* of the *Script Wizard* (Fig. 9.5) when the Report was created. If the Report produces no output, this field will be greyed out.

The *Save output as* field allows you to choose the location and name of the output document. It will default to a folder in the ARIS program file folders unless you specifically change it. If you tick the *Display result* checkbox, then once the document has been created, it will automatically be opened in the application associated with the selected *Output format*. Once the document is opened, you may save it with a new name and location. If the *Display result* checkbox is not ticked, the document will be saved with the chosen name and location, but you will have to manually locate and open it to see the result of running the Report.

Finally, you can click *Finish* and the Report will run. What happens next will depend on the actual Report. Some reports will run will no further display and then open the output document. Others will display additional dialog boxes generated by the Report Script itself to capture further configuration information. Some examples of Reports Scripts, their additional dialog boxes and their output are given in Chapter 16 which describes those Reports useful for database administration.

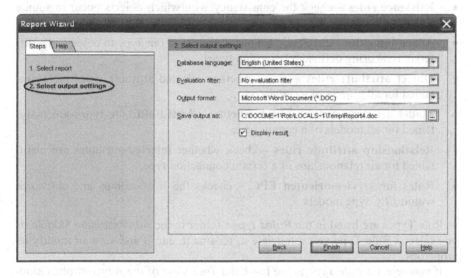

Fig. 9.7 Report Wizard Select Output Settings Dialog Box

9.4   Semantic Checks

9.4.1   Creating Semantic Checks

Semantic Checks consist of two parts: the *Rule Types*, which are programmed using the *Script Editor* and contain a number of *Rules*, and the *Profiles* which can be
configured to use existing *Rule Types* (and their *Rules*) or can be programmed in
the *Script Editor*.

There are two categories of Rule Types. *Pre-defined* Rule Types have fixed
Rules which can only be modified using the *Script Editor*, they comprise:

- **Structure Rules** – check the relationships and structures within models of
  specific types,

- **Assignment Rules** – check the relationship of an object definition to its assigned models.

Extendable Rule Types have Rules that can be configured by displaying their
properties and using the *Edit rule Dialog Box*, they comprise:

- **Existence rules** – check the consistency with which objects occur in source
  and target models,

- **Allocation rules** – check allocations of objects of one type to objects of a different type using defined relationship types,

- **Object attribute rules** – check whether selected attribute types are maintained for all objects of a certain type,

- **Model attribute rules** – check whether selected attribute types are maintained for all models of a certain type,

- **Relationship attribute rules** – check whether selected attributes are maintained for all relationships of a certain connection type,

- **Rules for service-oriented EPC** – checks the relationships and structures
  within *EPC* type models.

Rule Types are listed in the ***Rules types*** folder in the *Administration Module*. If
you select a Rule Type you can delete it, rename it, edit it and view or modify its
properties.

If you select a *Rule Type* in the left-hand *Tree View* of the *Administration Module* you will notice a set of *Rules* is displayed in the right-hand pane. These Rules
are not contained in the Rule Type folder, but are defined in the program script of
the selected Rule Type. You can delete, rename and view or modify the properties
of Rules.

You can't edit a Rule directly, because it is created by the script defined in the
Rule Type. However, for Extendable Rule Types, and if the script in the Rule
Type allows it, you can configure the Rule or create a new Rule using the *Rule
Type Wizard* for that particular Rule Type.

9.4.2 Creating New Rule Types

To create a new Rule Type:

1. Select the **Rules types** folder in the *Administration Module*,

2. Right-Click > <u>N</u>ew or click the New button on the
   Evaluations Toolbar.

   The *Rule Type Wizard* will now guide you through configuring a Rule Type
(we will look at this in the next section) and when you click <u>F</u>inish it will create a
new, empty, Rule Type. To create the program code for the Rules you will need to
edit the Rule Type with the *Script Editor* (Right-Click > <u>E</u>dit).

9.4.3 Modifying Rule Type Settings

To configure the setting of an existing Rule Type:

1. Select the Rule Type in the **Rules types** folder in the *Administration Module*,

2. Right-Click > Prop<u>e</u>rties or click the Properties button on the
   Evaluations Toolbar.

   The *Rule Type Wizard* will now allow you to change the Rule Type configuration (the dialog boxes are the same as those displayed when creating a new Rule
Type). Even if you have not created the Rule Type Script yourself, and have no intention of using the *Script Editor*, you can still make useful changes to Rule Type
configuration using the *Rule Type Wizard*.

General

In the *General Dialog Box* (Fig. 9.8) you can enter the usual <u>L</u>anguage, <u>N</u>ame and
<u>D</u>escription information and if we view the properties of an existing Rule Type we
will also be able to see the allocated <u>I</u>dentifier (GUID).

   Ticking the *Additional data checkbox* allows you to choose to display additional
object dialog boxes that will determine target models and objects to be used as
comparisons for Semantic Checks. If you tick either of these boxes, you are required enter information in the *Notes* fields to provide instructions on how to select these comparison models or objects.

Context

If you are creating a new Rule Type, the <u>N</u>ame field in the *Context Dialog Box*
(Fig. 9.9) will allow you to choose whether the Semantic Check will be run on a
group, model or object. If you are modifying an existing Rule Type, the context
will have been already determined when the Rule Type was created and the box
will be greyed out.

If models or objects have been selected in the *Name* field, the *Types* box allows you to choose which specific types of models or objects the Semantic Check can be run on. Now click <u>N</u>ext.

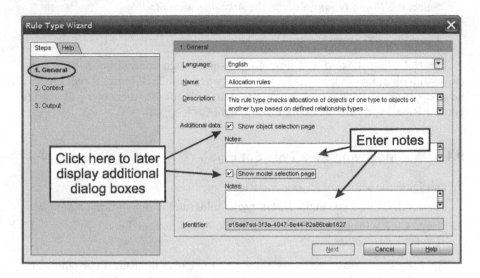

Fig. 9.8 Rule Type Wizard General Dialog Box

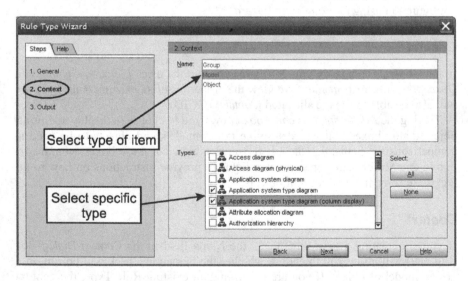

Fig. 9.9 Rule Type Wizard Context Dialog Box

Output

The results of a Semantic Check can be presented in one of three ways:

- A documented report,
- Information marks on a model,
- Improvement proposals.

In the *Output Dialog Box* (Fig. 9.10) you can choose any combination of these outputs, but information marks and improvements proposals will only work if the specific Rule Type script supports them.

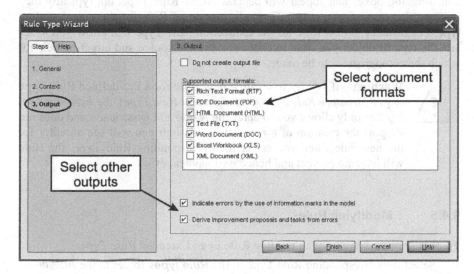

Fig. 9.10 Rule Type Wizard Output Dialog Box

Unless you have ticked the *Do not create output file* checkbox, you can select which documents types the report can be presented in using the *Supported output formats* box. If you select more than one type, the user will be given a choice of these when the Semantic Check is run (see Section 9.4.8).

Some Rule Types can display comments or information marks on a model to show where modelling conventions have not been adhered to. Ticking the *Indicate errors by the use of information marks in the model* checkbox will display these marks if the Rule Type supports it.

Some Rule Types can directly generate improvement proposals based on errors found when the Semantic Check is run. Ticking the *Derive improvement proposals and tasks from errors* checkbox will produce proposals if the Rule Type supports it.

Click <u>N</u>ext to save the Rule Type.

9.4.4   Creating New Rules

The ability to create new Rules for a particular Extended Rule Type is dependent on the script of the Rule Type. To create a new Rule:

1. Select the Rule Type for which you want to create a new Rule in the **Rules types** folder in the *Administration Module*,

2. Right-Click > <u>N</u>ew or click the New button on the *Evaluations Toolbar*.

The *Rule Wizard* will appear for the selected Rule Type. The number and format of dialog boxes that appear will depend on the Rule Type, but typically they will enable you to create a specific configuration of Rule for the corresponding type. For instance, a new Rule for the **Existence** Rule Type will allow you to select the type of object you want to check for and the source and target models for which the comparison is to be made.

 Warning – if you try to create a new Rule for a Pre-defined Rule Type (e.g. a *Structure Rule Type* or *Assignment Rule Type*), the *Edit Rule Dialog Box* only allows you to enter the *Name* and *Description* and does not support the creation of a new rule. Although you will see an entry for the new rule when you select the corresponding Rule Type, the Rule will have no content and hence will have no effect.

9.4.5   Modifying Rules

To configure the settings of an existing Rule in an Extended Rule Type:

1. Select the corresponding Rule Type in the **Rule types** folder in the *Administration Module*,

2. Select the Rule in the right-hand pane,

3. Right-Click > Prop<u>e</u>rties or click the Properties button on the *Evaluations Toolbar*.

As described above, the *Rule Wizard* will appear for the selected Rule Type and allow the configuration of the rule to be modified as allowed by the script of the Rule Type.

9.4.6   Creating New Profiles

The creation of Rule Types and Rules described above provides a set of checks that can be carried out on various ARIS items (groups, models, objects, etc). It would be tedious for users to have to pick the combinations of these to be used each time they wanted to run a Semantic Check, so *Profiles* can be created to define sets of checks to be carried out. Profiles can be created by individual users to carry out their favourite checks or by a database administrator to ensure models comply with corporate modelling conventions. The script of the Profile can also be modified directly in the *Script Editor*.

To create a new Profile:

1.   Select the **Profiles** folder in the *Administration Module*,

2.   Right-Click > New or click the New button on the *Evaluations*
     Toolbar.

The *Profile Wizard* will now guide you through configuring a Profile (we will look at this in the next section) and when you click Finish it will create a new Profile which be listed in the **Profiles** folder. If you wish, you can now directly edit the Profile with the *Script Editor* (Right-Click > Edit).

 Warning – if you edit the script of a Profile directly with the *Script Editor* you may not be able to configure it in future using the *Profile Wizard*.

 Hint – users can manually select their own combinations of Rules when they run the Semantic Check by selecting the **User-defined** Profile.

9.4.7   Modifying Existing Profiles

To configure the settings of an existing Profile:

1.   Select the corresponding Profile in the **Profiles** folder in the *Administration Module*,

2.   Right-Click > Properties or click the Properties button on the
     Evaluations Toolbar.

The *Profile Wizard* will appear and guide you through configuring the Profile as described below.

General

The *Profile Wizard General Dialog Box* (Fig. 10.11) allows us to set the familiar Language, Name and Descriptions boxes and to view the Identifier (GUID) of saved Profiles.

In addition, the *Can be selected from* box allows us to choose if the Semantic Check will be run on groups, models or objects. Click Next to continue.

Select Rules

The *Select Rules Dialog Box* (Fig. 9.12) allows us to select the Rules the Semantic Check will run.

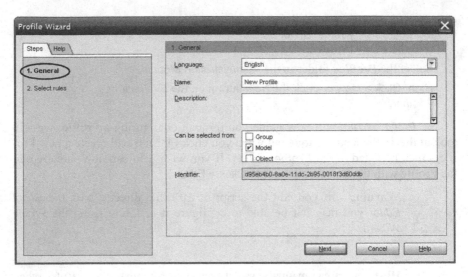

Fig. 9.11 Profile Wizard General Dialog Box

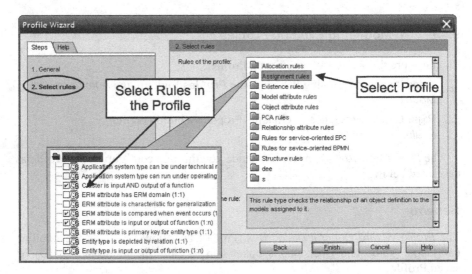

Fig. 9.12 Profile Wizard Select Rules Dialog Box

The *Rules of the profile* box shows folders for all of the Rule Types previously defined. Opening the Rule Type folder will list all of the Rules for that Rule Type. You can then put a tick in the box of those Rules you wish to run.

 Expert Tip – although you can select any number and combination of Rules for a Profile, it is best to select a limited number of related Rules so the results are not overcomplicated and confusing to the user.

Once you have selected all the Rules you want, click Finish. The Profile folder will be updated and the right-hand pane will list all those Rules that have been selected.

 Hint – you can't directly edit or view the properties of the Rules listed in the right-hand pane of the *Administration Module* for a Profile selected in the **Profiles** folder in the left-hand pane. To edit or view them you need to find the corresponding Rule entry in the **Rule types** folder.

9.4.8   Running Semantic Checks

Semantic Checks can be run in the *Explorer Module* or *Designer Module*, depending on the ARIS item you wish to run it on. To run a Semantic Check, select a group, model or object and do any of the following:

- Evaluate > Start semantic check from the *Main Menu*,
- Right-Click > Evaluate > Start semantic check,
- Click the Start semantic check button the *ARIS Toolbar*.

The *Semantic Check Wizard* will guide you through running the check.

 Expert Tip – if you frequently use the same Semantic Checks, you can avoid the need to keep using the *Select profile Dialog Box* and the *Select output settings Dialog Box* by creating a Macro (see Section 9.5) and assigning this to the *Main Menu* or a button on the *ARIS Toolbar*. You can also configure Macros to run a Semantic Check automatically on an ARIS event (e.g. saving a model).

Select Profile

In the *Select profile Dialog Box* (Fig. 9.13), choose the Profile you want to run. The pre-defined Profiles contain sets of Rules that you (or another user) have previously selected to be run when the Profile was created. However, if you want to run different combinations of Rules, you can do this without having to define a new Profile by selecting the **User-defined** option.

If you choose a pre-defined profile and click Next you will be taken to the *Select output settings Dialog Box* (see next section).

If you chose the **User-defined** option and click Next, you will go to the *Select rules Dialog Box*. This is very similar to the *Profile Wizard Select Rules Dialog Box* described above (Fig. 9.12) and allows you to choose which combination of rules you want to run. Click Next when you have chosen the Rules and you will normally be taken to the *Select output settings Dialog Box* (see next section). In some cases, depending on the Rules you have chosen, there may be further dialog boxes before you get to the *Select output settings Dialog Box*.

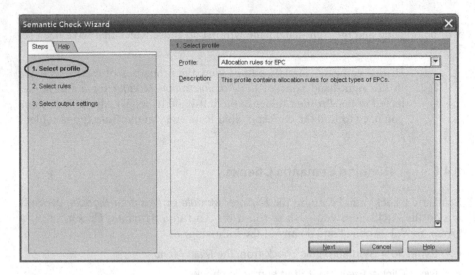

Fig. 9.13 Semantic Check Wizard Select Profile Dialog Box

Select Output Settings

The *Select output settings Dialog Box* for Semantic Checks is the same as for Reports described above in Section 9.3.2 and shown in Fig. 9.7. It enables you to select the format of the documented output of Semantic Checks. An example output is shown in Fig. 9.14.

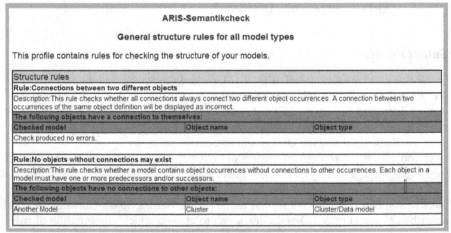

Fig. 9.14 Example Semantic Check Output

Running the Semantic Check may also produce information marks on a model or Improvement Proposals depending on the settings in the *Rule Type Wizard Output Dialog Box* (Fig. 9.10).

9.5 Macros

Macros allow the running of Reports or Semantic Checks to be simplified by pre-defining the information normally entered in the *Evaluation Start Dialog Boxes*. The Macro can either be started manually by allocating it to the *Main Menu* or *ARIS Toolbar*, or be triggered automatically when some ARIS event occurs (e.g. a model is saved).

Rather than using pre-existing Reports or Semantic Checks, '*User-defined*' Macros can be created using the *Script Editor*. Generally, user-defined Macros are used when some sort of output from ARIS is required. When automated modelling tasks change models or objects, but have no direct output, Transformations can be used instead (see Section 9.6).

 ARIS 7 – some of the Reports provided in ARIS do not create any output, but manipulate models and objects. In ARIS 7, many of these reports could be created using Transformations, but these were not available prior to ARIS 7, so Reports were used instead.

ARIS 7

9.5.1 Creating Macros

To create a new Macro:

1. Select a category sub-folder in the **Macros** folder in the *Administration Module* where you want to create the new Macro,

2. Right-Click > New or click the New button on the *Evaluations Toolbar*.

The *Script Wizard* will now guide you through configuring a Macro (we will look at this below) and when you click Finish it will create a new macro in the selected folder.

If you have created the Macro to run an existing Report or Semantic Check you will be able to run the Macro straight away. If you wish, you can edit it with the *Script Editor* (Right-Click > Edit), but this is not essential. You cannot normally edit any of the pre-defined Macros provided with ARIS using the *Script Editor* as they are protected.

If you selected a *User-defined macro* in the *Script Wizard Contents Dialog Box* (see Fig. 9.17, below), then when the Macro is saved you will have to edit it and create the necessary programming script before it can be run.

 Hint – you cannot create a Macro in the top level **Macros** folder, but only in a *category* sub-folder. To create a category folder, select the **Macros** folder, Right-Click > New > Category and enter a name in the Create category Dialog Box.

9.5.2   Modifying Macro Settings

To configure the setting of an existing Macro:

1.   Select the Macro in the **Macros** folder of the *Administration Module*,
2.   Right-Click > Properties or click the Properties button on the
      Evaluations Toolbar.

The *Script Wizard* will now allow you to change the Macro configuration (the dialog boxes are the same as those displayed when creating a new Macro). Even if you have not created the Macro yourself, and have no intention of using the *Script Editor*, you can still make useful changes to Macro configuration using the *Script Wizard*.

General

The *General Dialog Box* for creating Macros is the same as described for Reports (see Fig. 9.3) and allows you to enter the content of, and choose the *Language* in which you want to maintain, various entries such as the *Name*, *Description*, *Author*, etc. The *Version* and *Identifier* fields are maintained automatically by ARIS and will be populated once a new Macro has been saved. The *Version* field shows in which version of ARIS the Macro has been created.

Context

In the *Context Dialog Box* (Fig. 9.15) you can select how the Macro will run and on what items. There are three options for how the Macro will be run shown at the top of the dialog box:

- *Without context*,
- *Event*,
- *Database item context*.

The *Without context* option means the Macro is to be run manually and can be run at any time without the need to select any ARIS item. Typically this can only be used with a *User-defined macro* which has been designed to run in this way.

The *Event* option allows the Macro to be configured to run when something in ARIS happens (e.g. a model is saved). You can choose the particular ARIS events that will be the trigger for the Macro by clicking the Select event button. The *Select event Dialog Box* (Fig. 9.16) lists all the events that can be used and you can select one or more events and click OK.

 Warning – it is important to make sure the chosen triggering events for Macros are relevant to the Evaluation Script the macro will run and also to make sure that automatic running macros are not too intrusive for the user.

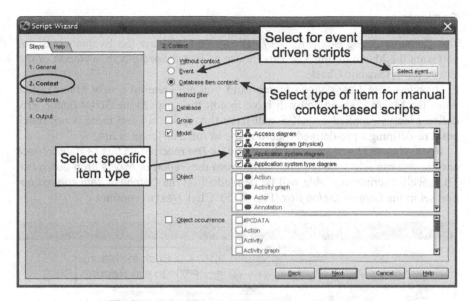

Fig. 9.15 Script Wizard (Macro) Context Dialog Box

The *Database item context* option allows the Macro to be run manually and be associated with the chosen item type so the Macro will only appear as an option, when that type of item is selected and the Evaluate > Start macro command is run. Select one or more checkboxes for the required types of item. If you select *Model*, *Object* or *Object occurrence* you can further select the specific item types.

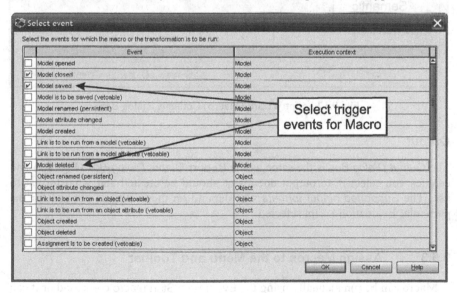

Fig. 9.16 Select Event Dialog Box

Contents

The *Contents Dialog Box* (Fig. 9.17) allows you to select the Evaluation Script you want the Macro to run. You can choose a *User-defined macro*, a *Report* or the *Profile* for a Semantic Check.

If you choose *User-defined macro* (and you are creating a new Macro), then when the Macro is saved you will have to edit the script in the *Script Editor*. Pre-define Macros supplied by ARIS will have this option set and there is not much point re-defining a pre-defined Macro name to run a different script.

If you choose *The macro runs this report* or *The macro runs this semantic check* option, you can select the required script from the *Report* or *Profile* drop-down list. The specific scripts available will be dependent on the *Database item context* option set in the *Context Dialog Box* (Fig. 9.15). Click <u>N</u>ext to continue.

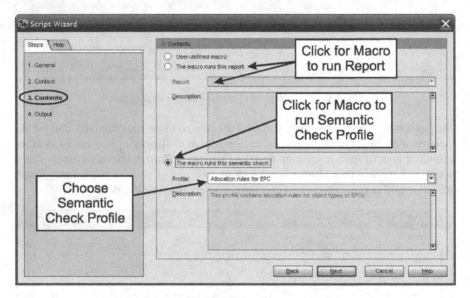

Fig. 9.17 Script Wizard (Macro) Contents Dialog Box

Output

The *Output Dialog Box* is the same as the Report *Output Dialog Box* (Fig. 9.5) and enables you select if an output document should be created and what format to use. The *Supported output formats* will depend on those outputs defined for the particular Evaluation Script selected.

9.5.3   Assign Macros to the Menu and Toolbar

A Macro can be run manually using the Ev<u>a</u>luate > Start <u>m</u>acro command or it can be allocated to the *Main Menu* and *Right-Click Menu* or the *ARIS Toolbar*.

To allocate a Macro, select Ev<u>a</u>luate > <u>C</u>onfigure macros from the *Main Menu*. The *Assign Macros Dialog Box* (Fig. 9.18) will display all the defined *Macros* on the current *Server*. Tick either or both of the *Menu* or *Toolbar* boxes to choose where the Macro entry will appear. You can also choose the icon that will be used for the button on the *ARIS Toolbar*, or displayed alongside the menu entry, from the drop-down list in *Icon* field.

Click OK and the Macro entry will be added to the toolbar or menus. If you ticked the *Menu* checkbox, an entry for the selected Macro will be added under the Macros sub-menu on the *Main Menu* underneath the Ev<u>a</u>luate command and also in the Macros sub-menu on the Ev<u>a</u>luate *Right-Click Menu*.

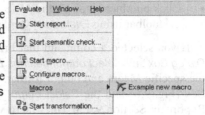

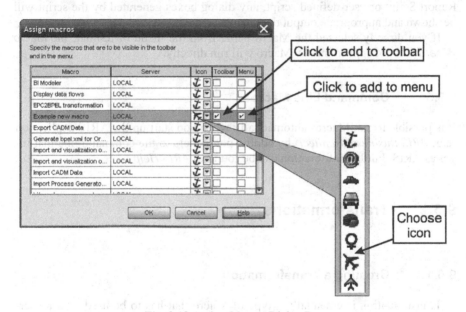

Fig. 9.18 Assign Macros Dialog Box

9.5.4   Running Macros

To run a Macro, select the ARIS item for which you want the Macro to run and do any of:

- Ev<u>a</u>luate > Start <u>M</u>acro from the *Main Menu* and choose the required Macro in the *Macro Wizard*,

- Right-Click > Ev<u>a</u>luate > Start <u>M</u>acro and choose the required Macro in the *Macro Wizard*,

- Click the *Macro* button on the ARIS Toolbar and choose the required Macro in the *Macro Wizard*,

- Ev<u>a</u>luate > <u>M</u>acros > <macroname> from the *Main Menu* (or *Right-Click Menu*), where the Macro has been added to the menu using Ev<u>a</u>luate > <u>C</u>onfigure macros,

- Click on Macro icon on the ARIS Toolbar where the Macro has been added to the toolbar using Ev<u>a</u>luate > <u>C</u>onfigure macros.

If you selected a command that brings up the *Macro Wizard*, the *Select macro Dialog Box* and *Select output settings Dialog Box* will appear to allow you to select the specific Macro and output format. These are similar to the *Select report Dialog Box* (Fig. 9.6) and the *Select output settings Dialog Box* (Fig. 9.7) described for Reports in Section 9.3.3. The Macro will now run and if the Macro is based on a Report Script or user-defined script, any dialog boxes generated by the script will be shown and appropriate output documents created.

If you directly selected the Macro name from the menu or toolbar, the *Macro Wizard* will not appear and the Macro will run directly.

9.5.5   Command Line Macros

It is possible to run Macros automatically when you start up the ARIS application (e.g. *ARIS Business Architect*) by adding parameters to the command line that invokes ARIS. Further information can be found in *ARIS Help*.

9.6   Transformations

9.6.1   Creating a Transformation

A Transformation is essentially a type of Macro that has to be used with a user-defined script. It cannot generate any documented output, so Transformations tend to be used to perform automated modelling tasks such as transforming one model type into another.

Transformations can be started manually using the Ev<u>a</u>luate > S<u>t</u>art transformation command, or triggered automatically when some ARIS event occurs (e.g. a model is saved). Unlike Macros, Transformations cannot be added to the *Main Menu* or *ARIS Toolbar*.

To create a new Transformation:

1. Select the category sub-folder in the **Transformations** folder in the *Administration Module* where you want to create the new Transformation,

2. Right-Click > <u>N</u>ew or click the New button on the *Evaluations Toolbar*.

The *Script Wizard* will now guide you through configuring a Transformation (we will look at this in the next section) and when you click Finish it will create a new Transformation in the selected folder. You can now edit the Transformation with the *Script Editor* (Right-Click > Edit).

> **Hint** – you cannot create a Transformation in the top level **Transforma-tions** folder, but only in a *category* sub-folder. To create a category folder, select the **Transformations** folder, Right-Click > New > Category and enter a name in the Create category Dialog Box.

General

The *General Dialog Box* for creating Transformations is the same as described for Reports (see Fig. 9.3) and allows you to enter the content of, and choose the Language in which you want to maintain, various entries such as the Name, Description, Author, etc. The Version and Identifier fields are maintained automatically by ARIS and will be populated once a new Transformation has been saved. The Version field shows in which version of ARIS the Transformations has been created.

Start Context

The *Start Context Dialog Box* for Transformation is the same as the *Context Dialog Box* for Macros (see Fig. 9.15). There are three options shown at the top of the dialog box:

- Without context,
- Event,
- Database item context.

These define whether the Transformation is to be run manually without the need to select any ARIS item, when something in ARIS happens (e.g. a model is saved) or to be run manually and associated with a chosen item type.

The Event option allows the Transformation to be configured to run when something in ARIS happens (e.g. a model is saved). You can choose the particular ARIS events that will be the trigger by clicking the Select event button. The *Select event Dialog Box* (Fig. 9.16) lists all the events that can be used and you can select one or more events and click OK.

If you choose the Database item context option, it will be associated with the item type chosen so the Transformation will only appear as an option when that type of item is selected and the Evaluate > Start transformation command is run. Select one or more checkboxes for the required item types and if you select Model, Object or Object occurrence you can further select the item types if you wish. Click Next to continue.

Execution context

The *Execution Context Dialog Box* (Fig. 9.19) allows you to choose which types of item the Transformation script will transform. This is different from the *Start Context Dialog Box* which defines what item must be selected to start the Transformation Script. For instance, if you wished to convert all of the objects of a certain type in particular type of model into another type of object, you would select the model type in the *Start Context Dialog Box* and the object type in the *Execution Context Dialog Box*.

Select the type of Database item in the top box (e.g. model, object or object occurrence) and select the specific item types you want to include in the Types box. Some types of item (e.g. specific object types) may also have Subtypes you can select. Click Next to continue.

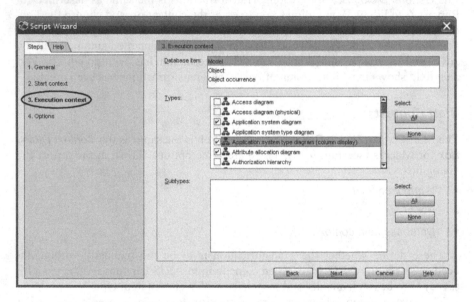

Fig. 9.19 Script Wizard (Transformation) Execution Context Dialog Box

Options

The *Options Dialog Box* (Fig. 9.20) displays five types of options the users could be asked to select when the Transformation is run. By ticking the appropriate checkboxes you can select which options will be used. By clicking the Settings button you can define the *Name* and *Description* for the option as well as other details such as the Access Privileges required to run the Transformation.

Setting these options requires a detailed knowledge of the Transformation Script and what it does. Click Finish and the Transformation will be saved.

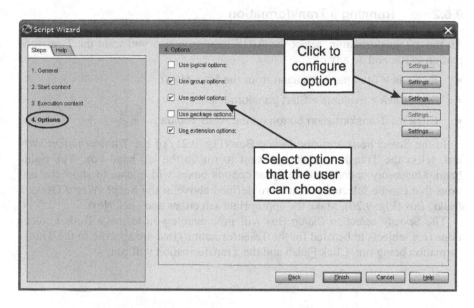

Fig. 9.20 Script Wizard (Transformation) Options Dialog Box

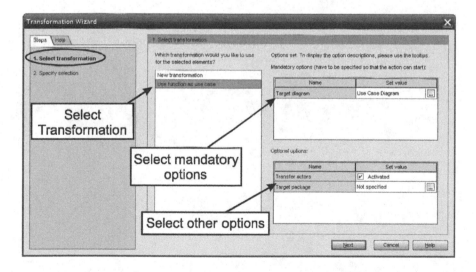

Fig. 9.21 Transformation Wizard Select Transformation Dialog Box

9.6.2   Running a Transformation

To run a Transformation, select the ARIS item on which you want the Transformation to run and do any of:

- Evaluate > Start transformation from the *Main Menu*,
- Right-Click > Evaluate > Start transformation,
- Click the Transformation button on the ARIS Toolbar.

In the *Select transformation Dialog Box* (Fig. 9.21) of the *Transformation Wizard*, select the Transformation you want to run in the left-hand box. The right-hand, *Mandatory options* and *Optional options* boxes will update to show the options that can be selected which were defined above in the *Script Wizard Options Dialog Box* (Fig. 9.20). Make the appropriate selections and click Next.

The *Specify selection Dialog Box* will now enable you to make further selections (e.g. objects to be used for the Transformation) that are specific to the Transformation being run. Click Finish and the Transformation will run.

Chapter 10   Database Administration

This chapter looks at the important tasks needed to manage ARIS servers and databases. In particular, it looks at the privileges and accounts needed to carry out administration and important topics such consolidation, merging and using the ARIS Admintool.

10.1   The Need for Administration

Most people who invest in the ARIS Platform will want to use it for modelling complex organisations. You may well have many modellers and process designers working on an ARIS Business Server and it is likely you will very quickly build up a large number of models. As soon as you have more than a few basic models you will need to become involved with some or all of the administration activities shown in Table 10.1.

Will we discuss the majority of these in this chapter, but administration of ARIS databases relies heavily on the following important topics described in detail in other chapters:

- User Administration (Chapter 11),
- Configuring the ARIS Method (Chapter 12),
- Method Filters and Evaluation Filters, (Chapter 14),
- Defining and Using Templates (Chapter 15),
- Queries (Chapter 5),
- ARIS Evaluations (Chapter 9).

10.2   Administrative Accounts and Privileges

10.2.1   Passwords, Accounts and Privileges

Administration is carried out with *ARIS Business Architect* using the *Administration Module*. Depending on the exact activity you wish to carry out, different administrator privileges are required.

Administrator privileges can be allocated in three ways:

- Administrator Passwords (server level),
- System Account (database level),
- Function Privileges (user/database level).

Table 10.1 Server and Database Administration

Administration Topic	Administration Activities
Server Connection	• Add server, • Remove server, • Change server administration passwords.
Server Configuration	• Conventions, • Method, • Queries, • Evaluation.
Database Management	• Create database, • Delete database, • Backup, • Reorganise, • Restore, • Statistics, • Export / Import, • Merge.
Database Configuration	• Users, • Font Formats, • Languages, • Properties, • Attributes.
Database Administration	• Managing group structure, • Access Privileges, • Model and object management, • Libraries, • Consolidating objects.

These privileges work in a hierarchical way. At the bottom level are *Function Privileges* which are granted to particular database Users and allow specific activities to be carried out on a database. The range of Function Privileges is described in Section 10.2.2.

The next level of privileges is assigned to Users who log in with the **system** account or with a User Account that has been created as a system account. System accounts have all the Function Privileges by default, but also have additional rights (e.g. can reorganise and backup databases). If the **system** account password has not been changed, then people who log into a database using the default *User name* and *Password* will automatically login as the **system** user and have all the Function Privileges.

The highest level of privileges are allocated to people who have the Administrator Passwords described in Section 10.2.4. People with the *Database Administrator* password can carry out database activities at the server level (e.g. creating and deleting databases).

If the Administrator Passwords have not been changed from the default values (see Table 10.4), then all Users will have the privileges associated with them.

Table 10.2 shows which alternative privileges can be used to give access to specific administration commands.

Table 10.2 Administrator Commands and Privileges

Administration Operation	Administrator Password	Function Privilege	Account
Create, Delete, Rename Database	Database Administrator		
Copy, Paste Database	Database Administrator		
Reorganise Database	Database Administrator		System
Backup Database	Database Administrator		System
Restore Database	User account User account		
Add, Delete Languages		Database Management	System
Add, Delete Font Formats		Font Format Management	System
View Users		Show User Management	System
Add, Delete Users		User Management	System
View Statistics	See Note 1	See Note 1	See Note 1
Edit Database Attributes		Database Management	System
Configure Database Properties		Database Management	System
Import, Export, Merge		Database Export	System

Note 1: ARIS Help says that Database Administrator (*sic*) Function Privilege is required, but in fact it works without any privileges.

10.2.2   Function Privileges

Function Privileges (Table 10.3) are assigned to individual users by someone using the **system** account or by a User who themselves has the *User Management*
privilege.

The procedure for assigning Function Privileges is described in detail in
Chapter 11. Users can be given any combination of Function Privileges and it is
usually preferable to allocate privileges this way rather than giving many people
access to the **system** account (see Section 10.2.3).

Table 10.3 Function Privileges

Privilege	Use
Change management	Manage change proposals submitted by other users (e.g. modify proposals, propose measures, give feedback, set priorities, and define responsibilities).
Database export	Merge (copy and paste) parts of one database into other databases (the privilege is required for both databases). Import and Export database content.
Database management	Manage languages for the database (create, edit or delete). Edit database attributes.
Font format management	Manage database fonts (create, edit, delete).
Method changes	Can change the appearance of objects and connections (e.g. *Fill color*, *Line Weight*, etc). **Note**: a User can apply pre-defined Templates without this privilege.
Prefix management	Manage the Identifier Prefix available in the database (create, edit delete). **Note**: this is assigning the Prefix for the database – assigning the Prefix to users requires *User Management* privilege.
Show user management	Allows a user to see the list of Users and User Groups defined for the database and view their Properties. **Note**: to create, edit or delete User Accounts and User Groups requires *User Management* privilege.
User management	Manage Users and User Groups (create, change properties, delete).

10.2.3   System Account

The default "**system**" User Account is a special account of type "*System user*" which has all of the Function Privileges, but also has additional rights (e.g. can reorganise and backup the database) that even a User with all the Function Privileges does not have.

When you use a **LOCAL** database you will normally use the **system** account by default and hence have all the necessary privileges. When you are using an ARIS Business Server, then only a limited number of people will have access to the **system** account. The default passwords for the System account are:

- User name = "system",

- Password = "manager".

10.2.4   Administration Passwords

The Administration Passwords (Table 10.4) allow actions to be carried out at the server level that affect all databases.

Table 10.4 Administrator Accounts and Passwords

Privilege	Use
Database Administrator	Database Backup, Restore, Delete, Copy, Paste, Rename, Reorganise.
	Default = "DBADMIN".
Configuration Administrator	Open Configuration folder, change ARIS Method or Conventions (Filters, Font Formats, Languages, Templates).
	Default = "CFGADMIN".
Scripts Administrator	Open Evaluations folder, create Reports, Macros, Transformations, and Semantic Checks.
	Default = "SCRIPTADMIN".
Business Publisher Administrator	Open Business Publisher Server.
	Default = "BPADMIN".

You don't actually log in with the Administration Passwords. When you try and carry out an operation requiring an Administration Password on your **LOCAL** server or an ARIS Business Server, the default passwords in View > Options [Login] will be compared with the actual server passwords. If the passwords match then the operation will be carried out, if not, then you will be asked to provide a password. Once a valid password match has been made you will have the privileges it provides for the rest of the session while you are using that server. You cannot log out of an Administrator Password, if you no longer want to have its privileges, you will have to shutdown and restart ARIS.

 Warning – once you have correctly entered the Database Administration password to carry out an administration operation (e.g. to create a database) you will have those administration privileges for the rest of the ARIS session. This means you can carry out another operation (e.g. deleting a database) without being asked for the password again.

Changing the Administration Passwords

To change an Administration Password (e.g. the *Database Administrator*), select the server name in the *Administration Module* and either:

- File > Change password > Database administrator,
- Right-Click > Change password > Database administrator.

Now enter the *New password* and *Confirm password* in the Change password (database administrator) Dialog Box. You will notice that you have to know the *Current password* to be able to make this change.

If you wish you can change the default password to be the same as the new password by ticking the *Add to defaults* checkbox. You will now automatically have the password enabled whenever you connect to this server.

Changing the Default Administration Passwords

If you don't wish to be prompted for the Administration Passwords when you carry out an administration activity on a server, you can store the passwords in the appropriate field of the Administrator Passwords area of the *View > Options [Login] Dialog Box* (Fig. 10.1).

 Expert Tip – when working on an ARIS Business Server it is best to disable the default Administration Passwords (remove the tick from the *Use defaults* checkbox in the *View > Options [Login] Dialog Box*) until you need them so you do not inadvertently carry out server level operations.

 Warning – once you have successfully carried out an administration operation with a valid *Database administrator* password then, even if you disable the use of default Administration Passwords, some operations (e.g. deleting a database) will still work for the remainder of the session without again asking for the Administration Password.

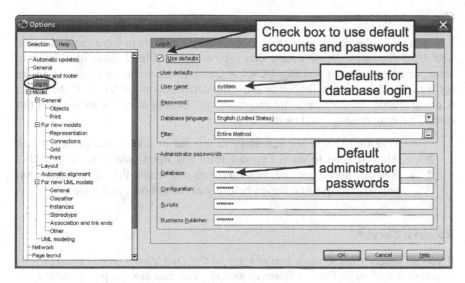

Fig. 10.1 View > Options [Login] Dialog Box

10.3   Server Administration

10.3.1   Server Connection

Add Server

To connect to an ARIS Business Server, select **ARIS Network** in the *Tree View* of the *Administration Module* and do either of:

- File > Server > Add server,
- Right-Click > Add server.

In the *Add ARIS Business Server Dialog Box* enter the *Server name or IP address*. The name of the server will now appear in the *Tree View* beneath the **ARIS Network**.

You can enter the server details at any time, irrespective of whether you are actually connected to the network. If you are connected to a network, you can check whether the server connection is valid by ticking the *Test connection* checkbox.

Connecting to a Server

You can make the connection to a server whose details you have entered in the *Add ARIS Business Server Dialog Box* (above) by double-clicking on the server name, or by selecting it and Right-Click > Open. If the server is available on the network, the *Tree View* will open to show the databases on the server. If the server is not available, or the details are incorrect, an *"Unable to find a server with this name"* warning message will be displayed.

 Warning – it is not necessary to log out or disconnect from a server. All you need to do is Log out from any open databases. If you click Remove server (see below), then you will delete the server details and will have to use Add server before you can connect to it again.

Remove Server

If you no longer want to see a server entry in the *Tree View* you can remove it by selecting it and Right-Click > Remove server. You can always put it back again using the Add server command.

Change Server Administration Passwords

The use of the Server Administration Passwords and how to change them is describe above in Section 10.2.4.

10.3.2   Server Configuration

The following items can be configured at the server level and effect all the databases on the server; each is described in their own chapters as shown:

- Conventions:
    - Filters (Chapter 14),
    - Font Formats (Chapter 15),
    - Languages (Chapter 15),
    - Templates (Chapter 15),
- Method (Chapter 12),
- Queries (Chapter 5),
- Evaluations (Chapter 9):
    - Reports,
    - Macros,
    - Transformations,
    - Semantic Checks.

Warning – ARIS Method changes affect all databases on the server. You should be particularly careful of importing Method Filters that have associated Method changes as these could cause unexpected effects on existing Filters and databases.

10.4   Database Management

10.4.1   Create Database

To create a new database on a server go to the *Administration Module*, select the server and do any of:

- File > New > Database,
- Right-Click > New > Database,
- Click on the New button on the *ARIS Toolbar*.

You will need to know the *Database Administrator* password and have stored it as a default password (see Section 10.2.4) or enter it when prompted. Now enter a *Name* for the database in the *Create database Dialog Box* and click OK. The new database name will appear in the *Tree View* underneath the server name.

You can now double-click on the database name to open it.

Warning – if you create a database on an ARIS Business Server you should immediately change the *system* User password to prevent any unauthorised access. You may also wish to consider creating a second, emergency, system account as described in Chapter 11.

10.4.2   Open and Close Database

To open a database, double-click on its name, or select it in the *Explorer Module* or *Administration Module* and Right-Click > Open or Right-Click > Log in.

If you double-clicked on it or used the Open command and the *system* user password is the same as the default password entered in the View > Options [Login] Dialog Box, the database will be opened and the icon next to its name will show a right-facing arrow.

If the password is different to the default, or you used the Log in command, the *Login Wizard* will prompt you for the *User* name and *Password*.

To close a database, select it and Right-Click > Log out.

10.4.3   Delete Database

To delete a database, make sure you are logged out of the database (its icon should show a small database icon without a right facing arrow), select it in the right-hand pane of the *Administration Module* and do any of:

- Edit > Delete,
- Right-Click > Delete,
- Click on the Delete button on the *ARIS Toolbar*.

   You will be asked to confirm that you really want to delete the database. To delete a database you will need to have the *Database Administrator* password.

 Warning – you are strongly advised to Backup the database (see Section 10.4.7) before deleting it as, once deleted, there is no way to recover it.

10.4.4   Rename Database

To rename a database you will need to have the *Database Administrator* password. Make sure you are logged out of the database and select it in the right-hand pane of the *Administration Module* and do any of:

- Edit > Rename,
- Right-Click > Rename,
- Press F2.

 Warning – in *ARIS Business Architect* you can only use letters and numbers when creating or renaming a database. Names may contain special characters if imported from a backed-up file which has had its name created in ARIS Toolset or changed in Microsoft Windows. You will not be able to rename such a database without deleting the special characters.

10.4.5   Copy and Paste Database

You can copy a database on a server, or between networked servers, using the copy and paste commands:

1. Select the database,
2. Edit > Copy or Right-Click > Copy,
3. Select the server,
4. Edit > Paste or Right-Click > Paste.

If the database is copied and pasted on the same server, the copy of the database will have the same name as the original appended with a sequence number (e.g. "*test*" becomes "*test(1)*"). To copy a database you will need to have the *Database Administrator* password on both source and target databases.

10.4.6 Reorganise Database

When object or connection occurrences are deleted from an ARIS model, the object or connection definitions are not immediately removed from the database, even if they are not used in any other models.

Object definitions remain visible in the ARIS group in which they were created (or moved to) and occurrences of these objects can be placed into models. If an object is deleted from a group (i.e. select it and Right-Click > Delete), then it will be completely deleted from the database after an appropriate warning message. If the object has occurrences in any models, a second warning message will be given and only when confirmed will the object definition and all its occurrences be deleted.

In a similar way, the relationship definition for a connection will remain in the database, even after all occurrences of the connection have been deleted from models. Unlike objects, it is not possible to see the relationship definition in the group structure, however you can still see the relationship by viewing the *Properties [Relationships] Dialog Box* of one of the objects it was originally connected to.

 Expert Tip – you can tell when a relationship definition no longer has any connection occurrences in models by selecting the relationship in the *Properties [Relationships] Dialog Box* of one of the objects it was originally connected to and looking at the Go to button. If the button is greyed out there are no model occurrences.

If no action were taken, all these unused object and relationship definitions would start to fill up the database and take up valuable storage space. They can be removed by using the Reorganize command. Select the database in the *Administration Module* and do either of:

- File > Database > Reorganize,

- Right-Click > Reorganize.

To reorganise a database you will need to have the *Database Administrator* password or to log into the database using the *system* account. After an appropriate warning message, any object or relationship definitions without occurrences in models will be deleted. You may wish to Backup the database before reorganisation.

When the reorganisation is complete, if any items have been deleted, you will be given the option to view a log of the results of the reorganisation in the *Reorganization results Dialog Box* (see Fig. 10.2). If any unused objects are being edited when the database is reorganised, these will not be deleted and will be listed in the *Reorganization results Dialog Box*.

Warning – if you have manually created objects in the *Explorer Module*, or have created library objects that are not yet used in models, they will be deleted if the Reorganize command is run. If you want to preserve as yet unused objects, paste them into a '*library model*' to ensure they have at least one model occurrence.

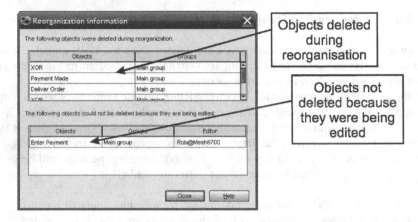

Fig. 10.2 Reorganization Results Dialog Box

10.4.7   Backup Database

The contents of ARIS databases are automatically updated on your *LOCAL* server or an ARIS Business Server as models and objects are saved during editing. You can manually save a copy of an ARIS database onto your PC's hard disk to create a backup or to transfer the database to someone else. To create a database backup, select the database in the *Explorer Module* or *Administration Module* and do either of:

- File > Database > Backup,
- Right-Click > Backup.

   The *Select file Dialog Box* will ask you to choose a location on your hard disk to save a file in "*.adb" format. This is a compressed file format that you can electronically save to other storage media or transfer by email. You can accept the default file name which is the same as the current database name or choose a different name. To Backup a database you will need to have the *Database Administrator* password or to log into the database using the *system* account.

Expert Tip – if you plan to backup and send a database to another user, you may also need to send a copy of the Method Filter you used to create the database (see Chapter 14 for information on exporting Method Filters).

10.4.8   Restore

To load a database previously saved to your hard disk using the Ba<u>c</u>kup command, select the server name in the *Administration Module* and do either of:

- File > Ser<u>v</u>er > <u>R</u>estore,
- Right-Click > <u>R</u>estore.

You will need to have the *Database Administrator* password. The database will now be loaded onto the server and will appear under the server name with the same name as the file name used to backup the database.

The database will be loaded with the same User Accounts as it had on the server from where it was backed up.

Warning – if you <u>R</u>estore a database onto an ARIS Business Server that was originally the result of a Ba<u>c</u>kup from *LOCAL* server, make sure you immediately change the *system* account password to prevent any unauthorised access.

If the database was created on another server using a specific Method Filter, you may also need to import that Filter (see Chapter 14) to ensure the correct items are visible.

Warning – if a database makes use of User-defined symbols that have been applied using an ARIS Method change on another server, make sure you import the related Method Filter before you run the <u>R</u>estore command to load the database. Otherwise you may find the custom symbols do not appear in the restored database.

Expert Tip – you cannot <u>R</u>estore a database with the same name as an existing database. To restore such a database, either Re<u>n</u>ame the existing ARIS database or change the filename of the database to be restored.

10.4.9   Statistics

The S<u>t</u>atistics command allows you to view the numbers of the following items in a database:

- Attributes,
- Connection occurrences,
- Connections,
- Font Formats,
- Groups,
- Languages,

- Models,
- Object occurrences,
- Objects,
- User Groups,
- Users.

To view the statistics, log into a database and in the *Administration Module*, select the database name and do either of:

- File > Database > Statistics,
- Right-Click > Statistics.

The *Create database statistics Dialog Box* (Fig. 10.3a) will allow you to choose which of the statistics you want to view. Right-click to choose Select all or Deselect all. Tick the appropriate boxes, click OK and the *Database statistics Dialog Box* will display the selected statistics (Fig. 10.3b).

 Bug – ARIS Help says that the *Database Administrator* password is required to view database statistics, but in ARIS 7.02 any User can view database statistics without any special passwords or privileges.

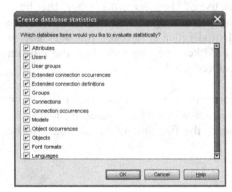   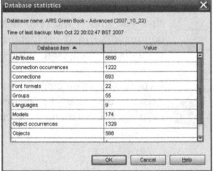

a) Create database statistics   **b) Database statistics display**

Fig. 10.3 Database Statistics

10.4.10   Export and Import

You can import and export models in standard interchange formats so as to exchange models with other modelling tools. Two formats are provided:

- XML (eXtended Markup Language) – all ARIS files,
- XMI (XML Metadata Interchange) – UML files.

XML

XML defines a format for how information can be interchanged. It defines the *syntax* of a language, but doesn't say anything about the meaning of the information (the *semantics*). To exchange information using XML, the vendors of both the tools will need to agree what information will be transferred using XML and how each tool will interpret it. Such an interchange can only be successful if both tools are capable of representing some or all of the same information in their modelling environment. You can also use XML to transfer information between ARIS databases, but it is better to use the Merge command (see Section 10.7).

XMI

XMI provides a semantic definition for interchanging UML (Uniform Modelling Notation) object-oriented models between different tools. It uses XML has the underlying exchange format and uses a DTD (Document Type Definition) model to define the document structure and the legal elements and attributes that convey the semantic meaning of the information. The semantics for importing and exporting ARIS UML models are described in the xmi_UML14.dtd file which is located in the Tools/UML directory of the ARIS installation CD.

Export

To export a model, select it in the *Explorer Module* and do either of:

- File > Export > as XML file or File > Export > as XMI format,
- Right-Click > Export > as XML file or Right-Click > Export > as XMI format.

The *XML Export Wizard* or the *Perform XMI Export Wizard* will guide you through selecting the appropriate export options.

Import

To import an existing XML or XMI file, select a group in the database in which you want to import the file and do either of:

- File > Import > XMI files or File > Import > XML files,
- Right-Click > Import > XMI files or Right-Click > Import > XML files.

Then select the location of the file on your hard disk.

10.4.11   Merge

You cannot directly copy and paste models, objects or groups between databases. However, you can Merge items from one database into another. This effectively is the same as a copy and paste, but provides more control over how items are transferred and how conflict resolution is handled. The Merge command is described in detail in Section 10.7.

10.5   Database Configuration

10.5.1   Introduction

Once we have created a database (see Section 10.4.1) it is very tempting to start using it straight away. However, there a few things we should configure before starting to use the database in earnest:

- Users,
- Font Formats,
- Languages,
- Properties (e.g. Identifiers).

These are especially important if the database is on an ARIS Business Server and will be used by other process modellers.

10.5.2   Users

If you use ARIS on your local PC and you are the only person to access your ARIS database, then there is no need to configure User Accounts. You can leave the default settings in the *View > Options [Login] Dialog Box* so that you always login with the **system** account and have full privileges (see Section 10.2.3). If you wish, you may change the **system** account password to provide some access security for your database, but that is normally all you need to do.

However, if you are setting up a database on an ARIS Business Server to allow collaborative modelling, it is essential to set up User Accounts for each person and to control their *Access Privileges* to various database groups. You can also assign *Function Privileges* to different Users to control what administrative tasks they can perform (see Section 10.2.2).

Setting up and configuring User Accounts and Access Privileges is a major topic and is described in detail in Chapter 11.

10.5.3   Font Formats

Introduction to Font Formats

In many software applications running under Microsoft Windows you can set the appearance of text by selecting from a wide range of different fonts. In ARIS, a User's ability to select any font they wish is restricted in order to create a standard 'look and feel' and to allow the application of corporate modelling conventions.

ARIS *Font Formats* are defined by the Database Administrator at the database level and can be applied to attribute text through model, object and connection appearance properties. Thus Users can only gain access to those fonts that have been selected by the Database Administrator (specifically someone with *Font format management* Function Privileges).

Creating New Font Formats

When a database is first created it will only have a single Font Format, the **Standard** Font Format, normally Arial 8pt; to create additional ARIS Font Formats:

1.   Login to the database using the **system** account or a User Account that has *Font format management* Function Privileges,

2.   Select the *Administration Module*,

3.   Select the **Font format** folder, underneath the database name,

4.   Right-Click > New > Font format or click the New button.

In the *Create font format Dialog Box* (Fig. 10.4), select the *Language* for which you want the Font Format to be available and enter a *Name* for the Font Format. You can choose any name you wish, but it is important to make the name meaningful to the different people who may be working on your database.

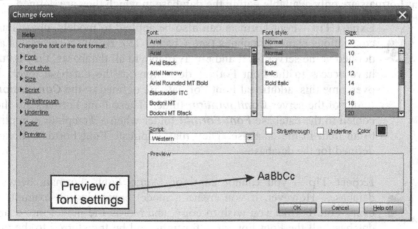

Fig. 10.4 Create Font Format Dialog Box

The *Preview* area provides a sample of the text. To change the style of the Font Format, click the Change font button. The *Change font Dialog Box* (Fig. 10.5) will now allow you to choose the font from the standard font set currently available in Microsoft Windows.

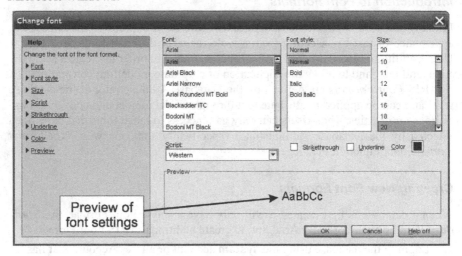

Fig. 10.5 Change Font Dialog Box

Click OK and you will return to the *Create font format Dialog Box*. The *Preview* area will update to show the new Font Format style. If you tick the *Default font* checkbox this Font Format will be used as standard for all ARIS attributes in that database unless you specifically choose a different Font Format. A default Font Format can be defined for each *Language*.

Click OK again and the new Font Format will appear in the right-hand pane. It is now available to be applied to any attribute placement selected in the database. Font Formats are only available within the database in which they are defined.

 Expert Tip – Font Formats can also be applied to models, objects and connections using Templates (see Chapter 15). Because Templates are defined at the server level and are available to all databases, they do not have access to the Font Format definitions at the database level. To overcome this, additional Font Formats are defined in the **Conventions** folder of the server **Configuration** folder. These Font Formats are then copied to the database **Font Format** folder when a Template is applied to an item in the database. They may duplicate Font Formats already defined for the database.

 Expert Tip – you cannot copy or Merge Fonts Formats between databases. However, if you create a model containing an example of every Font Format you wish to copy, and Merge the model into a new database, all the Font Format definitions will be transferred to the new database. You can then delete the transferred model.

Editing Font Formats

To change an existing Font Format, select the **Font Formats** folder in the *Administration Module*, select the Font Format you wish to change in the right-hand pane and:

- Right-Click > Prope_rties or click the Properties Button.

The *Properties – Font Format Dialog Box* will appear which is almost identical to the *Create font format Dialog Box* (Fig. 10.4). You can change the Font Format style by clicking the _Change font button and making the changes in the *Change font Dialog Box* (Fig. 10.5). The *Properties [Font format] Dialog Box* has one additional function; pressing the _Reset button will revert the Font Format style to the default Font Format defined for the chosen language.

In addition to changing the properties of the Font Format, you can also set its attributes by selecting the Font Format and Right-Click > _Attributes. The *Attributes Window* will allow you to change the *Name* of the Font Format as well as adding values for the *Description/Definition* and *Full name* attributes.

You can also change the name of a Font Format using Right-Click > Re_name (F2), delete it using Right-Click > _Delete and set it as the default Font Format using Right-Click > _Default font format.

10.5.4   Languages

Introduction to Languages

If you are creating process designs for a global organisation, you may well want to create standard processes that are used in all countries. While the visible process flow is likely to be easily understood, irrespective of language, it is unreasonable to expect everyone to understand the attribute values presented in a single language. ARIS provides for this by not only providing a user interface in different languages, but also allowing the attributes of all ARIS items (e.g. models, objects, etc) to be maintained in multiple languages.

Designers can create the process using the corporate standard language and translators can then create attribute values in a variety of other languages. Users can easily switch between languages and ARIS Reports and ARIS Web Publishing output can be generated in the chosen language.

Creating a New Database Language

When a database is first created it will typically have five languages already available (English, French, German, Japanese and Spanish).

To create additional languages:

1. Login to the database using the **system** account or a User Account that has *Database management* Function Privileges,

2. Select the **Languages** folder, underneath the database name,

3. Right-Click > New > Language or click the New button.

In the *Create language Dialog Box* (Fig. 10.6), choose the new language from the *Select language* list.

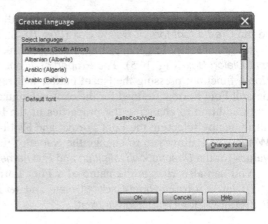

The *Default font box* beneath shows a preview of the Font Format that will be used as the default (e.g. the **Standard** Font Format) for this language. To change the Font Format, click the Change font button and choose the Font Format style from the *Change font Dialog Box* (Fig. 10.5). Click OK and the Language will now be displayed in the right-hand pane.

Fig. 10.6 Create Language Dialog Box

Once a Language has been created, you can change its default Font Format by selecting the Language and Right-Click > Properties or click the Properties Button. You can also change the Font Format by selecting the Font Format you want to be the default and using the *Properties [Font format] Dialog Box* (see above).

Logging in With a Different Language

When a User logs into an ARIS database using the *Login Wizard* (i.e. not using the *User defaults* set in the *View > Options [Login] Dialog Box*), the *Select filter and language Dialog Box* will allow the User to choose from the languages defined by the Database Administrator. All attribute values (including the names of groups, models and objects) will now be displayed in the chosen language.

? **Question** – why do all my groups and models have the name (**untitled**) and the labels on my objects appear blank?

Answer – you have logged into a database, selecting a language for which no attribute values have been maintained. Log out and then log back in and choose a different language.

Expert Tip – changing the language when logging in does not change the language of the ARIS user interface or the language in which attribute type names, object types and other ARIS Method information is displayed. If you selected multiple languages when you installed ARIS, you can select in which language to display the user interface and ARIS Method information using the *Languages* entries in the *View > Options [General] Dialog Box.*

Maintaining Multiple Languages

The values of attributes of groups, models, objects and connections will be displayed in the language chosen when a User logs in. However, it is possible using the *Attributes Window*, to display and edit attributes in any of the languages defined by the Database Administrator.

To display attributes in an additional language, select the item for which you want to display attributes and Right-Click > Attributes (F8). The *Attributes Window* will be displayed as shown in Fig. 10.7a with a single column for attribute values in the default language (i.e. English). To display another language, select the column header of the existing column and Right-Click > Insert language or click on the Insert language button. Choose the required language from the *Select languages Dialog Box* and click *OK*. A new column for the chosen language will displayed at the right-hand side of the *Attributes Window (*Fig. 10.7b).

a) Attribute Window
with a single language

b) Attribute Window
with multiple languages

Fig. 10.7 Attributes Window with Multiple Languages

You can display as many languages as you wish provided they have been defined by the Database Administrator. You can now directly compare the attribute values in different languages and enter appropriate translations. To remove a language column, select the column header and Right-Click > Remove column.

10.5.5   Properties

A database has properties just like any other ARIS item. To display database properties: login to the database, select its name in the *Administration Module* and do any of:

- Edit > Properties,
- Right-Click > Properties,
- Click the Properties button on the *ARIS Toolbar*.

The *Properties Dialog Box* will allow database properties to be viewed and set for:

- *General*,
- *Header and Footer*,
- *Identifiers*,
- *Logo Management*,
- *Method Filter*,
- *Page Layout*.

 Question – why can I only see the *General Dialog Box* within the database *Properties Dialog Box*?
Answer – if you view database *Properties* in the *Explorer Module*, only the *General Dialog Box* is visible. To view all dialog boxes, use the *Administration Module*.

General

The *Properties [General] Dialog Box* (Fig. 10.8) provides information on the database and server name, the User Account that has been used to log into the database and the Method Filter and Language in use. The same information can also be viewed as a tool tip by hovering your mouse over the database name.

Header and Footer

The *Properties [Header and footer] Dialog Box* (Fig. 10.9) allows you to define the information that will be shown in the header and footer of the pages produced when models are printed.

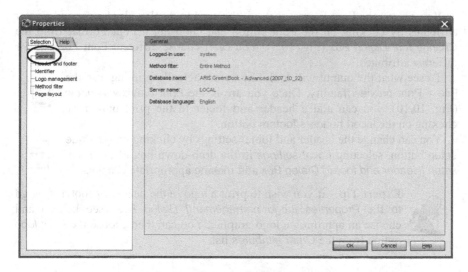

Fig. 10.8 The Properties [General] Dialog Box

There are three *Header* and *Footer* boxes at the top of the dialog box allowing you to set what will appear on the left, centre and right-hand sides of the pages. To select an attribute for printing, click in one of the *Header* and *Footer* boxes, then double-click on one of the attribute entries in the *Model and database attributes* or *Other attributes* lists. The chosen attribute will be displayed in the selected *Header* or *Footer* box. You can have a line drawn to separate the model display from the header or footer by ticking the *Separate headers and footers with lines* checkbox.

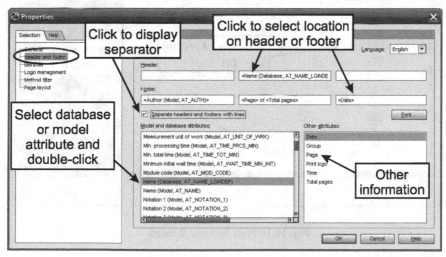

Fig. 10.9 Properties [Header and Footer] Dialog Box

You can set the Font Format that will be used to display all *Header* and *Footer* attributes by clicking on the Font button and choosing a Font Format from the *Change font Dialog Box* (Fig. 10.5). You can't choose different Font Formats for different attributes.

To see what the output will look like before actually printing, use the File > Print preview facility. Once you are in the *Print preview Window* (Fig. 10.10), you can add a header and footer to the print output by clicking on the Insert headers/footers button.

You can change the header and footer settings by clicking on the Page setup button, selecting *Local settings* in the drop-down box of the *Page setup [Header and footer] Dialog Box* and making appropriate changes.

 Expert Tip – if you wish to print a logo in the header or footer, first go to the *Properties [Logo management] Dialog Box* (see below) and choose an appropriate logo graphic. You can then choose the *Print logo* option from the *Other attributes* list.

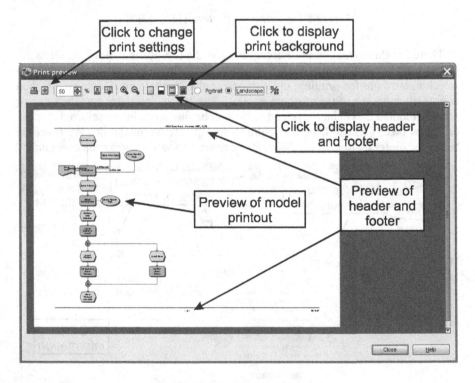

Fig. 10.10 Print Preview Window

Identifiers

The *Properties [Identifier] Dialog Box* (Fig. 10.11) allows one or more *Identifiers* to be defined that, when enabled, can be assigned to all new items (users, groups, models, objects, etc) created in the database. The *Identifier* is available as an attribute and can be used to provide a pseudo-unique reference for every item (easier to read than a GUID) which can be used for database administration. The *Identifier* value consists of a set of up to 20 alphanumeric characters (the *Prefix*) followed by an automatically allocated sequential number (e.g. xxxxx1234).

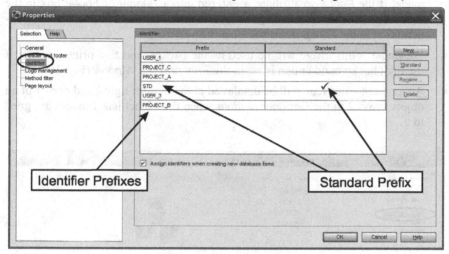

Fig. 10.11 Properties [Identifier] Dialog Box

When a database is first created, a single identifier with the prefix **STD** is defined. The **STD** prefix is automatically assigned to each User Account and you can also create additional prefixes and manually associate them to specific User Accounts (see Chapter 11). If the *Assign identifiers when creating new database items* checkbox is ticked, then whenever a User creates a new item (e.g. a model, object or connection, etc) it will automatically be assigned an identifier with the Prefix associated with the User.

To add another identifier prefix, click the New button and in the *Create prefix Dialog Box* enter the new *Prefix*. The *Prefix* can have up to 20 characters although it is best to limit it to a more manageable number. If you click the Standard checkbox, this prefix will become the standard prefix for all items. Click OK and the *Properties [Identifier] Dialog Box* will now show the new identifier in the list. You can rename or delete an existing prefix by selecting it and clicking on the Rename or Delete buttons.

 Expert Tip – if a prefix is deleted, any Users who had that prefix assigned to them will revert to using the standard database prefix. Any items that have an identifier with that prefix already allocated to them will retain that identifier.

You can choose any prefix to become the standard prefix by selecting it and clicking the Standard button.

Logo Management

The *Properties [Logo management] Dialog Box* (Fig. 10.12) allows you to select three different graphics options:

- *Print logo* – this image will be displayed in the header or footer of a printed model if the *Print logo* attribute is entered into a *Header* or *Footer* box in the *Properties [Header and footer] Dialog Box* and the Insert headers/footers option is set in the *Print preview Window* (Fig. 10.10),

- *Wallpaper* – this image will be used as the background to a printed model if the Print background option is set in the *Print preview Window* (Fig. 10.10),

- *Assignment* – this icon will be displayed at the bottom right-hand corner of an object symbol in the *Designer Module* when the object has a model assigned to it.

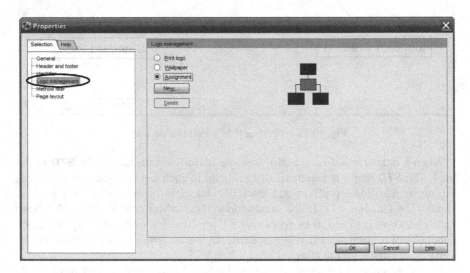

Fig. 10.12 Properties [Logo Management] Dialog Box

To set one of the options, click its radio button and the current graphic assigned to this option will be displayed. If no graphic is visible, then none has been selected; click on the New button and choose an appropriate graphic file. If you no longer want to use that graphic, click the Delete button to remove it (you cannot remove the *Assignment* graphic – a graphic must always be selected).

Method Filter

The *Properties [Method filter] Dialog Box* (Fig. 10.13) allows you to select the Method Filter that will automatically be assigned to any new User or User Group that is created. Select a Filter from the drop-down box and the description of the Filter will be shown beneath it.

You can assign an alternative Filter, or several Filters, to User Accounts and User Groups using the *Properties [User/Method filter] Dialog Box* (see Chapter 11).

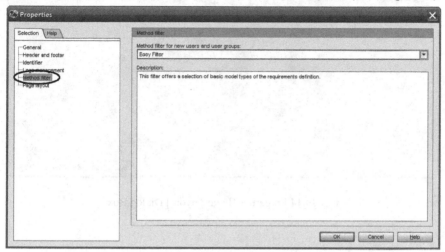

Fig. 10.13 Properties [Method Filter] Dialog Box

Page Layout

The *Properties [Page layout] Dialog Box* (Fig. 10.14) allows you to set the margins of printed model pages. If you tick the *Show navigation marks* checkbox, then when the model spans more than one printed page, arrows will be placed at the edges of the pages showing the page number of the adjacent page.

You can also access these settings by clicking on the Page setup button in the *Print preview Window*.

10.5.6   Attributes

To display the attributes of a database, select the database name in the *Explorer Module* or the *Administration Module* and do any of:

- Edit > Attributes,
- Right-Click > Attributes,
- Click the Attributes button on the *ARIS Toolbar*.

The *Attributes Window* will display a range of attributes that can be set to help manage the database.

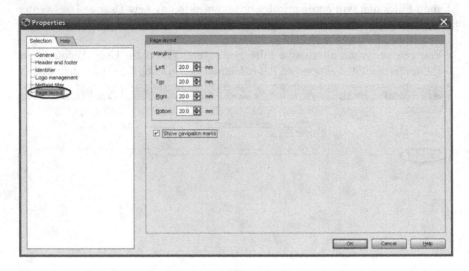

Fig. 10.14 Properties [Page Layout] Dialog Box

10.6   Database Administration

We have now configured the database ready for use, but it is still completely empty of content. Before we start creating models (and objects) it is worth giving some thought to the structure and management of the database contents.

10.6.1   Managing Group Structure

A *Group* is the ARIS name for a folder containing models or objects. The topmost group in the database is called, by default, **Main Group**. You can change the name of this (or any other group) by selecting it in the *Explorer Module* and Right-Click > Rename or by pressing [F2].

You may store all of your models in **Main Group**, but normally you will want to create a hierarchy of groups in which to structure your models. You can create a new group by selecting an existing group in the *Explorer Module* and Right-Click > New > Group or by pressing the Create Group button. The new group will be created in the selected group.

You can delete an existing group by selecting it and Right-Click > Delete. If the group is not empty you will be warned and given the option to delete it anyway or to cancel the delete.

Warning – you should be careful about deleting groups with content. You should check that both the models and objects in the group are no longer required and be certain the objects do not have occurrences in models elsewhere in the group structure.

The exact format of your group structure will depend on the nature of your modelling project. However a typical structure might follow a level-based process hierarchy similar to that shown in Fig. 10.15.

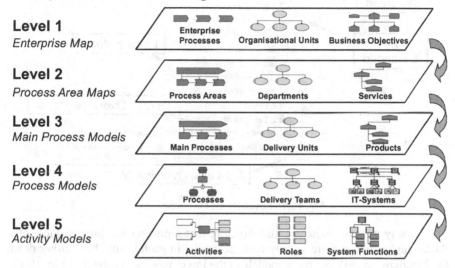

Fig. 10.15 Level-Based Process Hierarchy

The highest levels of the hierarchy typically contain *Value-added chain diagrams* which have further *VACDs* or *EPCs* assigned to them representing increasing levels of detail. Fig. 10.16 shows the first three levels of a group structure that could be used to replicate such a hierarchy.

In **Main Group** there is a single **Business Overview Model** (usually a *VACD* or a *Structuring model*) providing an overview to the database and providing assignment links to the more detailed models. In the overview model there are three Level 1 Functions (**Direct the Business, Manage the Business** and **Operate the Business**). We can also see that in **Main Group** there are groups for each of these functional areas. If we look at the expanded group for **Operate the Business** we can see it also has a *VACD* model and sub-groups representing the sub-processes of **Operate the Business** that would be shown in the **Business Overview Model**.

Drilling down again by expanding the Level 2 group, **Deliver Product**, we can see there is now an *EPC* for **Deliver Product** and further Level 3 sub-groups which will contain more detailed *EPCs* that are decompositions of the Level 2 *EPC*.

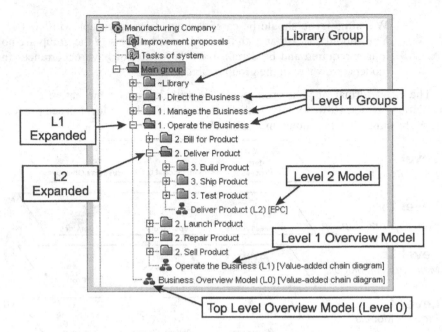

Fig. 10.16 Level-Based Group Structure

This way we can create a group structure that replicates our process hierarchy. At the higher levels there is only a single model in each group, but further down the hierarchy we will see more models in the lower groups as shown in Fig. 10.17.

 Expert Tip – the naming convention in the example shows group names starting with the hierarchy level number and the model names ending with the level number. This is so you can use the Find command to locate models with similar names and order them alphabetically without the level number distorting the sort order. Alternatively you can put the level number at the front so they are sorted by level.

10.6.2   Libraries

When we add resource objects (e.g. *Organizational unit types*, *Application system types*, etc) to models we normally use these to represent entities in our business (e.g. Sales Ordering System). These objects normally support many of our processes and when creating these resource objects it is important not to create duplicate objects with the same name. The power of using ARIS relationships is it enables us to ask questions such as: "tell me all the tasks supported by this IT system" or "tell me all the data accessed by this department". It is only possible to carry out this analysis if, each time we model a resource, we ensure we use an *occurrence copy* of the same object definition.

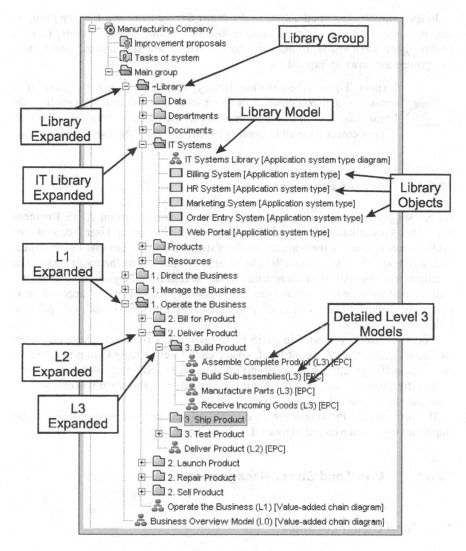

Fig. 10.17 Expanded Group Structure

A good way to manage resource objects is to create a library of similar objects by placing them all in a single group. It is then easy to re-use these objects and there is less temptation to create new ones each time. You can create a structure of library groups in your database as shown in Fig. 10.16 and appoint a Model Librarian (see Chapter 3) who creates and manages resource objects on behalf of all users. Typically, you would give the Librarian full 'write' access to these groups, but all other Users would only have 'read' access so they could incorporate them into their models, but not change the definition of the objects.

In the example described above, under **Main Group** there is a **Library** group in which we can store the various resource objects we want to use (e.g. *Application system types* and *Organizational unit types*). These are sub-divided into further sub-groups as shown in Fig. 10.17.

Expert Tip – when storing library objects in a library group it is recommended you create a library model containing one of each of the library objects. This will prevent any of the objects being deleted if they are not currently used in another model and the database is reorganised.

10.6.3   Access Privileges

As we suggested earlier, if you are setting up a database on an ARIS Business Server to allow collaborative modelling, it is essential to set up User Accounts for each person to control their access to the various database groups. For instance, you may want all of your modellers to be able to view all of the modellers in the database, but you may want to restrict 'write' access for changing models to specific modelling teams. You may want to completely restrict 'write' access to certain parts of the database to 'freeze' processes after a product launch or a particular IT system release.

Access control is provided in ARIS by User Access Privileges. These privileges can be set at the User Account level, where each User or User Group is given access to specific groups; or at the group level, where each group is made available to specific User Accounts or User Groups. The effect is the same whether you set access at the User level or group level.

Because Access Privileges are so directly related to User Administration, this important topic is described in more detail in Chapter 11.

10.6.4   Model and Object Management

Model and Object Location

Setting up a group structure and assigning Access Privileges provides a good framework for managing the models and objects in your database. Of course, not everyone will always adhere to your structure and over time you may wish to change the structure or tidy up items that have become misplaced.

An important concept to grasp is that object definitions do not necessarily live in the same groups as the models in which they have occurrences. When a model is created, and new objects are created by putting their symbols in the model, their object definitions will be stored in the same group as the model. If the same object is re-used in another model in another group, then an object occurrence will be placed in the model, but the object definition will stay in the group where it was first created. Furthermore, if a model is moved from one group to another, any object definitions originally associated with it will not automatically move with the model. You can see that over time objects become spread around the group structure with no particular relationship to the location of the models in which they have occurrences.

Moving Objects

You may well ask if it matters that objects become spread around the group structure. For the most part it doesn't. However, as we saw above in Section 10.6.2, it is important that resource objects can re-used and the best way to do this is to move them into library groups. You can move them by dragging and dropping them in the *Explorer Module* or by cutting and pasting them (don't use copy and paste otherwise you will create duplicate objects). You can also use the Find command (see Chapter 5) to identify specific types of object or objects that have specific attributes maintained.

For the remainder of the objects (e.g. Functions, Events and Rules) there is no obvious logic to where they should be located so it is normally best to leave them wherever they happen to be.

Moving Models

You can move a model from one group to another by selecting it in the *Explorer Module* and dragging it to a new group. You can also cut and paste the model to a new location. When you move the model, only the model will be re-located and the object definitions for objects with occurrences in the model will stay wherever they happen to be in the group structure.

If you want to move a model to a new group and also want to move all the objects that have occurrences in the model to the same group, you can use the Move here with objects command:

1. Select the model in the *Explorer Module*,
2. Right-click the mouse and drag the model to the new group,
3. Release the mouse key,
4. Select the Move here with objects command.

The model and all its objects will be moved to the new group, provided you have 'write' Access Privileges for the source and target groups for the model, and the groups containing all the object definitions for the object occurrences in the model. If any of the objects are in groups with read-only access (e.g. objects in library groups), these will not be moved, thus preserving any deliberately set group structure (e.g. a library).

10.6.5   Consolidating Objects

Introduction to Consolidating

Although the use of library groups helps promote the reuse of resource objects, rather than the creation of new objects, it is inevitable that, over time, you will end up with duplicate objects with the same or similar names. The task of finding these duplicate objects and replacing them all with a single object is made much easier by the Find and Consolidate commands.

Once we have found a set of objects with the same name, we can replace all these objects with one of the objects whose definition we have chosen to be the *master object*. After the Consolidate command has been executed, the remaining single object definition (based on the master object) will have taken on all of the relationships, assignments and attributes of all of the redundant objects which it replaced.

Finding Objects for Consolidation

To locate objects with duplicate names, use the Find command (see Chapter 5 for more detail). Select a group for which you want to find duplicate objects (or *Main Group* for the entire database) and Right-Click > Find.

In the *Standard Tab* of the *Find Dialog Box* (Fig. 10.18), select the *Objects with identical names* option in the *Find what* drop-down list.

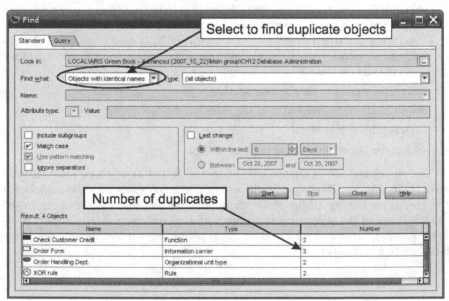

Fig. 10.18 Find Objects With Identical Names

You can refine the search criteria by selecting an object type in the *Type* list and by selecting the *Include subGroups*, *Match case* and *Ignore separators* options (see Chapter 5). Click Start and a list of all objects with identical names will be returned (Fig. 10.18).

The first entry shows there are two Functions with the name **Check Customer Credit**; this may be correct if the Functions are doing something similar in different parts of the process. However, it is good practice to ensure that no Functions have the same name and so, even if they are similar, it is best to try and use slightly different names. You can check where they are being used by viewing their Properties using the Consolidate command as we shall see below.

The second entry shows three *Information carriers* called **Order Form**; again this could be correct if we have three different order forms being used in different parts of the process. However, if it is in fact the same order form, then would want to consolidate the objects into a single object; if they are different, you should use different names.

The third line shows two *Organizational unit types* called **Order Handling Dept**. This is almost certainly incorrect as we will probably only have a single order handling department so let us consolidate these. Select the entry and Right-Click > Consolidate; the *Select object Dialog Box* of the *Consolidation Wizard* will open (Fig. 10.19).

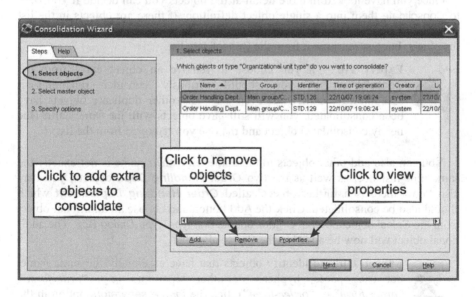

Fig. 10.19 Consolidation Wizard Select Object Dialog Box

Question – why do I always see a large number of *Rule* objects (e.g. *XOR*) listed when using the Find command with the *Objects with identical names* option?

Answer – as with any object, when it is first placed in a model the name of the Rule defaults to the object type (e.g. *XOR*). With most objects we then rename it to give it a more meaningful name. In theory we should do the same with *Rule* objects, but in practice we rarely do and hence we see a lot of *Rule* objects with identical names. These can be ignored.

Select objects

The *Select object Dialog Box* (Fig. 10.19), shows each of the individual object definitions of the type selected that have duplicate names. The columns in the list provide further information (e.g. *Group, Identifier, Creator*, etc) that may help you to identify the object. If you want further information, for instance to know what models an object occurs in, you can select the entry in the list and click the Properties button. The normal *Properties Dialog Box* will be displayed and you can view the *Occurrences Tab* or *Relationships Tab* to find out more about the object.

Once you have looked in more detail at the objects you can decide if you want to Consolidate them into a single object definition. If there are objects in the list you don't want to consolidate, select them and click Remove. This does not delete the object, but just removes it from the Consolidate list.

Expert Tip – if you choose to remove an object entry from the Consolidate list, you should seriously consider renaming it straightaway. Otherwise, even after any other duplicate objects have been consolidated, you will still have objects with the same name (the newly consolidated object and the one you removed from the list).

You can also add other objects to the list, even if their name is not exactly the same. For instance, as well as the two **Order Handling Dept.** objects, you may also know there is a further object called **Order Handling Department** which should also be consolidated. Click the Add button and choose an additional object from the *Select objects of the 'Organizational unit type' type Dialog Box*. The additional object will now be added to the Consolidate list.

Expert Tip – to identify objects that have essentially the same name, but use spaces, hyphens or other separators (e.g. *"orderform"*, *"order form"* or *"order-form"*), tick the *Ignore separators* option in the *Find Dialog Box* (Fig. 10.18).

Once you are happy you have the correct set of objects to be consolidated, click the Next button.

Select Master Object

In order to consolidate the objects, we must choose one of the listed objects to be the *master object* whose definition will be used to replace the other objects. The *Select Master Object Dialog Box* (Fig. 10.20) lists the selected objects and you can choose the master by selecting an object and clicking the Use as the master button. The chosen object will be highlighted in red.

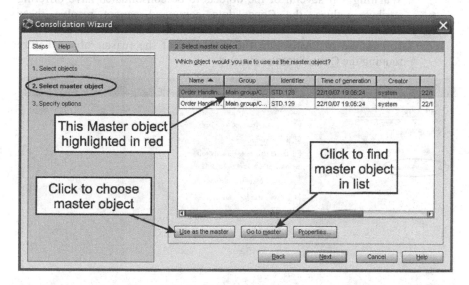

Fig. 10.20 Select Master Object Dialog Box

If you want more information about the objects in order to choose which is to be the master, you can again select an object and click the Properties button. If you want to change your mind about which object is the master, just select another object and click the Use as the master button. When you have chosen the master object, click Next.

 Expert Tip – to quickly locate the current master object in a long list of objects in the *Select Master Object Dialog Box*, click the Go to master button and the list will scroll to show the master object.

Specify Options

The different objects with the same name used to represent the same business entity (e.g. the same **Order Handling Dept.**) may have different attributes maintained or different values in those attributes. If we are to consolidate these multiple objects into a single object we have to decide how to handle these differing attributes.

If one of the redundant objects has an attribute maintained that is not maintained in the master object, then you can choose to have the value transferred to the master object by selecting the *Merge attributes* option in the *Specify options Dialog Box* (Fig. 10.21). This facility only works where there is a single redundant object with an additional maintained attribute or several redundant objects with the same attribute value.

 Warning – if several of the objects to be consolidated have differing attribute values, the Consolidate command cannot resolve these differences and the master object will not be updated. If this is the case you should manually edit the attributes of the master object before running the Consolidate command.

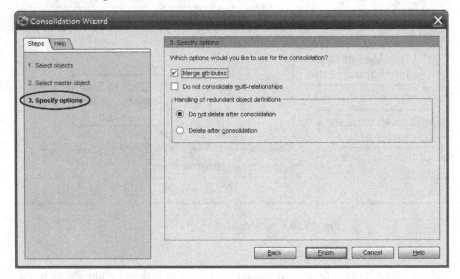

Fig. 10.21 Specify Options Dialog Box

When the Consolidate command is run, all occurrences of the redundant objects (i.e. those in the consolidation list not selected as the master object) will be replaced by occurrences of the master object with its attributes updated as described above. The objection definitions of the now redundant objects will remain in the database unless the Delete after consolidation checkbox is checked. Normally it makes sense to select this option as you don't want to have multiple objects with the same name remaining after consolidation.

 Warning – redundant objects that are no longer used after the Consolidate command is run, but have not been deleted because the Do not delete after consolidation option has been selected, will be deleted the next time the Reorganize command is executed. If you wish to keep these objects, make sure you place them in at least one model.

Select Variants

One situation where you may wish to have multiple objects with the same name is where you have made a *variant copy* of an object (see Chapter 8). For instance you may have used variants of an *Application system type* object to represent different releases of an IT System.

If you run the Find command with the *Objects with identical names* option, then variants with the same name will be also included in the *Select object Dialog Box* (Fig. 10.19). However, when you click Next, instead of going straight to the *Select Master Object Dialog Box*, the *Select variants dialog box* (Fig. 10.22) will specifically identify those objects with variants and allow you to choose if you wish to include these in the consolidation.

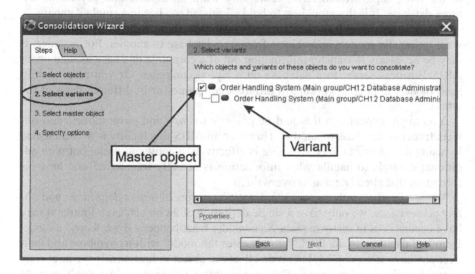

Fig. 10.22 Select Variants Dialog Box

Consolidation Report

In addition to performing consolidation by using the Find and Consolidate commands, you can also perform the same task using the *Consolidate* Report. This is especially valuable for large databases where there are likely to be many duplicate objects. It is quicker to run the report on the whole database and consolidate all objects at once than to individually have to select each duplicate object from the Find command and then run the Consolidate command on each one. The *Consolidate* Report is described in Chapter 16.

10.7   Merging Databases

10.7.1   Introduction to Merge

An ARIS database holds a collection of models that refers to a particular business, organisation, operational area or function, etc. If you wish, you can hold all your models in one database, or alternatively you can split your work into several different databases. The main criteria for deciding on how to structure your databases is that many operations such as process analysis, web publishing and many of the more sophisticated ARIS tools only work on models and objects in the same database. It is therefore best to hold all related models in a single database.

However you decide to structure you databases, there will be times when you want to transfer models and objects from one database to another. For instance, it may be necessary to transfer information out of a corporate database located on an ARIS Business server to a database on a laptop computer. Or you may wish to send models to people working in different companies or in different parts of the world.

You might expect that it would be possible to *copy* and *paste* models and objects from one database to another. However, in ARIS this facility is accomplished by using the *Merge* facility. Merging is effectively a copy and paste, but with additional controls to handle what information is actually transferred and how information that already exists is overwritten.

We are familiar with the important ARIS concepts of *object definitions* and *object occurrences*; we only have a single definition of an object, even though it may have occurrences in many models. So consider what happens if we 'copy' a model from one database to another. Not only does the model with its symbols and connections have to be copied, but so do all of the object definitions. If we now copy another model that has some of the same object occurrences, we don't want to create duplicates of the object definitions that were previously copied. We want to identify and re-use the existing definitions, only copying objects that don't already exist and then making sure the connections between the object occurrences and their definitions are all correctly established.

Now imagine we make some changes to these models. We add some new objects into the models (occurrences and corresponding definitions). We delete some connections and add some new ones, and we also change the attributes of some of the objects. What happens if we copy those models back into the original database? ARIS now has to work out how to integrate these changes into the original database. We don't want to create a set of duplicate objects; we want to recognise that some of the copied objects came from this database in the first place. If they haven't been changed we don't need to copy them. If they have changed we need to establish if the copied object should overwrite the original. If there are new objects these need to be added to the database.

You can see this is all quite complicated and is more than just the straight copy and paste you may be used to in Windows Explorer. However, this complication is managed for us by the ARIS *Merge* facility.

10.7.2   The GUID

The merge operation is based on the use of the GUID attribute. The GUID (Global Unique Identifier) is, as its name suggests, a completely unique identifier automatically allocated to every ARIS item as it is created (e.g. groups, models, objects, etc).

When a model or object, or any item with a GUID, is merged from one database into another, ARIS can tell by looking at the GUID, if that item already exists in the database. It can then compare its attributes, occurrences and relationships to see if the item is changed in anyway. It can then decide, based on the merge options, whether the item should be added to the database or whether it should update an existing item.

Thus a model and its related objects could be merged from one database to another; the model could then be edited, new objects added, other objects deleted and then transferred to yet another database. The model could be deleted and a new model created with the same name and having occurrences of some of the same objects. If this new model was now merged back into the original database, ARIS would be able to tell this was not the same model as before (despite the same name), but that some of its objects already existed and it could work out which of them had changed and what to do about it. No matter how many databases the model passed through, on different servers, in different organisations or in different parts of the World, ARIS would also be able to use the GUID to recognise items it had seen before.

10.7.3   The Merge Concept

Despite the complexity described above, the actual procedure for merging is effectively the same as performing a copy and paste. However, you need to be aware of what is actually going to happen.

When you merge a model from one database to another, all its object definitions will go with it. Those objects definitions may be located anywhere in the ARIS group structure of the original database (as we saw in Section 10.6.1). When the objects are transferred to the target database, the group structure that held those object definitions in the source database will be replicated in the target database. So not only will you see new models and objects, you may also see new groups unless they already existed in the target database.

If the models you chose to transfer have models assigned to their object occurrences, then you can choose to include these assigned models in the transfer as well. In this case the group structure that holds these assigned models and their related object definitions will also be transferred.

You can probably see that, if you have a database with a single high-level model with all other models linked to it through object assignments, then if you merge that single model into a new database and choose to transfer all assigned models, then in fact the entire contents of the database would go with it.

The converse of this also needs consideration. Transferring a single *EPC*, but without selecting assigned models, may not achieve the result you want if a lot of the detail is held in assigned *Function allocation diagrams*. One of the most important aspects of ARIS is the network of relationships between models and objects and so transferring a model from one database to another is never going to be as simple just copying and pasting a file.

 Warning – because of the way the Merge command works it is not possible to 'copy' a model from the source database into a specific group in the target database. The model will always be transferred into a group structure that is replica of the source database group structure.

The results of an ARIS merge can often be extensive and not always what you expect. Great care needs to be taken to think beforehand about what you want to achieve and want the results might be.

 Warning – because of the extensive effects of using the Merge command you are strongly recommended to backup both the source and target databases before running the command. It is important to backup the source database as well because people have been know to perform the merge in the wrong direction and overwrite the source database!

 Expert Tip – you can test the effect of a merge without actually performing it by selecting the *Merge preview* option (see below). An even better way is to first perform the merge into an empty database. This allows you to see exactly what group structure will be created and where models and objects will be located before you perform the merge on the target database.

You can select one or more groups, models or objects to be merged. If you select a model the merge will work as described above, taking with it all the necessary object definitions and groups. If you select a group, all the models and object definitions in the group will be transferred and each model will be processed to see what further models, objects and groups need to be transferred with it. Only if you just select object definitions will they be merged without anything else being transferred.

10.7.4   Making a Merge

To transfer items from one database to another:

1. Log into both source and target database, preferable as the **system** User,

2. In the source database, select one or more groups, models or objects,

3. Right-Click > Copy,

4. Select the target database name,

5. Right-Click > Paste as > Merge.

The *Merge Wizard* will now run and guide you through the merge options.

Question – why do I not see the Paste as > Merge option after I have made a copy and when I click on a group in the target database?
Answer – you must click on the target database name, not a group in the database.

Warning – because the Merge command both creates and transfers groups, models and objects into a replica of the source group structure, it must have Access Privileges to the required groups in the Target database; otherwise parts of the merge may fail. It is always best to run the Merge command when logged into both databases using the **system** User Account.

The *Select merge options Dialog Box* (Fig. 10.23) allows you to select how the merge will work. If you want all the model, object and connection attributes that are maintained (e.g. have values in the them) in the source database to be transferred to the target database, and to overwrite the existing attributes, then tick the *Yes* radio button in the *Do you want to merge source and target attributes* area. If you select *No* then the attributes won't be overwritten by default, but you can use the *Select conflict resolution Dialog Box* (Fig. 10.24) to choose what to do with attributes in the source and target databases that have different values.

When you select a model to be transferred (or a group containing models) you can also specify that any models assigned to objects in the selected models are transferred as well. You can enable this by choosing how many levels of assignment you want considered in the *Assignment level* box. So if you have a database with five levels of process hierarchy, you need to set the *Assignment level* to at least "*4*".

Later in the merge process, if you wish, you can choose the languages in which attribute transfers will be made. You can also choose to specify in which groups the conflict resolution options will apply. If you wish to select these extended options, select *Yes* in the *Do you want to configure the language and extended conflict resolution* area and the appropriate dialog boxes will appear later. Now click *Next*.

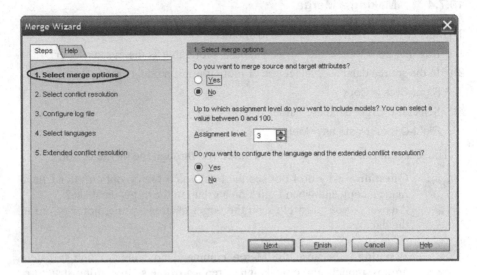

Fig. 10.23 Select Merge Options Dialog Box

As we saw above, the power of the Merge command is its ability to detect if items being merged into the database already exist and if they are different from the original items. In many cases you will want to update the target database with the new items, but that is not always the case and the *Select conflict resolution Dialog Box* (Fig. 10.24) allows you to choose how to handle conflicts.

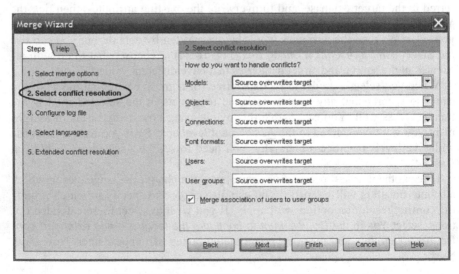

Fig. 10.24 Select Conflict Resolution Dialog Box

For each of *Models*, *Objects*, *Connections*, *Font formats*, *Users* and *User groups* you can select whether the *Source overwrites target* or if the *Target is preserved*. You can also choose whether the association between Users and User Groups should be updated by the merge by checking the *Merge association of user to user groups* checkbox. These options are applied to items anywhere in the target database. If you want items in specific groups in the target database to be overwritten, select the extended configuration option in the previous *Select merge options Dialog Box* (Fig. 10.23) and then choose the appropriate groups later in the *Extended conflict resolution Dialog Box* (Fig. 10.28). Now click *Next*.

The *Configure log file Dialog Box* (Fig. 10.25) allows you to choose what information will be displayed in the log file. The log file will be created automatically as a text file (see Fig. 10.26) and displayed when the merge is complete. You can choose *In which directory to create the log file* and also whether to *Overwrite existing file*.

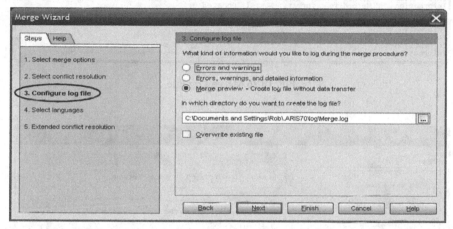

Fig. 10.25 Configure Log File Dialog Box

Perhaps the most useful option is the *Merge preview – create log file without data transfer*. As the name suggests, this enables you to see what items will be transferred as a result of the merge without actually carrying it out. The log file will be displayed showing the options selected and the complete list of items that will be transferred if the merge is run.

Click *Next* and, if you did not select the extended configuration option in the previous *Select merge options Dialog Box* (Fig. 10.23), the Merge command will now run. If you did select the extended option you will next be presented with the *Select languages Dialog Box* (Fig. 10.27).

At the top of the dialog box you can select which language will be used to display conflict resolution messages. This will only provide you with the language options you chose to install when you installed *ARIS Business Architect*. In the lower area of the dialog box you can select for which languages attributes are to be transferred from items in the source database to the target database. You can select specific language or the default *All languages*.

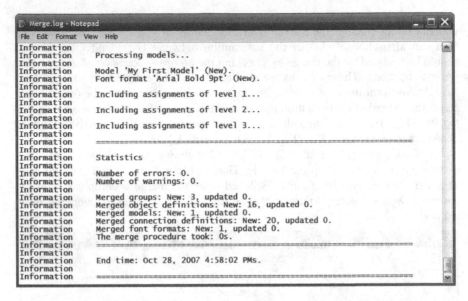

Fig. 10.26 Merge Log File

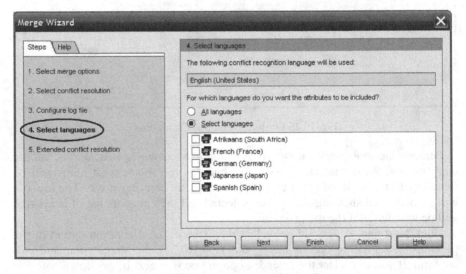

Fig. 10.27 Select Languages Dialog Box

The final *Extended conflict resolution Dialog Box* (Fig. 10.28) allows you to choose to prevent specified groups in the target data from being overwritten, irrespective of the conflict resolution options set earlier in the *Select merge options Dialog Box* (Fig. 10.23).

This is particularly useful if, for instance, you want to make sure objects in your library group are not overwritten by the Merging of new models into the database. In the *Tree View*, place a tick in the boxes of the groups you want to preserve.

 Warning – if you want to preserve sub-groups of selected groups in the *Extended conflict resolution Dialog Box*, make sure you tick the *Include subgroups* checkbox or specifically select the subgroups in the *Tree View*.

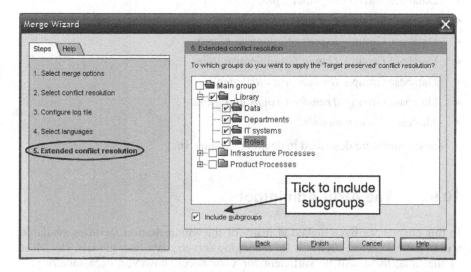

Fig. 10.28 Extended Conflict Resolution Dialog Box

Merge is a very powerful facility, but the results can be very drastic and it should be used with great care. Both the source and target databases should be backed up before the merge is run.

 Question – why are no models or objects transferred when I run the merge operation even though they are listed in the log file?
Answer – if the *Merge preview – create log file without data transfer* is selected the log file will show what items would be transferred, but no actual transfer takes place. Once you use this option, the *Merge Wizard* defaults to it next time unless you specifically change the option.

10.8   Administration Reports

There are a number of ARIS Reports that are useful for managing databases:

- Database – *Copying users and user Groups*,
- Database – *Database information*,
- Database – *Replace font formats*,
- Database – *Replace object types*,
- Database – *Replace symbol types*,
- Database Group – *Consolidate objects*,
- Database Group – *Export relationship matrix*,
- Database Group – *Output Group information*,
- Database Group – *Replace text attributes*,
- Database Group – *Transfer Groups and users*,
- Models – *Format models*.

These reports are described in detail in Chapter 16.

10.9   The ARIS Admintool

In this chapter we have looked at many of the administration facilities available within *ARIS Business Architect* for managing servers, database, models, etc. Most of the time, these will be sufficient for your needs, however, occasionally you may need to carry out tasks that are not available from within *Business Architect* (e.g. 'kill' a user's session). The *ARIS Admintool*, provides access to these commands outside of *ARIS Business Architect* and, on some rare occasions, maybe when your database is not responding, you may find the *ARIS Admintool* a useful last resort to backup the database or change a password.

The *ARIS Admintool* is installed with ARIS and is normally available from the ARIS Platform/Administration program group in Microsoft Windows. When run it displays a DOS style window (Fig. 10.29) with a simple prompt.

Appendix A shows all the commands available in the *ARIS Admintool*. You can list these commands when you are in the tool by just pressing the Enter key. To get help on any specific command, type Help followed by the command name. If you just type Help by itself it will list all the commands and their help descriptions.

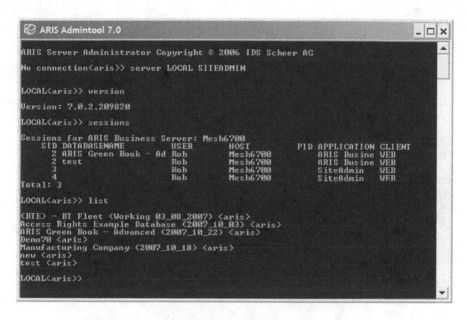

Fig. 10.29 ARIS Admintool

To start using the *ARIS Admintool* you need to connect to a server. Type the command Server followed by the server name (e.g. LOCAL). You will then be prompted for the server Site Administrator password. This password is different from any of the passwords described above in Section 10.2.4. It will have been set when the *ARIS Business Server* was installed and may have been changed by the Server Administrator.

 Expert Tip – the default Site Administrator password is SITEADMIN and this will be the password for your **LOCAL** server on your hard drive. You can enter the password when you enter the Server command; so to connect to your **LOCAL** server enter: Server LOCAL SITEADMIN.

 Expert Tip – you can change the Site Administrator password using the *ARIS Admintool*, but be careful to do it correctly otherwise you may block further access to site administration.

If you are connecting to an ARIS Business Server it is better not to enter the password on the same command line as the server name as it will be visible to anyone who looks at your screen (it is hidden if the server command prompts you for it).

You can now use any of the commands listed in Appendix A. When you are finished, type Exit and the *ARIS Admintool* window will close.

Chapter 11   User Administration

This chapter looks at how to create User and User Group Accounts. It describes how to assign various privileges to accounts and how to use Access Privileges to manage database access control.

11.1   Introduction to User Administration

11.1.1   The Need for User Administration

Many people will use ARIS in standalone mode on their local PCs. However, the real power of ARIS is realised when an ARIS Business Server is used to support collaborative design and modelling for an entire enterprise.

A small group of people working together may be able to work in an informal and unstructured way. However, when there are many modellers working on a large range of models, it is essential to provide some level of access control and structure. In particular, you will not normally want to provide all your users with write access to all the models and groups in your database. It is usually preferable to partition the database into project and library areas and only provide write access to groups of people who have specific reasons to edit those models. You may also wish to appoint a librarian who creates and manages resource objects (e.g. *Organizational unit types*, *Application system types*, etc) on behalf of all users.

Control over database access is provided in ARIS by establishing *User Accounts* and *User Groups* which allocate specific *'rights'* or *'privileges'* to those users including:

- Database access control,
- Passwords,
- User Group membership,
- Method Filters,
- Database management privileges,
- Group Access Privileges,

In addition to Access Privileges, *Function Privileges* (see Chapter 10) provide specific User Accounts with additional rights to undertake specialised database operations (e.g. *Change Management*) or provide privileges to others (e.g. *User Management*).

11.1.2   System Account

The default **"system"** User Account is a special account of type **"System user"** which has all of the *Function Privileges*. It is created automatically when a new database is created and is assigned the default *Database Administrator* and *Configuration Administrator* passwords.

When you use a **LOCAL** database, you will normally use the **system** User Account by default and hence have all the necessary privileges. However, when working with an ARIS Business Server it is normal to only have a limited number of people with **system** accounts and to assign specific, more limited, Function Privileges to other User Accounts.

Warning – when first setting up a networked ARIS Business Server, the password of the **system** User Account should be changed immediately to prevent any unauthorised access to the server.

Expert Tip – if you accidentally change the **system** User Account password, or forget it, you will not be able to access the database with sufficient privileges to undertake administration. To avoid this, create a second emergency **system** account on each database on the server. Test it works, share the password with the other system users, but avoid using it on a day-to-day basis. In this way, if one of the normal **system** accounts becomes unusable, or a **system** User Account is unavailable, someone can still access the database.

11.1.3   Strategy for User Management

It can be very tempting to just create User Accounts as and when people ask for them without a lot of thought about how they will be used. However, if you need to manage many users working on a large database it is important to give some thought to how you will organise User Accounts and User Groups.

The main privilege that needs to be considered is the group Access Privilege (see Section 11.5.2). This allows read, write or delete access rights (*rwd*) to be set for any group in the ARIS database. If all the groups a user requires access to are in a hierarchical tree, then it is easy to allocate rights in a single operation. However, if a user wants rights to a range of disparate groups spread throughout the database structure, this can result in a lot of management overhead. Furthermore, if the user no longer needs rights to a specific project area, or leaves the business and other people need to take over their work, it can be difficult to identify exactly what rights the person actually had (there are some ARIS Reports available for User Account management – see Section 11.6). Also if you wish to temporarily limit access to a particular area then, although it is relatively easy to deny access, it is difficult to restore access to a large number of different users.

A better approach is to structure your database in such a way that users will only need access to certain parts of it at any one time and then make use of User

Groups to allocate access. User Group Accounts are exactly the same as User Accounts in that they can be given (**rwd**) access to any group, but a number of User Accounts can be associated with a User Group.

For instance, you may wish to organise your database group structure on the basis of particular product design areas. Fig. 11.1 shows an example of such a structure with a group for **Product Processes** subdivided into **Product A**, **Product B** and **Product C**. The **Product B** group is further sub-divided into **Release 1** (which is '*frozen*') and **Release 2** which is undergoing further development.

You can then create User Groups (e.g. **Product_Group_A**) that have access to the specific project groups and assign the users who need to work on those product designs to the appropriate group. You can assign User Accounts to more than one User Group to provide access to different areas. As mentioned above, you may also wish to create library groups for **Data**, **Departments**, etc and assign a *Model Librarian* to manage these. Even if there is only a single person acting as librarian, it is still better to create a **Librarian** group and assign a User Account to it than to assign the specific Access Privileges to that person's User Account.

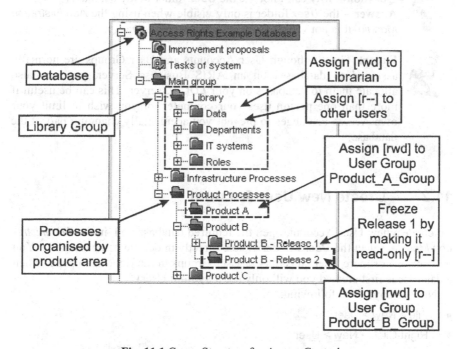

Fig. 11.1 Group Structure for Access Control

It is now comparatively easy to manage group Access Privileges for a particular User Account. For new users, you just need to identify which projects they need access to and then assign them to the correct groups. If they no longer need access to a particular product design, you just remove them from that particular group.

You can temporarily deny access to a project for all users by removing write access from the appropriate User Group. It is easy to restore access by restoring write access to the User Group.

Careful consideration of the structure of your database and how you will use User Accounts and User Groups to manage it, before you have too many users, will make your database administration task much easier.

11.1.4   Undertaking User Administration

To manage User Accounts you will need the *User Management* Function Privilege. You will have this by default if you login with the **system** account, but if not, another person with the *User Management* privilege can assign it to you.

User Accounts and User Groups are managed at the database level. They appear in the **Users** folder visible immediately under the database name when you are using the *Administration Module*.

Question – why can I not see the **User** folder in my database? **Answer** – the **User** folder is only visible when using the *Administration Module*, it is not visible from the *Explorer Module*.

Expert Tip – although User Accounts and User Groups are normally assigned to databases on an ARIS Business Server, you can also allocate them to databases on your **LOCAL** server. This can be useful if more than one person uses your computer, or you wish to limit your own Access Privileges to prevent you accidentally changing part of the database.

11.2   Create New User Account

To create a new User Account, open the required database and, in the *Administration Module,* select the **Users** folder visible directly under the database name. You will see one or more User Accounts or User Groups in the right-hand pane (when a database is first created you will only see a **system** User).

Now do any of the following:

- File > New > User,
- Right-Click > New > User,
- Click the Create user button on the *User Toolbar*.   Create user

The *User Wizard* (Fig. 11.2) will be displayed and guide you through the following dialog boxes:

- *Create user,*
- *User group association,*
- *Identifier,*
- *Function privileges,*
- *Method filter.*

Once a User Account has been created we can also configure:

- User Attributes – via the Attributes Window,
- Access Privileges – via the Properties Dialog Box.

11.2.1   Create User

The *Create user Dialog Box* (Fig. 11.2) allows you to enter a <u>U</u>ser name and <u>P</u>assword for the User Account. You should give careful thought to the allocation of <u>U</u>ser names and consider any security standards you may have in your organisation. If you leave the <u>P</u>assword field blank, the user will not have to enter a password.

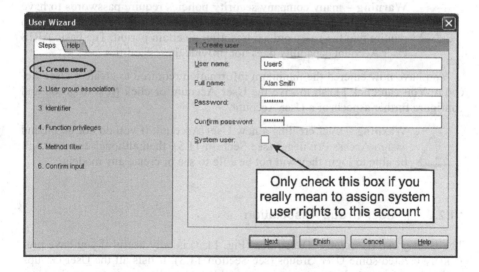

Fig. 11.2 Create User Dialog Box

Expert Tip – if there are no standards in your organisation for creating _User_ names and _Passwords_, you should agree a naming standard with the **system** users of other databases so you can recognise the same User Account in different databases. You may also wish to keep a central record.

 Expert Tip – you can _merge_ User Accounts and User Groups from one database to another so as to provide a user with the same _User name_ and _Password_ (see Section 11.4).

In addition to the _User name_, which the user enters, you can also enter a value into the _Full name_ field. This is only visible to the _User Manager_ and can be used to give a more meaningful (or unique) description of the User Account.

 Expert Tip – you can assign attributes to User Accounts and User Groups to provide additional identification information (e.g. _Telephone number, E-mail address_, etc) – see Section 11.2.7.

Finally, if you have logged in using a **System** User Account, there is a check-box that allows the new User Account to be created as a _System user_. You should use this option with great care. It is often better to give users specific Function Privileges rather than give them the full privileges of a **system** account.

 Warning – many company security policies require passwords to have a minimum length or a combination of letters and numbers. It may also require that the password expires after a certain period. The basic ARIS User Account capability does not provide these facilities.

You have now entered the minimum information required to create a User Account. You can click _F_inish to save the User Account or click _N_ext to go on and configure further aspects of a User Account.

 Warning – after creating a new User Account, if you do not go on and assign Access Privileges (see Section 11.5), then although the user will be able to login they will not be able to see or create any models.

11.2.2   User Group Association

The _User group association Dialog Box_ (Fig. 11.3) is only useful if you have previously created some User Groups (see Section 11.3). It lists all the User Groups in the database and allows you to choose which User Groups to assign the User Account to. You don't have to assign any User Groups or you can assign one or many.

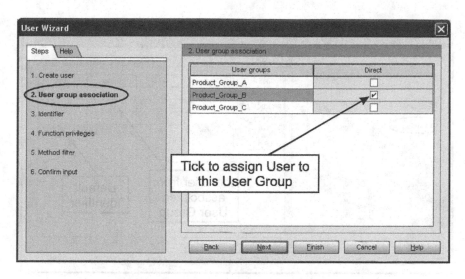

Fig. 11.3 User Group Association Dialog Box

11.2.3   Identifier

A database may have one or more *Identifiers* defined (see Chapter 10) that, when enabled, can be assigned to all new items (groups, models, objects, etc) created in the database. The *Identifier* is available as an attribute and can be used to provide a pseudo-unique reference for every item (easier to read than a GUID) which can be used for database administration. The *Identifier* value consists of a set of up to 20 alphanumeric characters (the *Prefix*) followed by an automatically allocated sequential number (e.g. xxxxx1234).

The Prefix can be assigned to a User Account or User Group so when a new user logs into the database, any new item they create will have an Identifier with their Prefix. User Accounts can be allocated a Prefix of their own, or any number of User Accounts and User Groups can share the same Prefix.

The *Identifier Dialog Box* (Fig. 11.4) allows the Prefix for the User Account to be selected. By default a User Account will be assigned the *Standard* Identifier Prefix (shown in the *Standard* column) which, if it has not been changed, will be "*STD*". The *Group* column shows the Prefix allocated to the User Groups and shows which User Groups the User Account belongs to.

By placing a tick in a box in the *Direct* column, a specific Prefix can be assigned to the User Account or User Group. Any Prefix can be chosen, even that of a User Group the User Account is not assigned to. The *Total* column shows all the Prefixes that are notionally assigned to the User Account (*Direct*, *Standard* or *Group*), but the *Direct* column indicates which Prefix will actually be used.

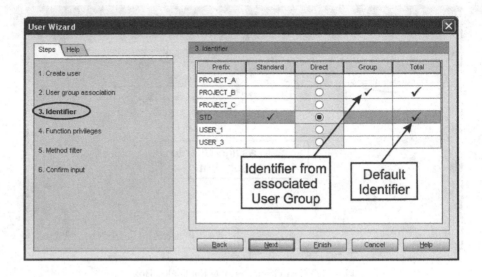

Fig. 11.4 Identifier Dialog Box

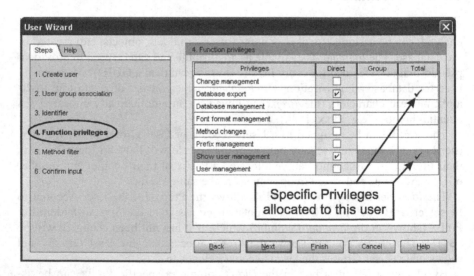

Fig. 11.5 Function Privileges Dialog Box

11.2.4   Function Privileges

The *Function privileges Dialog Box* (Fig. 11.5) allows any combination of the various privileges described in Table 11.1 to be assigned to the User Account by ticking the appropriate box in the *Direct* column. The User Account may also inherit Function Privileges through membership of one or more User Groups. These are shown in the *Group* column and the *Total* column shows the total combination of the privileges the User Account has been given.

 Warning – do not give too many Function Privileges to users who also undertake basic modelling roles; they may accidentally make unintended changes allowed by their enhanced privileges. Instead create a separate management User Account for them.

Table 11.1 Function Privileges

Privilege	Use
Change management	Manage change proposals submitted by other users (e.g. modify proposals, propose measures, give feedback, set priorities, and define responsibilities).
Database export	Merge (copy and paste) parts of one database into other databases (the privilege required for both databases). Import and Export database content.
Database management	Manage languages for the database (create, edit or delete). Edit database attributes.
Font format management	Manage database fonts (create, edit, delete).
Method changes	Change the appearance of objects and connections (e.g. *Fill color*, *Line Weight*, etc). **Note**: a user can apply pre-defined Templates without this privilege.
Prefix management	Manage the Identifier Prefix available in the database (create, edit delete). **Note**: this is assigning the Prefix for the database – assigning the Prefix to users requires *User Management* privilege.
Show user management	Allows a user to see the User Accounts and User Groups defined for the database and view their Properties. **Note**: to create, edit or delete User Accounts and User Groups requires *User Management* privilege.
User Management	Manage User Accounts and User Groups (create, change properties, delete).

11.2.5   Method Filter

The *Method filter Dialog Box* (Fig. 11.6) allows the Method Filters available to the User Account to be assigned by ticking the appropriate box in the *Direct* column. The User Account may also inherit Method Filter availability from any User Groups they are members of and are shown in the *Group* column. The *Total* column shows all the Method Filters available to the User Account.

When the user logs in, the *Select filter and language Dialog Box* of the *Login Wizard* will allow the user to select from all the available Method Filters in the drop-down box in the *Filter* field.

 Warning – be wary of assigning too many Method Filters to individual users. If you are using Method Filters to enforce modelling standards, users faced with a large choice of Filters may select the wrong one and thus compromise your standards.

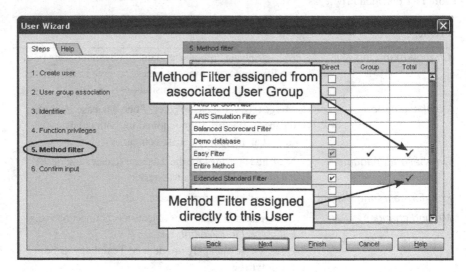

Fig. 11.6 Method Filter Dialog Box

11.2.6   Confirm Input

The final *Confirm input Dialog Box* (Fig. 11.7) does not require any input but summarises the User Account configurations that have been made. You can click Back to return and change settings or click Finish to save the User Account.

 Hint – once you have created a User Account you cannot edit it, but you can access its properties (Right-Click > Properties) to make changes to the account (see Section 11.2.8).

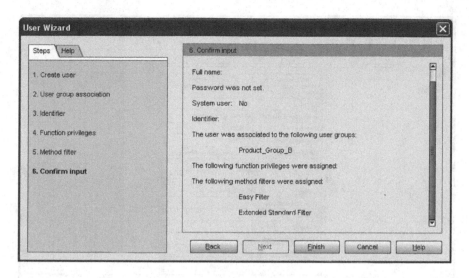

Fig. 11.7 Confirm Input Dialog Box

11.2.7 User Attributes

Once created, an ARIS User Account or User Group has attributes just like any other item. To view or edit its attributes do any of:

- Edit > Attributes,
- Right-Click > Attributes,
- Click the *Attributes* Button on the *ARIS Toolbar*.

The *Attributes Window* (Fig. 11.8) will allow you to enter useful values that can be used to more accurately identify the specific User Account or User Group. These attributes can also be reported on using an ARIS Report (see Section 11.6).

11.2.8 Editing User Accounts

Once a User Account has been created it is not possible to edit it directly, but you can change its configuration via its Properties (see Section 11.2.9).

 Hint – to change the name of a User Account or User Group, select it and Right-Click > Rename (F2).

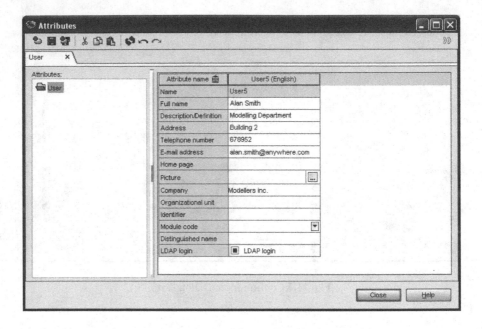

Fig. 11.8 The User Attributes Window

11.2.9   User Account Properties

To view or edit the Properties of a User Account do any of:

- Edit > Properties,
- Right-Click > Properties,
- Click the Properties Button on the *User Toolbar*.

The *Properties – User Dialog Box* (Fig. 11.9) provides a similar range of options to those available when the User was created:

- *Change Password*,
- *User group association* (see Section 11.2.2),
- *Identifier* (see Chapter 10),
- *Function privileges* (see Chapter 10),
- *Method filter* (see Section 11.2.5),
- *Access Privileges* (see Section 11.5).

The first *Change Password Dialog Box* allows you to change the password for a User Account. To avoid accidentally changing the password you have to deliberately tick the *Change password* checkbox and then enter the *New password* and *Confirm password*.

Hint – if a user forgets their password, there is no way to tell them what their password was. You will need to allocate them a new password.

Four of the options listed above work the same way as described for the *User Wizard* and are described in the sections shown. The setting of *Access Privileges* is the most important task in managing database access and is described in detail in Section 11.5.

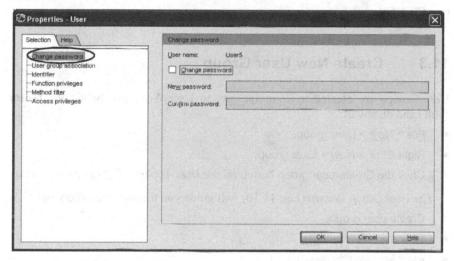

Fig. 11.9 Properties – User (Change Password) Dialog Box

11.2.10   Logining in as a User

Once a User Account has been created it can be used to log into the database. If the database is on an ARIS Business Server the password of the **system** User Account will almost certainly have been changed from the default and all users will be forced to login with their own credentials.

Expert Tip – you can force a new login to a database, rather than accepting the default *User* name and *Password,* by selecting a database and Right-Click > *Log in*.

The first screen of the *Login Wizard*, the *Enter user data Dialog Box* asks for the *User* name and *Password* that was set for the User Account in the *Create user Dialog Box* (see Section 11.2.1). The *Select filter and language Dialog Box* asks the user to choose a *Filter* from the range of Method Filters allocated to the User Account in the *Method filter Dialog Box* (see Section 11.2.5). The *Language* that can be selected in this dialog box is chosen from a list set for the current database (see Chapter 10); it is not set specifically for the User Account.

A user may change their own *Password* by:

1. Log into the database,
2. Select the database name in the *Administration Module* or *Explorer Module*,
3. Right-Click > Change password,
4. Enter the *Current password*,
5. Enter *New password* and *Confirm password*,
6. Click OK.

11.3   Create New User Group

User Groups are created in a similar way to User Accounts. Select the **Users** folder and do any of:

- File > New > User group,
- Right-Click > New > User group,
- Click the Create user group button on the *User Toolbar*.   Create user group

    The *User Group Wizard* (Fig. 11.10) will guide you through the following:

- *Create user group*,
- *User association*,
- *Identifier* (see Chapter 10),
- *Function privileges* (see Chapter 10),
- *Method filter* (see Section 11.2.5).

    The first two dialog boxes are slightly different to those for User Accounts and are described below.

    The remaining dialog boxes (*Identifier, Function privileges, Method filter*) perform the same function as for creating User Accounts and are described in the sections referred to. The only difference is they don't have *Group* and *Total* columns because you can only assign privileges directly to User Groups.

11.3.1   Create User Group

The *Create user group Dialog Box* (Fig. 11.10) is very simple. It just requires you to enter a *Name* for the group. As discussed in Section 11.1.3, a User Group will often be associated with a project, product or maybe a team.

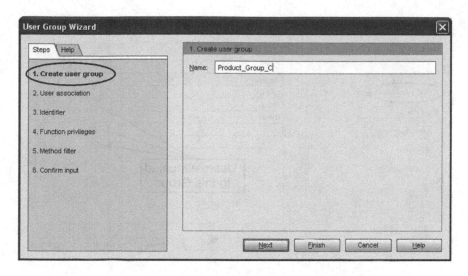

Fig. 11.10 Create User Group Dialog Box

You can't login as a User Group so there is no need for passwords. You cannot create a User Group as a *system* User Account, but you can assign the group any of the Function Privileges in the same way you can for a User Account (see Section 11.2.4). Any User Account assigned to the User Group will inherit all of the group's privileges.

11.3.2   User Association

The *User association Dialog Box* (Fig. 11.11) allows us to allocate User Accounts to the User Group. This is the complementary operation to associating a User Group to a User Account in the *User Group Association Dialog Box* of the *User Wizard*. It doesn't matter which way round we make the association, it is purely determined by which item we are creating and which other items are already in existence. Often you will need to swap between the two.

The *Users* column shows all the User Accounts defined in the database and you can place a tick in the *Direct* column to associate them with the current User Group.

11.3.3   User Group Attributes

The attributes for User Groups are rather limited and not normally maintained.

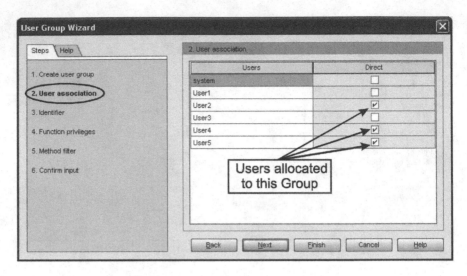

Fig. 11.11 User Association Dialog Box

11.3.4   User Group Properties

The Properties Dialog Box for a User Group allows us to view and maintain:

- *User association* (see Section 11.3.2),
- *Identifier* (see Chapter 10),
- *Function privileges* (see Chapter 10),
- *Method filter* (see Section 11.2.5),
- *Access Privileges*.

Database access control using Access Privileges will be described below (Section 11.5).

11.4   Merging Users

User Accounts and User Groups are stored in the database so if people want to use more than one database on an ARIS Business Server it will be necessary to create User Accounts on each database. A quick way to do this is to copy User Accounts and User Groups from one database to another using the ARIS Merge facility (see Chapter 10 for more on merging).

To merge User Accounts and User Groups:

1. Log into both databases using a *system* account or a User Account with *Database export* and *User Management* privileges,
2. In the *Administration Module* select the *User* folder in the source database,
3. Select the User Accounts and User Groups you wish to merge,
4. Press the left mouse key and drag the selected User Accounts and User Groups onto the target database name,
5. Release the mouse key.

The *Merge Wizard* will open and in the *Select merge options Dialog Box* accept the default options by pressing Next. In the *Select conflict resolution Dialog Box* you will need to decide if you want to copy the allocation of User Accounts to User Groups from the source database. This may or may not be relevant. If you do wish to copy the allocations, tick the *Merge associations of users to user groups* checkbox. Now click Finish and the User Accounts and User Groups will be copied to the target database.

Question – why can I not see the User Accounts and User Groups I have transferred using the merge facility in the *User* folder of the target database?

Answer – you will need to refresh the display (View > Refresh (F5)) to see the new entries in the folder.

Expert Tip – if you are managing User Accounts and User Groups for a large number of databases you may wish to create an administration database just to hold the master copies of all User Accounts. If you need to make a change to a User Account, for instance to change the password, you can make the change to the master account and then merge it into all the appropriate databases.

Expert Tip – you can also transfer part or all of the database group structure, along with the associated User Accounts and User Groups, from one database to another using the *Transfer groups and users* ARIS Report (see Section 11.6).

11.5   Database Access Control

11.5.1   Introduction to Access Control

The main use of User Accounts and User Groups is to control access to different parts of the ARIS database group structure. We discussed in Section 11.1.3 how we might structure a database based around product designs and how we might allocate User Groups to provide access to those areas.

Once we have created the required User Accounts and User Groups we now need to assign the Access Privileges to them. We can do that in one of two ways:

- Allocate access using User Account and User Group Properties,
- Allocate access using database group Properties.

It does not matter which of these approaches we use, it depends entirely on which is the most convenient. In practice, you may tend to use the User Group Properties when you have just created a new User Group and the database group Properties when you have just created a new database group. However, it is important to remember that when you create a new User Account or User Group, you must assign Access Privileges to the User Accounts (directly or via a User Group) before they can access the database group structure.

Question – why can I not see the *Access privileges Dialog Box* when I am creating a new User Account?

Answer – the dialog box is not visible in the *User Wizard* or *User Group Wizard*, but is accessed via the *Properties Dialog Box* once the User Account or User Group has been created.

11.5.2   User and User Group Access Privileges

If you have created a new User Account or User Group, and you already have your database group structure in place, you can now assign Access Privileges.

Warning – when a new User Account has been created you must assign Access Privileges to the User Account (directly or via a User Group) before the user can access the database group structure.

Normally, we assign Access Privileges to the User Group and then assign a User Account to the User Group. In special circumstances we may assign Access Privileges directly to a User Account, but in either case the procedure for assigning access is much the same. The privileges are shown as *read*, *write* or *delete* (***rwd***) and have the meanings shown in Table 11.2.

User Group Access Privileges

Using the *Administration Module*:

1. Select the User Group in the ***Users*** folder,
2. Right-Click > Properties,
3. Select the *Access Privileges Dialog Box*.

Table 11.2 Access Privileges

Privilege	Access Provided
No access (---)	• The user can see and navigate the database group structure, but cannot see the contents, • ARIS Reports cannot be run.
Read (r--)	• The user can see the contents of groups and can open and view models, • New models and objects cannot be created, • Existing models and objects cannot be edited, • Existing models and objects cannot be deleted, • ARIS Reports can be run.
Read + write (rw-)	• New models and objects can be created, • Existing models and objects can be edited, • Existing models and objects cannot be deleted.
Read + write + delete (rwd)	• Existing models and objects can be deleted.

The *Properties – User groups Access Privileges Dialog Box* is shown in Fig. 11.12. In the left-hand *Group* column is a *Tree View* of the database structure. The right-hand *Privileges (user)* column shows the Access Privileges that User Accounts assigned to the User Group will have.

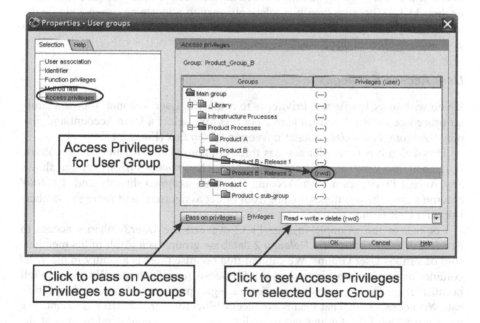

Fig. 11.12 Properties – User Groups Access Privileges Dialog Box

To add a new Access Privilege for the User Group:

1. Open the group structure in the *Tree View* until you can see the required group,

2. Select the type of access to be given to the User Account from the drop-down list in the *Privileges* field (e.g. *Read + Write (rw-)*),

3. Click on the *Pass* on privileges Button if you wish the User Group to have the same Access Privilege for all the sub-groups of the selected group.

You will now see the *Privileges (user)* column updates to show the selected Access Privilege for chosen database group.

 Warning – Access Privileges for a particular sub-group are only visible when the *Tree View* is expanded so the group is visible. If you collapse the *Tree View* so only the top group is visible, it may appear there are no Access Privileges assigned. You have to drill down to all levels to be sure.

 Expert Tip – if you want to check what Access Privileges are assigned to a particular database group, it is easier to do this from the database *Group Properties Dialog Box* than the *User group Properties Dialog Box*.

If access to other database groups is required, work through the group structure in the *Tree View* allocating access as appropriate. You can now see why it is better to create a database group structure based around simple access requirements (see Section 11.1.3), because then it is relatively easy to allocate access to a single database group, and pass on the privileges to the sub-groups, rather than to have to give access to lots of disparate database groups.

User Access Privileges

If you wish to assign Access Privileges to a specific User Account, follow a similar procedure to that described above but this time select a User Account and display the *Properties – User Access privileges Dialog Box* (Fig. 11.13).

This dialog box is simpler and has three columns. The left-hand Group column is again a *Tree View* of the database structure. The *Privileges (user)* column shows any Access Privileges a User Account has been assigned directly and the *Total* column shows the privileges arising from direct assignment and through membership of a User Group.

Looking at the example in Fig. 11.13 we can see **User3** inherits access to **Product A** and **Product B – Release 2** database groups as a result of his membership of various User Groups. We can tell this because there is an entry in the *Total* column for these groups, but not in the *Privileges (user)* column. We can also tell because, if we click on one of those database groups, the *Privileges* field will indicate **No access (---)**. That means no access 'directly' for that User Account. We can't tell which User Groups are providing access; we would need to look at the User Group Properties or the database group Properties to check this.

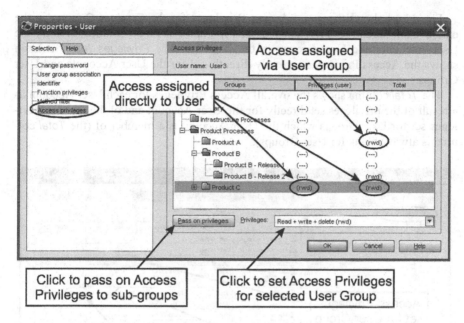

Fig. 11.13 Properties – User Access Privileges Dialog Box

We can also see **User3** has direct access to the **Product C** group. We can tell it is direct access because there are entries in both the *Privileges (user)* column and the *Total* column, and also if we click on the **Product C** group the *Privileges* field will indicate **Read + write + delete (rwd)**.

We can add direct access to any of the database groups by selecting them and changing the selection in the *Privileges* field. We can also allocate the privileges for that User Account to all the sub-groups of the selected group by clicking the *P*ass on privileges Button.

You can also remove any privileges directly allocated for the chosen User Account for the selected database group by changing the *Privileges* field. However, you cannot remove privileges assigned via a User Group; you will need to use the *User group Access privileges Dialog Box* to change the privileges for all User Accounts in the User Group or remove the User Account from the User Group.

11.5.3   Group Access Privileges

If you have created a new database group or group structure and want to allocate access to existing User Accounts or User Groups, then use the *User group Properties Dialog Box*. Select the database group in either the *Explorer Module* or the *Administration Module* and Right-Click > Prop*e*rties [Access privileges].

Fig. 11.14 shows the group Access Privileges for the **Product C** group in the example shown in Fig. 11.1. The *Name, Type* and *Full name* columns identify the User Accounts and User Groups in the database. The *Privileges (user)* column shows the Access Privileges currently directly set for the User Accounts and User Groups.

The *Total* column shows the overall Access Privileges for each User Account as a result of the privileges set directly for the User Account and of the Access Privileges set for User Groups which the User Account is a member of (the *Total* column is always blank for User Groups).

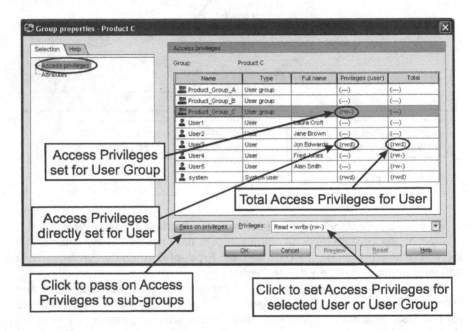

Fig. 11.14 Group Properties Dialog Box

To change the Access Privileges for the selected database group, select the User Account or User Group whose access you want to change and select the appropriate Access Privileges from the *Privileges* drop-down box. You can also click on the *Pass on privileges* to assign the same User Account or User Group privileges to all the sub-groups of the chosen database group.

To remove Access Privileges for a User Account you need to remove the Access Privileges from the User Account or from the User Groups from which it inherits them. If you want to remove an inherited Access Privilege from a specific User Account, but not from the other User Accounts in the User Group, you will have to restructure your User Group membership and maybe create a new group.

Question – why does the *Total* column not change when I remove some of Access Privileges in the *User group Properties Dialog Box*?
Answer – when removing Access Privileges you have to close and reopen the *User group Properties Dialog Box* in order to refresh the list.

Hint – when you create a new sub-group it will automatically inherit all the User Account and User Group Access Privileges of the parent group.

In the example shown in Fig. 11.14, **Product_Group_C** has (**rw-**) privileges set and **User3**, **User4** and **User5** are members of the group and inherit those privileges. In addition, **User3** has (**rwd**) privileges directly set, so its *Total* column shows (**rwd**) whereas **User4** and **User5** only show (**rw-**).

11.6   User Administration Reports

There are a number of ARIS Reports which are useful in managing User Accounts, User Groups and Access Privileges:

* Database – *Copying users and user groups*,
* Database – *Database information (Function Privileges)*,
* Database group – *Group Information*,
* Database group – *Transfer groups and users*.

These reports are described in detail in Chapter 16.

11.7   Lightweight Directory Access Protocol (LDAP)

Managing large numbers of User Accounts across many ARIS databases requires a lot of administrative overhead. You may also already have Usernames and Passwords assigned to your users for accessing other IT systems in your organisation. An alternative to using ARIS itself for managing users is to authenticate them using a *Lightweight Directory Access Protocol (LDAP)* server.

You may already have an LDAP server in your organisation or might wish to consider setting one up, however further discussion of LDAP is beyond the scope of this book.

Chapter 12 Configuring the ARIS Method

This chapter looks at the principles of configuring ARIS and provides an introduction to the contents of the ARIS Configuration group. It describes how to select configuration options and how to create and use a Reference Model. It described in detail configuring the ARIS Method.

12.1 ARIS Configuration

ARIS is a functionally rich tool and there are many different ways of using it to achieve the same business objectives. Each organisation will want to define its own way of using ARIS and will want to align it to their corporate identity. You will probably need to configure standards for the languages you use, the fonts you prefer and the look and feel of the model presentation. Furthermore, when a number of people in an organisation collaborate to create process designs, it is essential to create modelling conventions to ensure everyone can work together effectively.

 Expert Tip – in ARIS 7 it is possible to create new '*derived*' model types (with user-defined symbols and attributes) based on existing ARIS models. This feature is useful for creating different kinds of models for structuring big projects and for guiding users by providing models based on pre-defined modelling conventions.

ARIS 7

To change the *ARIS Configuration* we use the *Administration Module* in *ARIS Business Architect*. In the **Configuration** Group (Fig. 12.1) there are folders for:

- Conventions:
  - Filters,
  - Font Formats,
  - Languages,
  - Templates.
- Method:
  - Attribute type groups,
  - Attribute types,
  - Connection types,
  - Model types,
  - Object types,
  - Symbols.

The *Configuration* items that can be defined at the server level and applied to all databases on the server are summarised in Table 12.1. In this chapter we will look in detail at the principles of ARIS Configuration and how to change the ARIS Method. In Chapter 14 we will look at how to create Filters and in Chapter 15 we will look at how to create Templates.

Table 12.1 ARIS Configurations

Term	Meaning
Evaluation Filter	A Filter used by an ARIS Evaluation (e.g. Reports, Web Publishing, etc), in addition to the Method Filter applied to the database, to further limit the range of models, objects, symbols, relationships and attributes that are reported on or viewed.
Filter	Configuration Filters (*Evaluation Filters* and *Method Filters*) restrict the range of models, objects, relationships and attributes that are used.
Font Formats	The fonts used by all ARIS Templates on a server that are applied by the Templates to attribute placements. These are distinct from the Font Formats defined at the database level.
Languages	Languages available for Filters, Font Formats and Templates.
Method Filter	A Filter applied to an ARIS database limiting the range of models, objects, symbols, relationships and attributes that can be viewed and used.
Method	The underling definition or 'meta model' that defines the models, objects, symbols, connections and attributes used in ARIS. Many of these can be configured to create corporate standards.
Template	A graphic template that alters the appearance of ARIS models, but has no effect on the information modelled.

12.1.1 Method

Underlying ARIS is the *ARIS Method* or '*meta model'* that defines the models, objects, symbols, connections and attributes used in ARIS. Many aspects of the ARIS Method can be configured by users to create corporate standards that are applied to all databases on an organisation's ARIS Business Server:

- Rename attribute type groups,
- Rename attributes,
- Allocating attribute to attribute type groups,
- Rename connection types,
- Rename model types,

- Create new derived model types,
- Rename object types,
- Rename symbols,
- Create user-defined symbols and allocate them to objects types.

We will look at configuring the ARIS Method in Section 12.3.

12.1.2   Conventions

In addition to the ARIS Method, *ARIS Conventions* provide a way of configuring how ARIS appears to different users:

- Filters (see Chapter 14),
- Font Formats (see Chapter 15),
- Languages (see Chapter 15),
- Templates (see Chapter 15).

For instance, Method Filters can be applied to databases to restrict the range of models, objects, connections and attributes available to a user to a subset of those defined in the ARIS Method, while Templates can be applied to models and their contents to specifically determine their appearance.

12.1.3   Using ARIS Configuration

To make changes to the ARIS Configuration you will need to be a *Configuration Administrator*. If you are working on a **LOCAL** server on the hard disk of your PC you will normally have all the system and configuration rights and be able to make any changes you wish. If, however, you are working on an ARIS Business Server, then it is usual to restrict configuration rights to a few trusted users and to change the administration passwords. In that case you will need to know the new configuration password.

You can enter your *Configuration* password in the *Administration passwords* area of the *View > Options [Login] Dialog Box*. Entering the password here means you can make any configuration changes you wish to the server at any time. Alternatively you can leave the password at its default setting and then whenever you click on the **Configuration** group in the *Administration Module* of an ARIS Business Server, you will be asked for the password. The latter mode is probably the safer approach as it prevents you making accidental changes to the server configuration.

 Hint – if you change the *Configuration* password in the *View > Options [Login] Dialog Box* then, if you want to make configuration changes to your **LOCAL** server, you will need to enter the default configuration password "CFGADMIN" when prompted.

Once you have clicked on the **Configuration** group in the *Administration Module* you will see there are two groups: **Conventions** and **Method** (see Fig. 12.1). The **Conventions** group has subgroups for **Filters**, **Font formats**, **Languages** and **Templates**, while the **Method** group has sub-groups for the various elements of the ARIS Method that can be configured.

Clicking on a group in the *Explorer Tree* in the left-hand pane will display the contents of the group in the right-hand pane. You can normally click a button at the top of the right-hand pane, or on the *Right-Click Menu*, to Edit, create New, Delete, Duplicate, Rename, Export or display the Properties depending on the item selected.

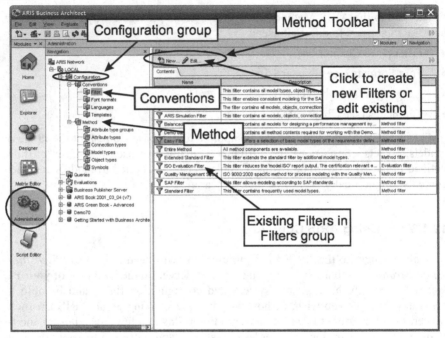

Fig. 12.1 The Configuration Group

12.2   The Principles of Configuring ARIS

12.2.1   Introduction

Defining and changing the configuration of ARIS is one of the most important tasks a *Configuration Administrator* has to perform. While the various tools needed to make the changes are relatively easy to use, a lot of thought and preplanning is required before any changes are made. It is essential to have a good understanding of the ARIS Method and the ARIS House and its Views.

12.2.2   The ARIS Method

One of the strengths of ARIS is the underlying ARIS Method. As mentioned above, the method defines the models, objects, symbols, connections and attributes used in ARIS.

The fact you are reading this advanced book should mean you are familiar with all the ARIS items and what they represent. A clear understanding of these is vital for correctly configuring ARIS. It is worth looking at Table 12.2 as a reminder of these important ARIS concepts.

Table 12.2 ARIS Items

Term	Meaning
Attribute	Information stored for different ARIS items (e.g. models, objects, connections, databases, User Accounts, User Groups, Font Formats, etc.).
Connection	The line connecting two objects in an ARIS model denoting an ARIS Relationship.
Database	A collection of related ARIS models stored on a server (distinct from the physical database application that ARIS uses for all storage).
Object	An ARIS representation of a real-world entity (e.g. task, organisation, system, data item, etc.).
Model	An ARIS diagram of a particular type (e.g. a data model, process model, etc.) comprising objects and connections stored in the underlying ARIS database.
Occurrence	An instance of an object used in one or more models.
Relationship	The ARIS representation of the interaction between real-world entities represented by ARIS objects.
Server	A file storage system on a PC or networked file server holding a set of ARIS databases.
Symbol	The visual depiction of an object in an ARIS model.

12.2.3   The ARIS House

The range of available models and objects define how you can use ARIS to model your organisation. So, in addition to providing a structured approach to modelling, ARIS is also an '*Architectural Framework*' that allows you to organise and present all of the information comprising an enterprise's architecture. Because such architectures are often large, this can result in very complex models. To manage this complexity, an Architectural Framework defines a standard set of model categories called '*Views*' each of which have a specific purpose.

The ARIS framework provides the concept of the '*ARIS House*'; a structuring view for all information on the enterprise (Fig. 12.2).

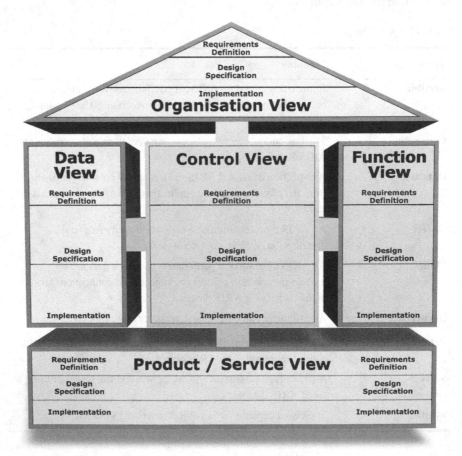

Fig. 12.2 The ARIS House With Five Views

- **Organisation View** – static models of the structure of the organisation. Includes: departments, people resources and roles in hierarchical organisation charts, technical resources (e.g. equipment, transport etc.) and communications networks.

- **Data View** – static models of business information. Includes: data models, knowledge structure, information carriers, technical terms and database models.

- **Function View** – static models of process tasks. Includes: function hierarchies, business objectives, supporting systems and software applications.

- **Product/Service View** – static models of the structures of products and services. Includes: product trees, products, services.

- **Process (Control) View** – dynamic models showing the behaviour of processes and how they relate to the resources, data and functions of the business environment. Includes: event-driven process chains, information flow, materials flow, communications diagrams, product definitions, flow charts and value chain diagrams.

The first four views concentrate on the structure of the organisation, while the Process View (also called the Control View) concentrates on the dynamic behaviour of the business process and brings together all the different elements of other views. We can use the ARIS Views to identify the different models we require to model our business.

12.2.4   Why Not Just Use the Entire Method?

So we have the ARIS Method, the ARIS House and the ARIS Views. You may think you could just use them as they stand without any further work. In principle you can, but in practice ARIS has developed over the years to provide a large range of model types for representing different aspects of a business. There are too many for any organisation to use them all, so we have to make architectural decisions about which ones are right for our organisation. Once we have decided which to use (see Section 12.2.6) we create Method Filters to restrict the range of models, objects, connections and attributes that will be available to our users (see Chapter 14).

 Expert Tip – while the *Entire Method* Filter allows you to view all the types of models, objects and connections, never use it for actual modelling work. Always use a Filter with a more limited range of items, otherwise you will find it impossible to create a set of consistent models.

Some of the different model types provide alternative formats for modelling the same sort of thing. For instance you could model data (the left-hand View of the ARIS House) using a *Technical terms model*, an *IE Data model*, an *eERM diagram* or a *UML Class diagram*. All of these are perfectly valid and will provide more or less the same information about your organisation, but which format you use may depend on the design standards used in your organisation, the personal preference of modellers or the clients for the models.

Other models may be very specialised and only relevant if you wish to specifically model those aspects of your business (e.g. *Risk diagram, SAP applications diagram, Competition model*, etc).

There is also an interaction between the object types and connection types you wish to use to represent your business and the model types you have to use to model them. For instance, while some objects are available in a wide range of models, certain types of relationships between those objects are only allowed in particular types of model. Hence, you will sometimes be forced to make use of model types you didn't initially select in order to represent the specific relationship you require.

The object and connection types made available in the ARIS Method provide a good set of basic business entities and relationships. However, they may not exactly match the types of entities that occur in your organisation or the terms you use to describe them. In earlier versions of ARIS there was not much you could do about this, but in ARIS 7 you can rename relationships, create your own specific model types and customise the look and feel of symbols and models.

 Warning – configuring ARIS to more closely match your business can be very beneficial in gaining acceptance for enterprise modelling. However the more you customise ARIS, the more work there is to administer it and to train new users. A careful balance needs to be struck.

12.2.5   Things to Consider

From the above discussion you can see there are many possible ways to configure how ARIS is used and how it appears. How should you decide what configuration changes to make? Consider some of the following to build up a picture of what models, objects and connections you need.

Scope

* **Modelling Objectives** – think about why you are using ARIS. You may just want to do some basic process modelling or you may want to produce a complete enterprise architecture.

* **Use of ARIS models** – will they be made available to the entire business or just used by an architecture team? Will you be using them to provide specifications to the IT department for automation? Maybe you want to generate IT implementations directly from process models, for instance using BPMN or BPEL.

- **Standards and Frameworks** – are there particular standards or frameworks applicable to your organisation? Do you want to use UML or BPMN? Maybe there are standard reference models you can make use of such as SCOR, ITIL, eTOM. Do you want to make use of frameworks such as Zachmann or DODAF?

- **Customers for Your Models** – who are they? Will they want to see actual ARIS models (in which case the look and feel may be important) or just results derived from them?

- **Model Detail** – how much detail is required? Will you need a hierarchy of detailed process models? Do they need to be supported by data models, product hierarchies, organisational charts, etc?

Considering these questions will enable you to start to define the scope of what you need to model with ARIS. It is always best to think beyond your immediate requirements. It is easier to design your ARIS configuration to support more than you currently need and then scope it down using Method Filters than to try and add things later.

Business Entities

Once you have an idea of the scope of your modelling work you can start to define the range of business entities and relationships you want to represent. For instance: process tasks, departments, IT applications, web pages, instruction documents, etc. If you are familiar with data modelling you can use a class diagram or an entity-relationship model to represent your business entities (see Fig. 12.3).

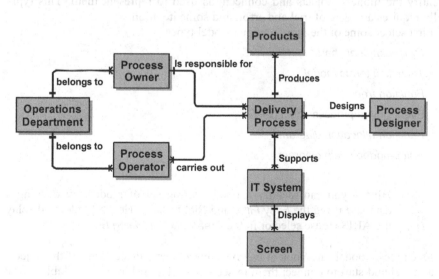

Fig. 12.3 A Business Entity-Relationship Diagram

Expert Tip – why not use ARIS to model your entity-relationship Diagram? Use an *IE Data model* or if you don't want to be as formal use the *Quick model*. It doesn't matter if these models are not part of your final ARIS configuration as only you will be using them.

Analysis Requirements

Identifying the relationships you require is frequently guided by the analysis that you may wish to perform on the model. For instance, if you think you may want to know all the departments involved in process steps that deliver a particular product, and who are supported by specific IT systems, then not only do you need to have objects representing all those things in an *Event-driven process chain* (*EPC*), you also need to have the correct relationships between them. Furthermore, if you then want to identify which person is technically responsible for those IT systems, you are going to need an additional model where you can model such a relationship.

It is very important to think through these requirements and add them to your entity-relationship model.

12.2.6   Choosing Models, Objects and Relationships

Once we have identified the basic concepts we wish to represent, we now need to identify the models, objects and connections used to represent them. This typically requires a degree of trial and error, and some iteration.

First select some of the more obvious model types:

- *Organizational chart,*
- *Technical terms model,*
- *Function tree,*
- Event-driven process chain *(EPC),*
- *Function allocation diagram,*
- *Value-added chain diagram.*

 Hint – you can identify a good starting set of models by opening a database using the *Easy Filter* and Right-Click > Ne<u>w</u> > <u>M</u>odel to display the ARIS House selector in the *Create model Dialog Box.*

Open these models and look at the available objects. Place some of the objects in a model and start to connect them to see what relationships are available. For a good guide to the more useful objects and relationships see Chapter 11 on "Objects and Relationships" in Davis and Brabänder 2007.

Hint – remember there maybe more object symbols available than initially visible on the *Symbols Bar*. Right-Click > Add symbols or F12 to display additional symbols in the Add symbols Dialog Box.

Compare the objects and relationships with those you defined in your entity relationship model. If you can't find any that match, try a Filter with more scope (e.g. the *Extended Standard Filter*). If you still can't find what you want, try the *Entire Method* or refer to the ARIS Method Help (Help > Method Help on the *Main Menu*). However, beware of introducing unusual objects and relationships. It is always best to keep things as simple as possible.

Expert Tip – the ARIS Method Manual provides detailed information on the ARIS Method and the full range of models, objects, connection and attributes, and how it is intended they are used. You can find this PDF file on your installation CD or typically at c:\Program Files\ARIS7.0\doc\en (where the last two letters represent your installation language (e.g. en for English)).

If you can't find exactly the object or relationship you need, look for something very similar. For instance, if you want to represent that a person '*owns*' a particular process, you may feel that the "*is technically responsible*" relationship between a *Person type* and a Function is close to what you want.

If you can find an object or relationship that is close to what you want, and appears in the right models, you have the option to change the Method by renaming the relationship (Section 12.3.7) or to create a user-defined symbol (Section 12.3.12) so that ARIS exactly matches what you want.

Expert Tip – if you want to model specific relationships which are meaningful to your business, but you think the model type in which they appear isn't going to be obvious to your modellers, you can create your own user-defined model (with a more meaningful model type name) based on the standard ARIS model (Section 12.3.8).

By using user-defined models, symbols, and renamed connections and by applying your own Templates you can create a very customised modelling environment. However, don't overdo this. It requires a lot more administration to maintain large degrees of customisation and you may need to provide specialist training as new users won't be familiar with these non-standard modelling conventions.

12.2.7   A Reference Model

It may occur to you while experimenting with various model and objects types, that the models you create are very useful. In fact, if you create a full set of models with all the objects and connections you want to use, you have created a *Reference Model* defining the specific implementation of the ARIS Method in your organisation.

Even better, you can make the *Type* attribute visible to label all the object and connection types and maybe use the *Remark/Example* attribute to describe any intended changes to connection names or symbols (See Fig. 12.4).

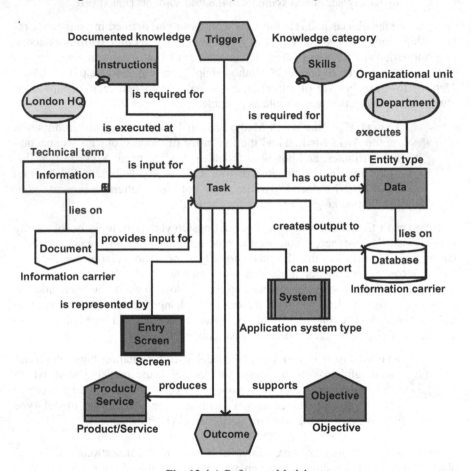

Fig. 12.4 A Reference Model

Prior to ARIS 7, Method Filters had to be created manually following the procedure described in Chapter 14. This was hard work for even the simplest Filter. Creating a Reference Model was an essential starting point. In ARIS 7, however, we can use the Reference Model to automatically generate the Filter, confident in the knowledge that it will exactly represent what we want. This is a huge labour saving advantage and we will see how to do this in Chapter 14.

12.3   Configuring the Method

12.3.1   Introduction to Configuring the Method

In many cases, Method Filters alone may be sufficient to configure ARIS for your needs. However, you may feel the models, objects and connections provided by default are not exactly what you want. You cannot add completely new items to the ARIS Method, but you can change the names and appearance of many items so they more closely match what you require. In this section we will look at how to:

- Rename attribute type groups,
- Rename attributes,
- Allocate attribute to attribute type groups,
- Rename user-defined attributes,
- Rename attribute units,
- Rename connection types,
- Rename model types,
- Create new derived model types,
- Rename object types,
- Rename symbols,
- Create user-defined symbols and allocate them to object types.

We make these changes in the *Method* subgroup of the *Configuration* group using the *Administration Module* in *ARIS Business Architect*. All of the changes you make in the ARIS Method will be reflected in the various dialog boxes of the Filter Wizard (Chapter 14) and hence renamed attributes, derived model types and user-define symbols, etc. will appear in the various dialog box lists when you create or edit a Method Filter.

We will now look at how to configure each of these aspects of the ARIS Method.

12.3.2   Renaming Attribute Type Groups

ARIS *Attributes* are organised into *Attribute Type Groups*. These attribute type groups are used to organise the display of attributes in the *Attributes Window* and in dialog boxes such as the *Select model attributes Dialog Box* in the *Filter Wizard*.

You can change the name of an attribute type group by:

1.   Select the **Attribute type groups** sub-group (Fig. 12.5) of the **Method** group in the *Administration Module*,

2.   Select the attribute type group you wish to rename in the *Contents Tab* in the right-hand pane,

3.   Right-Click > Re_n_ame, press F2, or select the Rename button on the *Method Toolbar*,

4.   Enter a new *Name* and press Enter.

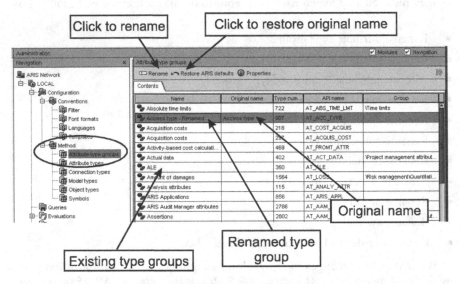

Fig. 12.5 Attribute Type Sub-group

The new name will appear in the *Name* field of the *Contents Tab* and the *Original name* field will show the old name. You can revert back to the original default name of the attribute type group by selecting it and Right-Click > Restore ARIS defaults or by selecting the Restore ARIS defaults button on the toolbar.

You can maintain the attribute type group name in multiple languages using the *Properties – Attribute type groups Dialog Box* (Fig. 12.6) to rename the attribute type group:

1.   Select the attribute type group in the *Contents Tab* in the right-hand pane,

2.   Right-Click > _P_roperties, press Alt+Enter, or select the Properties button on the *Method Toolbar*,

3.   Select the required *_L_anguage*,

4.   Enter a new value in *_N_ame* field and press Enter.

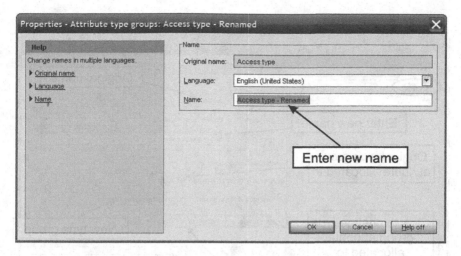

Fig. 12.6 Properties – Attribute Type Groups Dialog Box

12.3.3   Renaming Attributes

You can change the name of an attribute to be more meaningful to your organisation by:

1. Select the **Attribute types** sub-group of the **Method** group in the *Administration Module*,

2. Select the attribute type you wish to rename in the *Contents Tab* in the right-hand pane,

3. Right-Click > Re*n*ame, press F2, or select the Rename button on the *Method Toolbar*,

4. Enter a new *N*ame and press Enter.

The new name will appear in the *Name* field of the *Contents Tab* and the *Original name* field will show the old name. You can revert back the original default name of the attribute type by selecting it and Right-Click > Restore ARIS defaults or by selecting the button on the toolbar.

The **Attribute types** sub-group lists all attributes, irrespective of whether they are used for models, objects or connections. You can maintain the attribute type group name in multiple languages by using the *Properties – Attribute types Dialog Box* (Fig. 12.7). Select the required *L*anguage and enter a new value in *N*ame field.

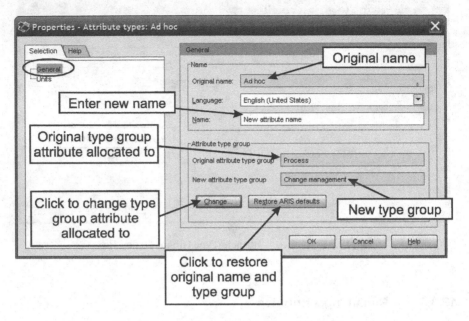

Fig. 12.7 Properties – Attribute Types Dialog Box

Hint – not all ARIS attributes can have their names changed and be allocated to other attribute type groups. Only those that can be configured are shown in the *Attribute types* sub-group.

12.3.4   Allocating Attributes to Attribute Type Groups

Most (although not all) attributes are organised into attribute type groups. You can see which group an attribute is allocated to by looking at the *Group* field in the *Contents Tab* (Fig. 12.5). Those attributes that aren't shown as being in a group are listed at the top level of an attribute display.

You can allocate an attribute to a new group using the *Properties – Attribute types Dialog Box* (Fig. 12.7):

1.   Select the ***Attribute types*** sub-group of the ***Method*** group in the *Administration Module*,

2.   Select the specific attribute type in the *Contents Tab* in the right-hand pane,

3.   Right-Click > Properties, press Alt+Enter, or select the Properties button on the *Method Toolbar*,

4. Click the Change button in the *Properties – Attribute types Dialog Box*,
5. Select the new group in the *Select attribute type group Dialog Box* (Fig. 12.8),
6. Click OK.

The *New attribute type group* field will show the new group and the *Original attribute type group* field will show where it was before. Click OK and the *Contents Tab* will update and show the new location in the *Group* field.

    Hint – when you move an attribute to a new group it is in fact copied into the new group and it will also remain in its original group. It is effectively an occurrence copy and both entries point to the same attribute.

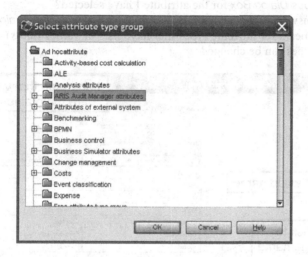

Fig. 12.8 Select Attribute Type Group Dialog Box

12.3.5   Renaming Attribute Units

There are a number of different types of attributes (e.g. Boolean, Text, Time, etc). Boolean and Value attributes have specific values (*units*) associated with them that can be chosen from a drop-down list. For instance, in the *ARIS Audit Manager attributes* group, the *Control frequency* attribute has values of "Annually", "Daily", "Monthly", etc.

You can change the names of the attribute units for those attribute types that have them from the *Properties – Attribute types [Units] Dialog Box* (Fig. 12.9):

1. Select the **Attribute types** sub-group of the **Method** group in the *Administration Module*,
2. Select the specific attribute type in the *Contents Tab* in the right-hand pane,

3. Right-Click > Properties, press Alt+Enter, or select the Properties button on the *Method Toolbar,*

4. Select the *Properties – Attribute types [Units] Dialog Box,*

5. Click on one of the entries in the *Value* list,

6. Click Modify or press F2,

7. Enter a new *Name* and press Enter.

The *Value* field will update to show the new name while the *Original value* field will show what it was before. Click OK to save the change.

 Question – why do I not see a *Units* entry in the *Properties – Attribute types Dialog Box* for the attribute I have selected?

Answer – the *Properties – Attribute types [Units] Dialog Box* only appears for attribute types that have lists of values (*units*) whose value names can be changed.

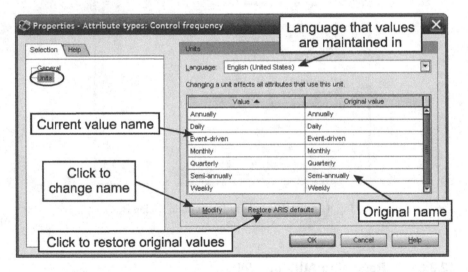

Fig. 12.9 Properties – Attribute Types (Units) Dialog Box

12.3.6   Renaming User Attributes

ARIS has a large range of attributes, many of which are associated with specific ARIS models, objects and applications. You cannot add new attributes to the ARIS Method, but there is a set of *User attributes* that you can rename for your own purposes and you can arrange them in *Free attribute type groups* which you can also rename. Follow the instructions in the section above to rename the User attributes and Free attribute type groups and then to assign these attributes to attribute type groups. The different types of free attributes are shown in Table 12.3.

Table 12.3 Free Attributes Types

Type	Meaning
User attribute Boolean	Binary values (e.g. "True" or "False") selectable with checkboxes. Values can be renamed.
User attribute Date	For holding dates in DD.MM.YY format. Can also be selected from a calendar tool.
User attribute Duration	Time period in DDDD.HH.MM.SS format.
User attribute Float	Positive and negative numbers with two decimal points.
User attribute Int	Positive and negative integer numbers.
User attribute Point in time	Start or end time in HH.MM.SS format.
User attribute Time	Time in HH.MM.SS format.
User attribute Text	Free multi-line text field.
User attribute Value	Values that can be selected from a drop-down list of 5 or 10 entries that can be renamed.

12.3.7   Renaming Connection Types

Connections are the *Relationships* between objects created by drawing a line between them in the *Designer Module*. The *Type* attribute of a connection is used throughout ARIS to refer to the connection (or Relationship). The *Type* attribute actually has two names associated with it:

- *Active name* – the connection as seen from the source object to target object; equivalent to the *Type* attribute.

- *Passive name* – the connection as seen from the target object to source object; not normally visible, but can be printed in ARIS Reports.

Both the *Active name* and *Passive name* can be changed from the *Properties – Connection types Dialog Box* (Fig. 12.10):

1.   Select the **Connection types** sub-group of the **Method** group in the *Administration Module*,
2.   Select the specific connection type in the *Contents Tab* in the right-hand pane,
3.   Right-Click > Properties, press Alt+Enter, or select the Properties button on the *Method Toolbar* ,
4.   Enter a new *Active name* in the *Properties – Connection types Dialog Box*,
5.   Enter a new *Passive name*,
6.   Click OK.

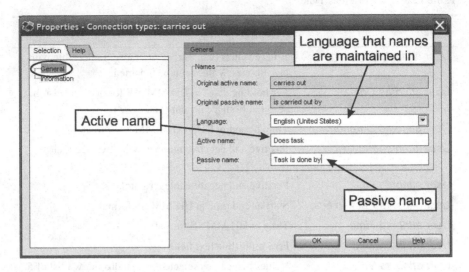

Fig. 12.10 Properties – Connection Types Dialog Box

You can maintain the connection type names in multiple languages by selecting the *Language* before you change the names. If you need to know between which objects the connection type occurs and in which model, look at the *Properties – Connection types [Information] Dialog Box* (Fig. 12.11).

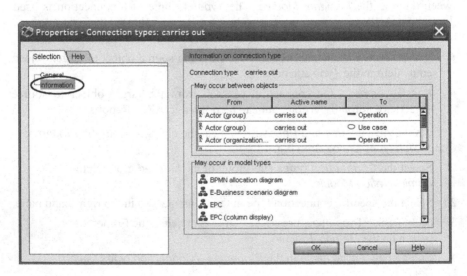

Fig. 12.11 Properties – Connection Types (Information) Dialog Box

After you click OK, the *Contents Tab* will update and show the new values in the *Active name* and *Passive names* fields. You can quickly change just the *Active name* by selecting it in the *Contents Tab* and Right-Click > Rename, pressing F2, or selecting the Rename button on the *Method Toolbar*.

 Warning – the *Type* attribute is used throughout ARIS to refer to the connection being made between objects. If you rename it, make sure that it is going to be meaningful to your users.

12.3.8 Renaming Model Types

The types of model available in ARIS are defined by the ARIS Method. They tend to have rather formal names such as *Application system type diagram, Value-added chain diagram, Technical terms model*, etc. You may find it useful to rename these model types to represent the terms used in your business, for instance, "*IT systems diagram*", "*high-level process model*" or "*information model*". To do this:

1. Select the **Model types** sub-group of the **Method** group in the *Administration Module*,

2. Select the model type you wish to rename in the *Contents Tab* in the right-hand pane,

3. Right-Click > Rename, press F2, or select the Rename button on the *Method Toolbar*,

4. Enter a new *Name* and press Enter.

You can also rename a model type by entering a new value in the *Name* field of the *Properties – Model types Dialog Box*. You can maintain the model type name in multiple languages by selecting the *Language* before you change the name.

 Warning – the model type is used throughout ARIS to select the type of model to create, to assign models to objects, etc. If you rename it, beware of making the name too specific to a particular application or business initiative; consider creating a derived model type (see next section) instead.

12.3.9 Creating Derived Model Types

We have seen above how we can rename model types so, for instance, we could rename the *EPC* as "*Process Model*". However, in practice we use many different types of process model in our business. We may have a "*high-level model*", an "*operational process model*" and a "*detailed level-4 model*". All of these use the basic *EPC* model, but we may wish to have a different range of object types and connections in each style of model.

In ARIS 7 we cannot create new model types, but we can create *derived model types*, based on an underlying ARIS model type. These have their own names and their own definitions in the Method Filter. For instance, our *"high-level model"* may just have Functions, Events, Rules and *Organizational unit types*, while our *"detailed level-4 model"* could have additional object types such as *Application system types, Technical terms, General resources*, etc.

Of course we could just use an *EPC* with all the required object and connection types as the basis for all of these models, but the advantage of having separate *derived model types* is that we can limit the objects, symbols, connections and attribute types to just those needed. This helps the users understand what the models are used for and helps enforce corporate modelling conventions.

We can also apply different default Templates to the derived model types (see Chapter 15). Using these in association with user-defined symbols (see Section 12.3.12) allows us to create different views (with a different 'look and feel') that we can tailor to our target audience.

To create a derived model type:

1.   Select the **Model types** sub-group of the **Method** group in the *Administration Module*,

2.   Select the model type on which you want to base the derived model in the *Contents Tab* in the right-hand pane,

3.   Right-Click > Ne<u>w</u> > <u>M</u>odel type, or select the New button on the *Method Toolbar*,

4.   Enter a new <u>N</u>ame in the *Create model type Dialog Box*,

5.   Press Enter.

A new model type will be created and entered in the *Contents Tab*. It will be based on the model type you selected which will be shown in the *Original name* field. The *Type* field will show that it is a *"derived"* model. You can maintain the model type name in multiple languages by selecting the <u>L</u>anguage before you change the name.

This derived model type will now appear in the *Filter Wizard* and you can configure it and use it exactly as you would any other model type.

If you no longer want this derived model type, select it in the **Model types** sub-group and Right-Click > <u>D</u>elete. You can only delete derived model types and not default ARIS model types.

 Expert Tip – if you delete a derived model type it will be automatically deleted from any Filters that use it. Any models of that type will not be lost, but will revert to the model type the derived type was based on.

 Warning – models that have reverted to the model type a deleted derived model type was based on may no longer be visible if the current Method Filter has not enabled the base model type. Use the **Entire Method** or add the base model type to the current Filter.

12.3.10   Renaming Object Types

As with models, the types of object available in ARIS are defined by the ARIS Method and have rather formal names such as *Application system type, Technical term*, etc. You may find it useful to rename these object types to represent the terms used in your business, for instance, "*IT system*", or "*Information*". To do this:

1. Select the **Object types** sub-group of the **Method** group in the *Administration Module*,
2. Select the object type you wish to rename in the *Contents Tab* in the right-hand pane,
3. Right-Click > Rename, press F2, or select the Rename button on the *Method Toolbar*,
4. Enter a new *Name* and press Enter.

You can also rename an object type by entering a new value in the *Name* field of the *Properties – Object types Dialog Box*. You can maintain the object type name in multiple languages by selecting the *Language* before you change the name.

 Warning – the object type is used throughout ARIS to select the type of object to create, etc. If you rename it, beware of making the name too specific to a particular application or business initiative; consider creating user-defined symbols (see next section) instead.

12.3.11   Renaming Symbols

Wherever an object has an occurrence in a model, displayed in the *Designer Module*, it is represented by a symbol. We are already familiar with the concept that an object type such as a Function or an *Organizational unit type* can have a number of different symbols. Some of the alternative symbols have the same meaning, but just provide a different appearance, while others can be used to convey different varieties of the basic object (e.g. the various different information carriers). You can rename a symbol by:

1. Select the **Symbols** sub-group (Fig. 12.12) of the **Method** group in the *Administration Module*,
2. Select the symbol in the *Contents Tab* in the right-hand pane,
3. Right-Click > Rename, press F2, or select the Rename button on the *Method Toolbar*,
4. Enter a new *Name* and press Enter.

You can also rename a symbol by entering a new value in the *Name* field of the *Properties – Symbols Dialog Box*. You can maintain the symbol name in multiple languages by selecting the *Language* before you change the name.

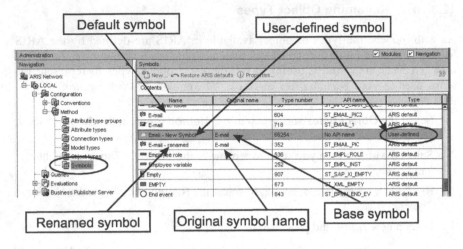

Fig. 12.12 Symbols Sub-group

 Warning – the symbol is used to refer to a particular object type and often has the same name as the object. If you rename it, be careful to make it obvious which object it refers to.

12.3.12 Creating User-defined Symbols

In addition to renaming existing symbols, you can create your own user-defined symbols using the *Symbol Editor* (see Chapter 13). Once you have created a user-defined symbol and saved it into your hard disk, you can add it to the Method and allocate it to an object type by:

1. Select an existing symbol in the *Contents Tab* of the **Symbols** sub-group (Fig. 12.12) on which you want to base your new symbol,

2. Right-Click > New > Symbol, or select the New button on the *Method Toolbar*,

3. Enter a new *Name* in the *Create symbol Dialog Box*,

4. Click Next,

5. Click on the *Browse* button in *Select graphic Dialog Box* (Fig. 12.13),

6. Navigate to the location where you saved your user-defined symbol,

7. Click Open.

The *Preview* area of the *Select graphic Dialog Box* (Fig. 12.13) will update to show an image of the new symbol alongside the original symbol on which it was based. Click Finish and the new symbol will be created and allocated to the object type that was associated with the base symbol. The user-defined symbol will be added to the *Contents Tab* and the *Original name* field will show on which symbol your new symbol was based. The *Type* field will now say "*user-defined*" to distinguish it from the ARIS default symbols.

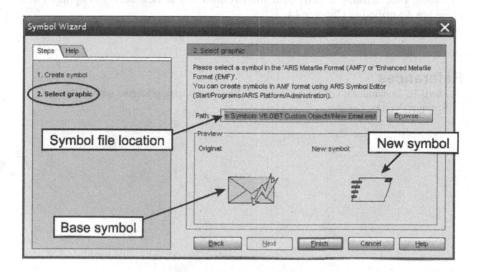

Fig. 12.13 Select Graphic Dialog Box

You can now configure a Filter to use this new symbol to represent the associated object type in the same way the symbol on which it was based could be used.

 Expert Tip – symbols representing the same object type may be used in different models and have different connection types (e.g. a Function in an *EPC* and a *Value-added chain* in a *Value-added chain diagram*). A user-derived symbol will take on the properties and usage of the symbol on which it was based.

 Question – why does the <u>N</u>ew button remain greyed out when I have selected a user-defined symbol in the *Symbols* sub-group?
Answer – you can only base a new symbol on an ARIS default symbol, not on a previously created user-defined symbol.

12.3.13   Saving Method Changes

The Method changes and additions described above are applied at the server level and automatically become available in any Filters created or edited on the server. If a Filter is subsequently exported from the server, any Method changes that have been selected in the Filter (e.g. selection of a model type that has had its name changed) will automatically be saved in the Filter.

When you import a Filter onto another server, all of the Method changes saved in the Filter will be applied to the server. The changes will add to or overwrite any existing method changes. There are a number of different options on the *Import filter Dialog Box* defining exactly how the Method on the new server is updated and these are described in Chapter 14.

References

Davis R, Brabänder E (2007) ARIS design Platform: Getting Started with BPM, Springer-Verlay, London.

Chapter 13   The Symbol Editor

This chapter described the Symbol Editor tool and how it can be used to created user-defined symbols that can be imported into ARIS and used to customise the ARIS Method.

13.1   Introduction

The *ARIS Symbol Editor* is a graphical drawing tool that enables you to create your own ARIS user-defined symbols. You can base the design of your symbols on existing ARIS symbols provided in the Symbol Editor library, you can draw new symbols from scratch using basic graphic shapes or you can import graphics files of various formats (e.g. GIF, JPEG, BPM, EMF, etc).

The Symbol Editor is not part of *ARIS Business Architect*, but is a separate application you can run from: Start/Programs/ARIS Platform/Administration.

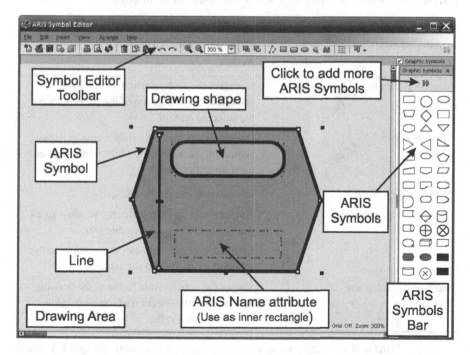

Fig. 13.1 The Symbol Editor Window

13.2   The Drawing Window

The main window of the Symbol Editor (Fig. 13.1) has an appearance similar to the *Designer Module* in *ARIS Business Architect*. At the top of the window there is the *Main Menu* and underneath it the *Symbol Editor Toolbar*. The buttons on the toolbar will be familiar from the *Designer Module*. At the right-hand side of the window is the *Graphic Symbols Bar*.

13.2.1   Scaling the Symbol View

The Vi̲ew sub-menu on the *Main Menu* has a set of commands for scaling the drawing area. The Zoom commands also have buttons on the *Symbol Editor Toolbar* and, in addition, the *Size of appearance* button allows the scale of the screen to be set directly using the drop-down box, either by selecting one of the pre-set values or by entering a new value followed by <Enter>. The operation of these commands is shown in Table 13.1 along with their shortcut keys.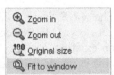

Table 13.1 Drawing Area Scaling Commands

Command	Shortcut	Action
Vi̲ew > Z̲oom In	<+>	Increases the scale of window area by 10% centred at the middle top of the window or on the selected symbol.
Vi̲ew > Z̲oom Out	<->	Decreases the scale of window area by 10% centred at the middle top of the window or on the selected symbol.
Vi̲ew > Original si̲ze		Resizes the window to 100%.
Vi̲ew > Fit to w̲indow		**Nothing selected** – rescales the window so all the symbols fit into the visible area.
		Symbol selected – rescales the window so the selected symbols fit in the visible area.
Size of appearance Button 110 %		Shows the current scale factor of the drawing area and allows selection of a pre-set value or overtyping of a value.

 Hint – if you have a mouse with a scroll wheel you can quickly zoom in and out of the drawing area by holding down the <CTRL> key and rotating the wheel. If you click on a symbol first, the zoom will be centred on the symbol.

13.2.2   The Overview Window

On the *Right-Click Menu* there is a command Right-Click > <u>O</u>verview window. Selecting this displays a small Overview Window on top of the drawing area which shows a view of the entire drawing space.

The *Overview Window* (Fig. 13.2) shows a white shaded area representing the current visible drawing area. As you scroll around the drawing area, or zoom in or out, the shaded area will also move or scale in synchronisation to give you a visual indication of the relationship between the visible area and the entire drawing space. If you click on the white area on the *Overview Window* and drag it around the window, the visible part of the drawing area will also move to make that part of the area visible. This makes it very quick to locate a particular part of a zoomed model.

You can alter the size of the *Overview Window* by dragging its sides and you can drag it around to the most convenient location. You can close it by clicking on the window close icon at the top right-hand corner of the window.

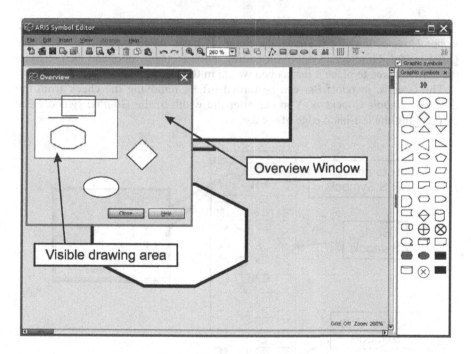

Fig. 13.2 The Overview Window

13.2.3   Window Properties

You can select the *Background colour* of the drawing area and the *Grid* size from the *Properties – Drawing area Dialog Box*. Make sure no symbols or shapes are selected and do any of:

- Edit > *Properties*,
- Right-Click > Properties,
- Press Alt+Enter.

The background colour only affects the drawing area and has no effect on the symbol itself.

The grid can also be turned on or off by selecting the Toggle grid button on the *Symbol Editor Toolbar*.

13.3   The Graphic Symbols Bar

The *Graphic symbols Bar* (Fig. 13.3), is analogous to the *Symbols Bar* in the *Designer Module*. Initially it shows the range of basic ARIS symbols used in the *Quick model*. To select a symbol for editing, click on the symbol and then click in the drawing area to place it just as you would in the *Designer Module*.

The *Graphic symbols Bar* can be turned off by removing the check from the *Graphic symbols Checkbox*. You can alter the width of the *Graphic symbols Bar* by dragging the left-hand edge of the bar.

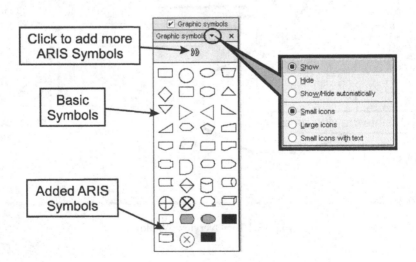

Fig. 13.3 The Graphic Symbols Bar

Alternatively you can minimise the bar and set it to appear automatically when you move your mouse to the far right-hand side of the window. To set the visibility of the *Graphic symbols Bar,* click on the down arrow next to the *Symbols* label in the *Graphic symbols Bar* title area and select from the Show, Hide, and Sho<u>w</u>/Hide automatically options (see Fig. 13.3).

You can alter the size of the symbol icons on the *Graphic symbols Bar* or additionally display the names of the symbols by selecting the down arrow next to the *Symbols* label and selecting <u>S</u>mall icons, <u>L</u>arge icons or Small icons wi<u>t</u>h text (Fig. 13.3).

 Expert Tip – you can find the *ARIS Symbol Number,* used to identify symbols, by hovering your mouse over the symbol on the *Graphic Symbols Bar.* A tooltip will appear showing the number of the symbol.

13.3.1 Adding ARIS Symbols to the Graphic Symbols Bar

To add an ARIS symbol not currently visible to the *Graphic symbols Bar,* click on the Add symbols Button at the top of the *Graphic symbols Bar* (or press F12). The *Add symbols Dialog Box* (Fig. 13.4) will show all the additional ARIS standard symbols.

You can double-click on a symbol to add it directly to the *Graphic symbols Bar* or select one or more of the symbols (use <CTRL>+left-click to select multiple symbols) and click the <u>A</u>dd Button. You can repeat this a number of times to choose the set of symbols you want to include in the *Graphic symbols Bar.* Once you have finished selecting all the symbols, click the Close Button. You should now see the ARIS symbols you chose added to the *Graphic symbols Bar.*

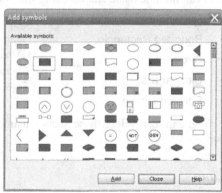

Fig. 13.4 Add Symbols Dialog Box

13.3.2 Removing a Symbol from the Graphic Symbols Bar

To remove an ARIS symbol from the *Graphic symbols Bar,* right-click on the symbol and select Remove <u>s</u>ymbol. The symbol is not deleted, but moved back to the *Add symbols Dialog Box* (Fig. 13.4). You can add it back to the *Graphic symbols Bar* as described above. The basic set of shapes visible when you open the Symbol Editor cannot be removed.

13.4   Creating a Symbol

You can build up the design of a symbol from one or more existing symbols, graphic shapes or imported graphics files (although this is not recommended). To start creating a new symbol click on the File > New > ARIS symbol command or use the File > Open > ARIS symbol to edit an existing symbol.

13.4.1   Using Existing Symbols

To use an existing symbol as the basis for a new symbol design, select the shape you want from the *Graphic symbols Bar* and click in the modelling area. Just like the *Designer Module* you cannot drag and drop symbols. You can configure the symbols bar to include any of the ARIS symbols as described in Section 13.3.1. You can add any number of symbols to build up a more complex, compound symbol.

13.4.2   Inserting Shapes

You can include basic shapes using the Insert menu:

- Rectangle,
- Rounded Rectangle,
- Circle/Ellipse,
- Circular arc,
- Polygon (lines).

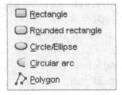

You can also select these shapes using the buttons on the *Symbol Editor Toolbar*.

Lines

To draw a line, select Insert > Polygon and click on the start point of the line. Move the mouse to the end of the line and double-click; a line will be drawn. To draw multiple lines, single-click at the end of the line segment and keep drawing new segments until the lines are finished, and then double-click at the end of the last line.

If you click the end of the last line at the start of the first line, a polygon will be created and filled with a default colour. You can change the fill colour using the *Properties – Graphic symbol Dialog Box* (see Section 13.5).

If you have selected an arc, you can choose whether to make the arc *Open* or *Closed*.

Editing Polygons

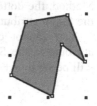

You can alter the shape of a polygon (e.g. shapes that are not
perfect circles or rectangles) that you have previously drawn or
placed in the drawing area. Click on the symbol and you will
see small white squares appear at each change of line direction.
Click on the square and drag it to move the position of the
connecting node.

Insert and Remove Angles

You can also add or delete connecting nodes to a polygon. To
add a node, click the symbol, hover the cursor over one of the
polygon's lines and Right-Click > Insert angle. A new white
node will appear in the middle of the selected line and you can
drag it to change the shape.

   To remove a node, select the symbol, hover your mouse over
the white square of the node you wish to remove and
Right-Click > Remove angle. The node will be removed and the line redrawn to
connect the adjacent nodes.

Circular Arc

Select Insert > Circular arc and click at the start and end points that represent the
radius of the arc. Initially a circle will be drawn, but if you continue to move the
mouse you can change the angle of the arc.

   You can select the *Properties – Graphic symbol/Circular arc Dialog Box* and
choose whether to make the arc *Open*, *Closed* or a *Pie* chart (see Section 13.5.4).

13.4.3   Inserting the Name Attribute

All ARIS symbols display the *Name* attribute by default, normally in the centre of
the symbol. When you create a user-defined symbol, the *Name* attribute will be
provided by default and will not normally be visible in the Symbol Editor. However, if you wish, you can specifically set the required location of the *Name* attribute and the boundary of its text box by specifically adding it to the symbol.

   Select a rectangle using the Insert > Rectangle command or
button and place the rectangle on your symbol where you want
the *Name* attribute to appear. Adjust the size of the rectangle to
set the area within which you want the text to be wrapped. Now
select the rectangle and Right-Click > Use as inner rectangle.
The outline of the rectangle will now change to a yellow dotted
line.

When you save the symbol and import into the ARIS Method, the dotted rectangle will now represent the area where the *Name* attribute will be displayed and the text wrapped.

Text is wrapp ed here

You cannot change the properties of the inserted *Name* attribute in the Symbol Editor; the appearance of the attribute will be set by ARIS.

13.4.4   Inserting Text

You can insert free text into the symbol using the View > Text command or by pressing the Insert text button on the *Symbol Editor Toolbar*.

To edit the text, select it, press F2 and overtype a new value. You can also edit the text in the *New text* area of the *Text properties Dialog Box* (Fig. 13.11) as well as change the text alignment and font.

13.4.5   Importing a Graphic File

You can import existing graphics to use as the basis for a symbol design using the File > Import graphic command. The *Import graphic* dialog box will allow you to choose an appropriate *File type*. You can then browse for the chosen file type and click the Import graphic button.

Hint – click on the *File type* drop-down box to see the range of file types that can be imported.

Expert Tip – you can edit an existing symbol file using the File > Open > ARIS symbol command. If you want to add a second symbol file to the drawing area, use the File > Import graphic command.

13.4.6   Setting the Display Order

If you create a compound symbol from a number of shapes and symbols you can select the order in which the shapes overlay each other using the commands in the Arrange menu:

*   Bring to front,
*   Send to back,
*   One level forward,
*   One level backward.

You can also click the Bring to front and Send to back buttons on the *Symbol Editor Toolbar*.

13.4.7   Aligning Shapes

If you create a compound symbol from a number of shapes and symbols you can select the way in which the shapes align with each other using the commands in the Arrange > Align menu:

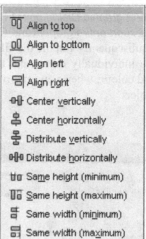

- *Align to top,*
- *Align to bottom,*
- *Align left,*
- *Align right,*
- *Centre vertically,*
- *Centre horizontally,*
- *Distribute vertically,*
- *Distribute horizontally,*
- *Same height (minimum),*
- *Same height (maximum),*
- *Same width (minimum),*
- *Same width (maximum).*

You can also select these commands from the Align button on the *Symbol Editor Toolbar.*

13.4.8   Saving and Resizing a Symbol

Every shape, symbol or graphic file placed in the drawing area will be combined and saved as a single symbol when you select the File > Save (Ctrl+S) or File > Save as command. The symbol will be saved in ".amf" format.

You can resize the symbol using the Edit > Resize command. The *Resize Dialog Box* will enable to change the *Width* and the *Height* and you can select to *Keep aspect ratio* the same by clicking the checkbox or return the symbol to the default size by clicking in the Scale to default size button. The default ratio depends on the size of the symbol chosen.

In practice, provided you keep the aspect ratio the same as the default ratio, it doesn't matter what size you save the symbol. When the symbol is assigned to an object type in the ARIS Method (based on an existing symbol) and subsequently used in a model, it will always appear the same size as the symbol for that object type on which it was based.

If you change the aspect ratio, the symbol will appear with the different ratio, but scaled to be the same width as the base symbol.

 Warning – if the symbol contains free text this will not be resized if the symbol is resized. Instead you will need to use the *Text properties Dialog Box* (Section 13.4.4) to change the font size.

13.4.9   Exporting a Symbol

You can export a symbol as a graphic file using the File > Export > As a graphic command. The file will be saved in ".emf" (Windows Enhanced Metafile) format.

The *Export graphic Dialog box* (Fig. 13.5) will allow you to *Export selected objects only*, *Export entire graphic* and *Export background*.

If you subsequently import the file, all the components used to create the file can still be individually edited and their properties changed. If you exported the background colour, when you import the file, the background will appear as a rectangular object.

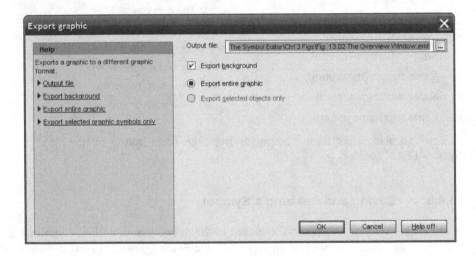

Fig. 13.5 Export Graphic Dialog Box

13.4.10   Undo and Redo

The Symbol Editor has multiple levels of *undo* and *redo* which enable you to revert back to any stage in the editing operation since the last time the symbol was saved. Undo and Redo are on the *Main Menu* under Edit and can also be selected from icons on the *Symbol Editor Toolbar*.

13.5   Symbol Appearance Properties

You can change the appearance of a symbol or its component parts (shapes, text, etc) using the *Properties – Graphic symbol Dialog Box*.

Select the symbol and do any of:

- Edit > *Properties*,
- Right-Click > *Properties*,
- Press Alt+Enter.

There are several sub-dialog boxes depending on the item chosen:

- *Colours,*
- *Scaling,*
- *Rotation,*
- *Circular Arc,*
- *Rectangle,*
- *Text Properties.*

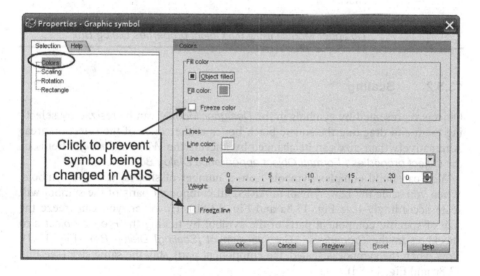

Fig. 13.6 Colours Dialog Box

13.5.1   Colours

The *Colors Dialog Box* (Fig. 13.6) allows you to change the appearance of the graphic component using the settings shown in Table 13.2.

The appearance of most symbols can be changed in the ARIS *Designer Module* using the *Object properties Dialog Box* or by applying a Template. If you don't want users to be able to change the appearance of a user-defined symbol, the *Freeze color* and *Freeze line* check boxes can be ticked.

Table 13.2 Symbol Properties / Colours

Command	Action
Fill color	Allows the background colour of a symbol to be chosen from the *Choose color Dialog Box*.
Freeze color	Prevents the selected colour being changed in the *Designer Module* using the *Object properties Dialog Box*.
Line color	Allows the outline colour of a symbol to be chosen from the *Choose color Dialog Box*.
Line style	Allows the outline of the symbol to be *Solid*, *Dashed* or *Dotted*.
Weight	Shows the weight (i.e. thickness and intensity) of the symbol outline and it allows it to be changed by entering a value or dragging the slider.
Freeze line	Prevents the selected line colour, style or weight being changed in the *Designer Module* using the *Object properties Dialog Box*.

13.5.2   Scaling

Objects represented by symbols in the *Designer Module* can be resized by selecting them and dragging the square black boxes at the edges of the selection area. Alternatively their size can be changed by altering the *Width* and *Height* fields in the *Object properties / Format/ Object appearance Dialog Box*.

You can build complex symbols from a number of shapes, text and symbols. When you scale the new symbol in ARIS, all component parts of the symbol will scale accordingly (see Fig. 13.8a and Fig. 13.8b). However, you can freeze the size of specific component parts of the symbol by ticking the *Freeze object size* checkbox in the *Properties – Graphic symbol [Scaling] Dialog Box* (Fig. 13.7). Now when the symbol is scaled, the component parts stay the same size (see Fig. 13.8c and Fig. 13.8d).

The position of the frozen component part, in relation to the whole symbol, can be fixed at various points (e.g. *Top left*, *Centred*, *Bottom right*) or by selecting *Free* and entering x and y coordinates.

An example of an existing ARIS symbol with frozen parts is the *Technical term*. As the symbol is scaled, the small icon at the bottom right of the symbol remains a fixed size, anchored to the bottom right-hand corner.

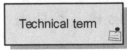

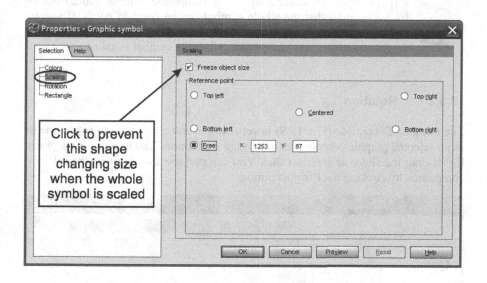

Fig. 13.7 Scaling Dialog Box

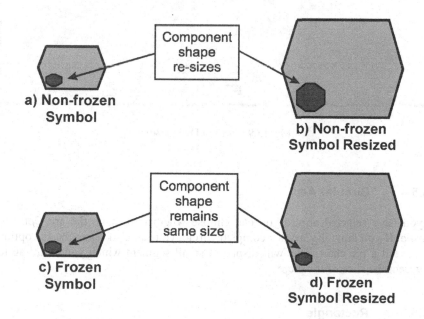

Fig. 13.8 Freeze Object Size Options

Expert Tip – the outer shape of a compound symbol should not be frozen in order that the whole symbol can be sized in ARIS. If you try to freeze the outer shape you will find the Symbol Editor deselects all the *Freeze object size* checkboxes when the symbol is saved.

13.5.3   Rotation

The *Rotation Dialog Box* (Fig. 13.9) is very simple and allows you to rotate one or more selected graphic components in a range from minus 180 to plus 180 degrees. Either drag the slider or enter a value. You can preview the effect on the selected component by clicking the Preview button.

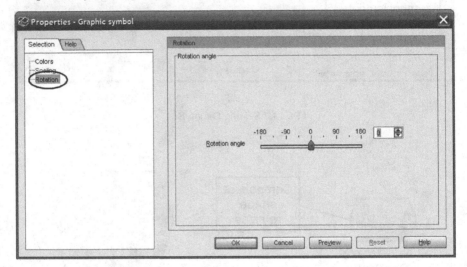

Fig. 13.9 Rotation Dialog Box

13.5.4   Circular Arc

If you have selected an arc you can choose whether to make the arc *Open* or *Closed*. If you draw the arc as a complete circle, you can also select the *Pie* option to make it a pie chart. This will display a small segment which you can drag to represent the slice of the pie.

13.5.5   Rectangle

The *Rectangle Dialog Box* (Fig. 13.10) only applies to symbols that are rectangles and allows you to set the radius of the corners of the rectangle. Either drag the slider or enter a value. You can preview the effect on the selected rectangle by clicking the Preview button.

The exact appearance of rounding of the corners will depend on the scaling of the symbol. If you check the *Constant rounding* option, the appearance of the rounding will look the same even if the symbol is scaled. If it is not checked, the rounding will be scaled as the symbol is scaled.

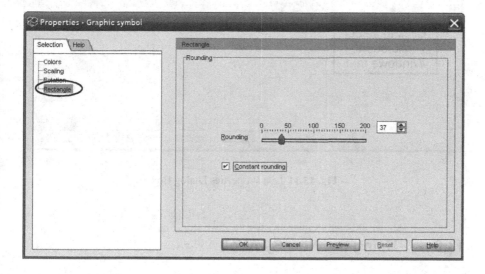

Fig. 13.10 Rectangle Dialog Box

13.5.6   Text Properties

The *Text properties Dialog Box* (Fig. 13.11) only appears when a free text component is selected. You can specify the *Alignment* of the text (*Left*, *Centered*, *Right*) and change the font using the Change font button. Fonts are selected from the *Change font Dialog Box* and you can select any of the fonts available in *Microsoft Windows*. Free text in symbols only affects the graphic appearance of the symbol and has nothing to do with the attributes of the object the symbol represents. The fonts used for free text have no connection with the Font Formats defined in ARIS.

To edit text, overtype the "text" entry in the *New text* area of the dialog box. You can also freeze the size and location of text components as described in Section 13.5.2.

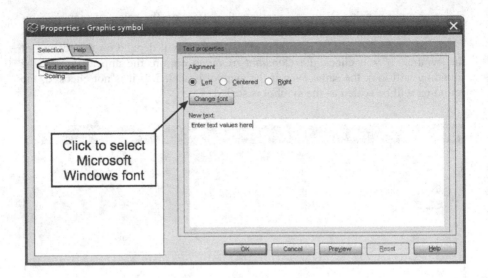

Fig. 13.11 Text Properties Dialog Box

13.6   Using the New Symbol

To use the user-defined symbol you need to add it into to the ARIS Method using the *Administration Module* in *ARIS Business Architect*. Go to the *Method/Symbols* sub-group of the *Configuration* group and add the new symbol based on an existing symbol for the object type you want the new symbol to represent. For a detailed description of adding new symbols see Chapter 12.

Warning – if you use the Symbol Editor to change the design of a symbol already used in the ARIS Method, you need to edit the symbol's entry in the *Method/Symbols* sub-group of the *Configuration* group in the *Administration Module* to update it with the new file. It won't update automatically, so edit the symbol and in the *Symbol Wizard* go to the *Select graphic Dialog Box* and click the Browse button to navigate to the updated version of the symbol file.

Chapter 14　　Method Filters and Evaluation Filters

This chapter discusses the importance of Method and Evaluation Filters and looks in detail at creating a new Filter and how to create a Filter directly from a Reference Database.

14.1　　The Importance of Method Filters

ARIS has many model types, many object types and a variety of relationships between those object types. There is also a large set of attributes available for each. Not every modelling task needs all these models, objects and attributes and working with all of these would make modelling unnecessarily complicated and prone to error. To simplify things ARIS provides '*Method Filters*' which limit the number of options available. By limiting the range of models, objects and relationships available to users, the *ARIS System Administrator* can both make the tool easier to use and also enforce corporate standards by implementing modelling conventions.

ARIS provides a number of standard Filters and any number of additional user Filters can be defined. Filters can be applied at the database level or be allocated to individual users or groups of users so as to only make visible the information relevant to them. The combination of user *Access Privileges* (see Chapter 11) and applied Method Filters can be used to precisely configure how users view and use ARIS. There is also the facility to create new symbols for existing objects and to define '*User attributes*' to describe the user's own information (see Chapter 12).

14.1.1　　Evaluation Filters

Method Filters limit which items users can see when creating and editing models in ARIS. However, an important aspect of Business Process Management is the way we present process designs to end users. In ARIS we can do this using *ARIS Evaluations* (including ARIS Reports) and by creating HTML pages using ARIS Web Publisher. The output from Evaluations will be constrained by the Method Filter applied to the particular database in use, but often we want to restrict even further the objects, relationships and attributes visible to a viewer of a report or web site. In particular, we often wish to constrain the list of attributes to just those the user may be interested in.

We can control what the viewers of ARIS Evaluations see by applying an *Evaluation Filter* at the point when the output is created. Evaluation Filters are exactly the same as Method Filters, but they are applied in addition to the Method Filter already in use. Thus a number of different Evaluation Filters can be used in conjunction with a single Method Filter to create a variety of output with different content, but based on the same database.

The creation of Evaluation Filters is the same as for Method Filters and hence I shall use the term *Filter* to apply to both except where explicitly stated. You may also see the term *Configuration Filter* used to refer to both.

14.1.2   Languages

Normally, the *Languages* used to display attribute placements are defined in specific ARIS databases. However, Filters are defined independently from ARIS databases and can be used in any database, so the *Administration Module* allows Languages to be defined for specific use within Filters (and Templates). These are stored in the **Conventions/Languages** sub-group of the **Configuration** group. When a Filter is applied to a database, any Languages required will be copied into the database.

Before creating a new Filter, check that the Languages you require are available. If not follow the instructions below.

Add New Languages

To add a new Language for use in Filters:

1.   Select the **Configuration / Conventions / Languages** group in the *Administration Module*,
2.   Right-Click > New > Language,
3.   Select the required Language from the *Create language Dialog Box*.

The right-hand pane of the *Administration Module* should update to show the new Language.

14.2   Creating and Editing Filters

14.2.1   Create Filter

To create a new Filter, select the **Filter** sub-group in the **Conventions** group and Right-Click > New or click on the New button at the top of the right-hand pane of the *Administration Module*. The *Filter Wizard* will open; it has 13 dialog boxes which are summarised in Table 14.1 and are described in the following sections.

Table 14.1 Filter Wizard Tabs

Dialog Box	Options
Select creation mode	• Customise Filter from scratch, • Create Filter from a database, • Merge Filters.
Create filter	• Name and Description, • Method Filter or Evaluation Filter.
Select model types	• Models to be included in the Filter.
Select object types	• Objects to be included in the Filter.
Select connection types	• Connection types to be included in the Filter, • Information on connection types.
Select symbols	• Symbol types to be used in model types.
Assign connection types	• Connection types between symbol types.
Select assignments	• Model types that can be assigned to object types.
Select model attributes	• Attributes included for models.
Select object attributes	• Attributes included for objects.
Select connection attributes	• Attributes included for connections.
Select attribute order	• The order attributes will be displayed in the *Attributes Dialog Box* or the *Attributes Tab* in the *Designer Module Properties Bar*.
Select symbol order	• The order symbols will be displayed in the *Symbols Bar*.

14.2.2   Edit Filter

You can edit an existing Filter by selecting it in the right-hand pane of the *Administration Module* and Right-Click > Edit or by clicking the Edit button. The same Dialog Boxes (Table 14.1) are used to edit the Filter.

You can also create a copy of an existing Filter using Right-Click > Duplicate and edit this to form the basis of a new Filter; adding new options or removing ones that you don't want.

14.2.3   Select Creation Mode

The *Select creation mode Dialog Box* (Fig. 14.1) has three checkboxes which allow us to choose which mode we are going to use to create the Filter.

In previous releases of ARIS it was necessary to define Filters from scratch or copy existing ones. However, since the introduction of ARIS 7 we are able to create a Filter automatically from a database. This is a very useful facility and we will look at it in detail in Section 14.3.

We can now also create a Filter by merging two existing Filters (see Section 14.4). Initially we will select the _Customize_ option to create a Filter from scratch. Now click _N_ext.

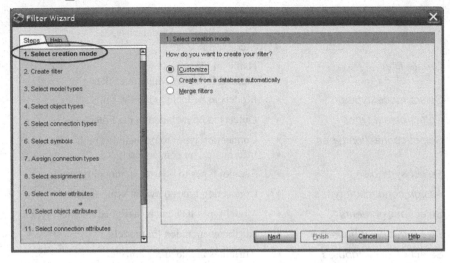

Fig. 14.1 Select Creation Mode Dialog Box

14.2.4   Create Filter

The _Create filter Dialog Box_ (Fig. 14.2) is similar to dialog boxes we are familiar with from other wizards and allows us to enter a _N_ame and _D_escription. We can also choose in which _L_anguage we would like to maintain the _N_ame and _D_escription and we can enter values in several languages by selecting another language from the drop-down box and entering different text in the _N_ame and _D_escription fields. You can get help on any of the entry fields by pressing the _H_elp button at the bottom of the dialog box.

Expert Tip – if the _L_anguage field does not show the language you wish to use, then go back to the **Conventions** group, select the **Languages** group and Right-Click > Ne_w_ > _L_anguage to add a new Language from the list shown.

The _GUID_ field will show the unique reference number allocated automatically to the Filter. It is initially shown as zeros, but once the Filter has been saved, the actual _GUID_ will appear if the Filter is later edited.

Expert Tip – if you subsequently make changes to the Filter it is useful to provide a version number in the _N_ame field and list the changes against the version number in the _D_escription field.

It may not be immediately obvious to you what the *Filter group* field does, but in fact it enables you to choose if the Filter is to be used a *Method Filter* or an *Evaluation Filter*. There is no difference in the way the Filters are defined and you can subsequently change a Filter from one type to another by editing it and changing the value in the *Filter group* field.

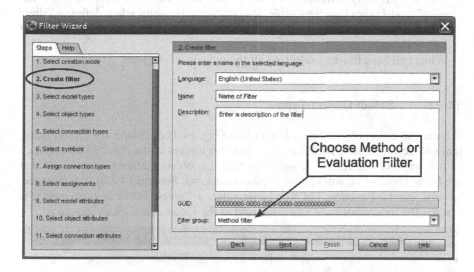

Fig. 14.2 Create Filter Dialog Box

When you have finished entering all the values, click Next.

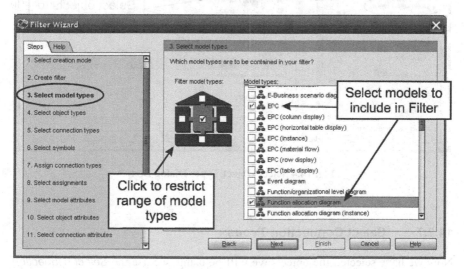

Fig. 14.3 Select Model Types Dialog Box

14.2.5   Select Model Types

The *Select model Types Dialog Box* (Fig. 14.3) allows us to choose which models will be available in our Filter. Click the checkboxes for one or more of the *Model types*. You can Right-Click to Select all or Deselect all models.

You are probably familiar with using the ARIS House selector to limit the range of model types that are visible. It is particularly useful when defining Filters as it allows you to quickly see if you have created appropriate models for each of the *ARIS Views*.

When you have finished selecting all the models, click Next.

14.2.6   Select Object Types

We use the *Select object Types Dialog Box* (Fig. 14.4) to choose the *Object types* that will be available in the Filter. Tick the checkboxes of the objects you require.

It is important to realise at this stage that it is objects rather than symbols that are being chosen (we will choose symbols later, see Section 14.2.8). For instance, we can select a Function, but we cannot select a *Value-added chain* because it is just a different symbol for a Function used in the *Value-added chain diagram*.

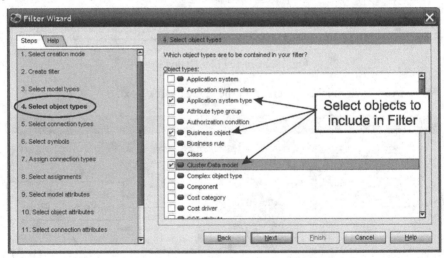

Fig. 14.4 Select Object Types Dialog Box

14.2.7   Select Connection Types

Now we have selected the objects we will be using, we use the *Select connection Types Dialog Box* (Fig. 14.5) to select the *Connection types* between the objects we wish to use.

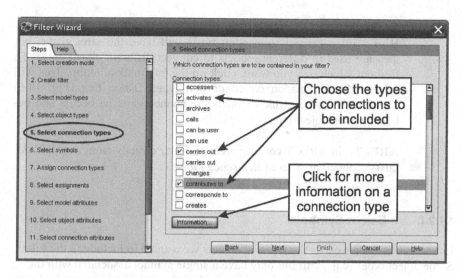

Fig. 14.5 Select Connection Types Dialog Box

This a more difficult dialog box to complete because there may be a large number of *Connection types* required and most people are not as familiar with them as they are with object types. Therefore it is important to plan ahead and work out exactly which *Connection types* you need, and in which models they will appear, before you use the *Filter Wizard*. The easiest way is to create a *Reference Model* to work out which connections you need.

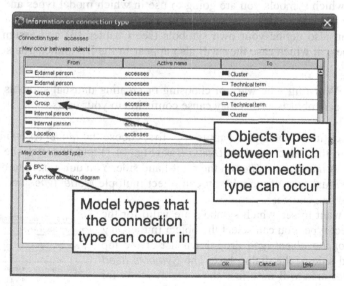

Fig. 14.6 Information on Connection Types Dialog Box

Hint – often several connection types will have the same name, but they are used in different models to connect different object types. To find out which one you want, click on the Information button. This will display the *Information on connection types Dialog Box* (Fig. 14.6) which will show in which models the connection type occurs and between which object types.

ARIS 7 – in ARIS 7 you can create a Filter directly from an ARIS database containing a set of *Reference Models*.

ARIS 7

14.2.8   Select Symbols

In Section 14.2.6 we chose the types of objects we wanted to include in the Filter. Some object types (e.g. *Position*) only have a single symbol associated with them, but most have a variety of symbols, some of which are specific to particular types of model. For instance, a Function has 16 different symbols that can be used in an *EPC*, but only 5 that can be used in a *Value-added chain diagram*.

Some of the alternative symbols have the same meaning, but just provide a different appearance. For instance the *Organizational unit type* object has an oval symbol or an oblong symbol. On the other hand, some symbols have an entirely different meaning (e.g. the *Control* symbol based on a Function) and will have different connection types with other objects. Because of this, it is essential to plan carefully which symbols you are going to use in which model types and, again, a Reference Model can play a valuable role here.

You can also define your own symbols (see Chapter 13) and assign these to object types, in which case they will also appear in the list and can be selected in the Filter.

Warning – be wary of choosing or creating unusual symbols to represent objects as this may cause confusion to your users.

To select the symbols you want to use, first choose the *Model types* in the left-hand list in the *Select symbols Dialog Box* (Fig. 14.7) and then tick the boxes of the *Symbols used by the filter* on the right-hand side. You don't have to do this for each individual type of model; you can select multiple *Model types* and select all their objects in one go.

If you want to see which symbols are valid for the same object type, you can select the object in the *Only symbols of the object type* drop-down list at the top right-hand side of the dialog box. The *Symbols used by the filter* area will now just show the symbols for that object type. To return to showing all the symbols, select *[No constraint]* from the list.

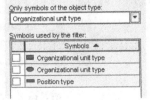

The list is shown in alphabetical order, but you can reverse the sort order by clicking on the list header. The upward-facing arrow will change direction to show the sort order.

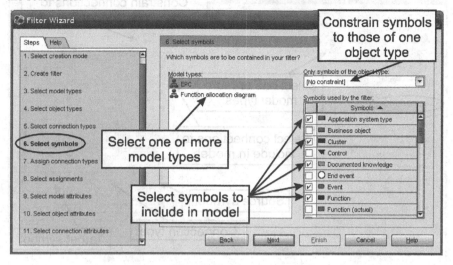

Fig. 14.7 Select Symbols Dialog Box

 Expert Tip – when selecting multiple model types, not all symbols will be valid in all types of model, in which case the checkbox will show a blue square in it. If you then tick this box, the symbol ⬛ will be selected for all the models in which it is valid.

 Hint – if you have already selected the symbols for one type of model (e.g. an *EPC*) and want to use the same symbols in another model type (e.g. a *Function allocation diagram*), select both model types and the symbols that are common to both model types and have already been selected in the first model (the *EPC*) will be shown with a blue square in the checkbox. Now click all of these boxes (so a tick is now displayed) to select the same symbols for the second model (the *FAD*).

14.2.9   Assign Connection Types

The *Assign connection Types Dialog Box* (Fig. 14.8) allows us to select which of the connection types we defined in the *Select connection Types Dialog Box* (Fig. 14.5) will be used between the symbol types we selected in the *Select symbols Dialog Box* (Fig. 14.7) in the types of models selected in *Select model Types Dialog Box* (Fig. 14.3). In principle this is fairly straightforward, but as you can imagine, the more types of models, symbols and connections we have selected, the more connection types we will have to select. More than any other dialog box in the *Filter Wizard*, this is the one that requires the most care and planning.

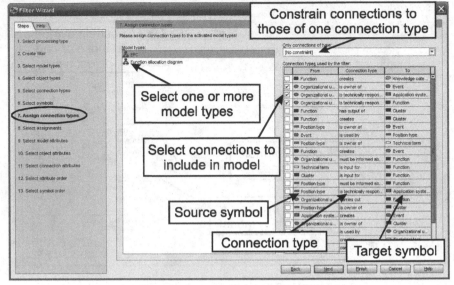

Fig. 14.8 Assign Connection Types Dialog Box

Again we can select one or more models in the left-hand *Model types* area and select the *Connection types used by the filter* in the right-hand list. Only connection types common to all selected model types will be shown.

 Hint – selecting multiple model types only makes sense with models that are very similar, for instance the various types of *EPC* and the *Value-added chain diagram*. If you select very different model types (e.g. an *EPC* and an *Organizational chart*), you will find there are no common connection types.

The list of connection types can be very long, so in order to help find the right connection you can constrain the list to specific connections types using the *Only connections of type* drop-down list, or you can sort the list by source object, target object or connection type. To sort the list, click on the column header; a small arrow indicates whether the sort order is ascending or descending and you can click the column header again to change direction.

 Hint – the *Filter Wizard* window cannot be maximised, but you can re-size it by dragging its edges to allow more of the list entries to be visible at once.

 Hint – click on the header of the left-hand column containing the tick boxes to sort the list to show all the selected connection types at the top of the list. Click again to show the unused connection types at the top.

Warning – many pairs of objects have several valid connection types between them and often have connections in both directions. Be careful to select the right connection type.

Expert Tip – the names of connection types can be changed to be more meaningful to your organisation by configuring the ARIS Method (see Chapter 12). If you rename connections, the new names will appear in the *Assign connection Types Dialog Box.*

Once we have finished selecting all the required connection types we have basically finished the main element of configuring what appears in the models defined by the Filter. We can now continue to select some of the other aspects of how models are used.

14.2.10   Select Assignments

One of the important aspects of ARIS is the ability to create hierarchies or frameworks of connected models. As we know, we make links between models by assigning models to the objects that have occurrences in a model. The *Select assignments Dialog Box* (Fig. 14.9) allows us to select which assignments allowed by the ARIS Method will be available in the Filter. As with all Filter configurations, we cannot create new types of assignment not allowed by the ARIS Method.

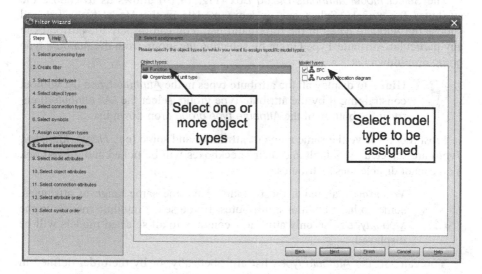

Fig. 14.9 Select Assignments Dialog Box

Expert Tip – model assignments are made to object definitions. They will appear in all models that have occurrences of those objects, no matter what symbol is in use. You cannot choose to have assignments in one model type, but not in another, although you can change the properties of individual models and model types so the *Assignment Icon* is not visible.

Select one or more *Object types* in the left-hand list and select the *Model types* that will be assigned to them in the right-hand list. Only *Model types* common to all selected *Object types* will be displayed.

Hint – selecting multiple object types only makes sense with objects that are very similar, for instance the various types of objects representing organisational elements. If you select very different object types you will find there are no common assignments that can be displayed.

14.2.11   Select Model Attributes

All ARIS items (models, objects and connections, etc) have attributes associated with them. The next four dialog boxes enable us to select which attributes we want to be visible and the order in which they appear in various dialog boxes and lists. The names of many attributes, and the attribute type group in which they are listed, can be changed by configuring the ARIS Method (see Chapter 12).

The *Select model attributes Dialog Box* (Fig. 14.10) allows us to choose the attributes for models. Select one or more models in the *Model types* list and choose the *Attribute types* in the right-hand list. You can display the attributes in any particular Attribute Type Group by selecting the group from the *Attribute type group* drop-down list.

Hint – to display all the attribute types in the *Attribute types* list without constraining it by the attribute type group, select the (*All attributes*) entry at the bottom of the *Attribute type group* drop-down list.

Most models have the same range of attributes and some (e.g. *Name, Identifier, Type*) are selected by default and their checkboxes will be ticked and greyed out. You cannot disable these attributes.

Warning – although most models have the same range of attributes, some do have additional attributes. If you select multiple models in the *Model types* list, only attributes common to all selected models will be displayed.

You can sort the *Attribute types* list alphabetically, or by the order defined in the ARIS Method, by using the *Sorting* drop-down list.

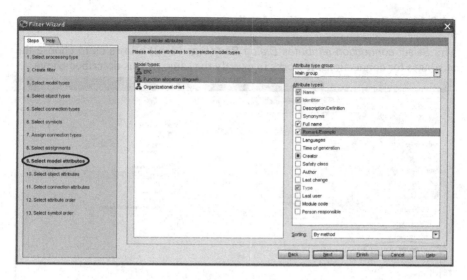

Fig. 14.10 Select Model Attributes Dialog Box

14.2.12 Select Object Attributes

The *Select object attributes Dialog Box* (Fig. 14.11) allows us to choose the attributes for objects. It works in exactly the same way as described above for models.

Again, most objects have the same range of attributes and similar comments about default attributes and warnings about selecting multiple *Object types* apply.

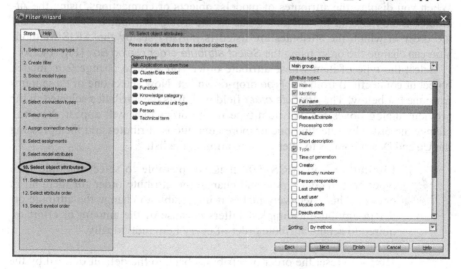

Fig. 14.11 Select Object Attributes Dialog Box

14.2.13   Select Connection Attributes

The *Select connection attributes Dialog Box* (Fig. 14.12) allows us to choose the attributes for connections. It works in exactly the same way as described above.

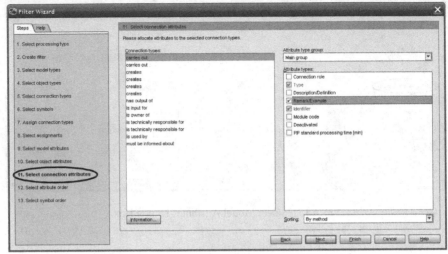

Fig. 14.12 Select Connection Attributes Dialog Box

14.2.14   Select Attribute Order

When you display the attributes of models, objects or connections, using the *Attributes Dialog Box* or the *Attributes Tab* in the *Designer Module Properties Bar*, the order in which the attributes are listed is initially set by the ARIS Method. You can change the order using the *Select attribute order Dialog Box* (Fig. 14.13).

Select the type of item whose attribute order you wish to change (e.g. model, object or connection) from the *Type* drop-down list. Now select one of these items from the list below. The *Attribute order* field now lists the attributes selected in the previous dialog boxes for that item type in the order they will appear. You can change the order by selecting one or more contiguous attributes and then pressing the *Up* and *Down* buttons to alter their position in the list.

 Limitation – in ARIS 7.02 it is not possible to select multiple item types (e.g. model types) and change the attribute order for them all in one go. This effectively makes it impossible to change the attribute order in any but the simplest Filters because of the amount of effort required to set the attribute order of every item individually.

 Hint – to reset the order of attributes back to the default defined by the ARIS Method, click the *R*eset order button.

Expert Tip – it is generally best to set the availability and order of all common attributes for all items of the same sort to be the same (e.g. set all common attributes for all objects to be the same). Unless there is a real need, maintaining different attributes for, say, different object types requires a lot of effort.

When you have changed the attribute order for one type of item (e.g. objects), then select a new entry in the *Type* drop-down list and make the changes for that item.

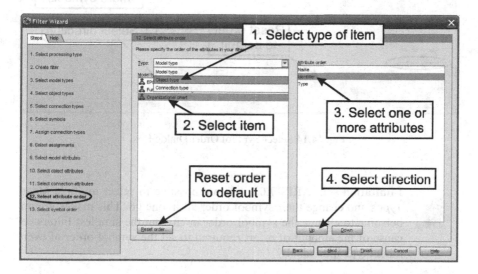

Fig. 14.13 Select Attribute Order Dialog Box

14.2.15   Select Symbol Order

Finally we can select the order in which symbols appear in the *Symbols Bar* (sometimes called the *Modelling Toolbar*) in the *Designer Module*. The order initially defaults to that defined by the ARIS Method, but we can change the order using the *Select symbol order Dialog Box* (Fig. 14.14). This is valuable if you find that in your organisation you use some objects more than others and you prefer to have them at the top of the list.

Select the type of model in the *Model Types* field. The *Symbol order* field now lists the symbols in the order they will appear in the *Symbols Bar*. You can change the order by selecting one or more contiguous symbols and pressing the Up and Down buttons to alter their position in the list. The order they will be shown in the *Symbols Bar* is left to right and then top to bottom.

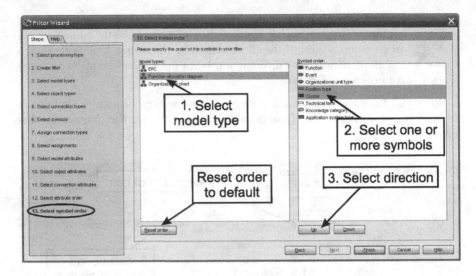

Fig. 14.14 Select Symbol Order Dialog Box

 Limitation – in ARIS 7.02 it is not possible to select multiple *Model Types* and change their symbol order all in one go. This makes it cumbersome to change the symbol order in any but the simplest Filters because of the amount of effort required to set the symbol order of every model type individually.

 Hint – to reset the order of symbols back to the default defined by the ARIS Method, click the Reset order button.

 Hint – not all of the symbols will initially appear in the *Symbols Bar*. Only a certain number are visible. Symbols can be added or removed using Right-Click > Add symbols or Right-Click > Remove symbol. The number of symbols initially visible is controlled by the ARIS Method and cannot be configured.

Congratulations, you have now created a Filter and you can click Finish to save it.

14.3   Creating a Filter from a Database

Section 14.2 showed how to create a new Filter from scratch. While it is important to understand how to do this, there is in fact a much easier way. We can create the Filter automatically from a set of Reference Models contained in a Reference database.

14.3.1   Creating Reference Models

All we have to do to create a Filter automatically from a set of Reference Models is to create a database containing all the models, objects, symbols, connections, attributes, etc, we want to appear in the Filter.

We need to create models that define all the different aspects of a Filter described in Section 14.2 with the exception of *Select attribute order* and *Select symbol order* (see Section 14.3.3).

The important thing to keep in mind is that you need to think of all the different combinations of objects, symbols and connections you need. The easiest way to do this is to create some specific models to define particular aspects of the Filter rather than try and include everything in one model. Table 14.2 shows some typical Reference Models you might create to define a Filter for basic process modelling.

Table 14.2 Type Reference Models

Model	Filter Definition
EPC (structure)	Structurally relevant objects (e.g. Functions, Event, Rules) and the different process structures they can be combined to create (see Fig. 14.15).
EPC (relationships)	Structurally non-relevant objects (e.g. *Application system type, Organizational unit type, Technical term*, etc) and their range of connections types with Functions (and possibly Events) (see Fig. 14.16).
EPC (assignments)	One of each type of object for which you want to allow assignments with the objects assigned to their appropriate Reference Models. Some object types can be assigned to several model types (e.g. a Function to an *EPC*, a *Function allocation diagram* and a *Value-added chain diagram*).
FAD (relationships)	The object and connection types required for a *Function allocation diagram*. Normally this will be a copy of the contents of the *EPC* (relationships) model.
Application System Type Diagram	*Application System* object types and the hierarchical connections between them.
Organizational chart	*Organisation* object types and the hierarchical connections between them.
Technical Terms Model	The hierarchical connections between *Technical term* objects.
Value-added chain diagram	The *Value-added chain* symbols and their connections to other object types.

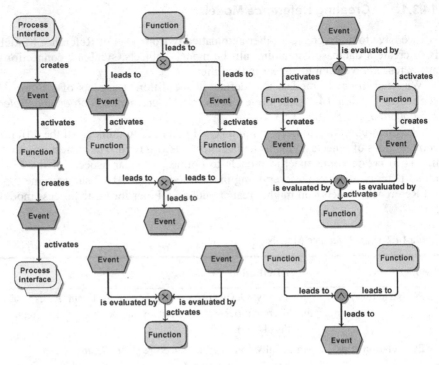

Fig. 14.15 EPC (structure) Reference Model

 Warning – always create your Reference Models in a database which has the **Entire Method** Filter applied, otherwise you may inadvertently limit the definition of your Filter.

 Expert Tip – there is no need to create models that represent or even look like a real process. Although you may be tempted to create one huge *EPC* with all of the required information, provided you create models containing all the required items, you can create as many models as you wish and structure them in a way that is easy to maintain.

 Warning – when we create normal process models we will often create a *lean EPC* containing the process flow and use the *Function allocation diagram* to contain all the relationships to other objects (e.g. *Application system type, Organizational unit type, Technical term*, etc). When creating Reference Models you must put all the required objects and connections in both the *EPC* and *FAD*. If you just put resource object relationships in the *FAD* reference model, then they will not be defined in the Filter for any *EPC*.

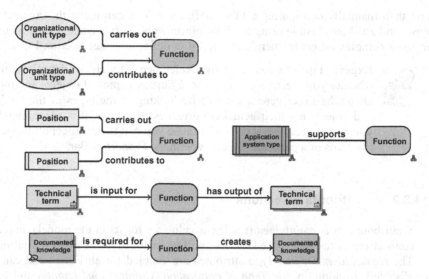

Fig. 14.16 EPC (relationships) Reference Model

In Table 14.2 we have used *EPCs* for attribute and assignment definitions because the *EPC* can display all of the basic process modelling objects. For complex Filters with many different object types, the *EPC* will not be able to display all the objects and you will need to use a range of models.

 Warning – you must create one or more Reference Models for every type of model you wish to include in the Filter and all the Reference Models of a particular type must collectively contain every symbol and connection type you wish to see in that model type. The fact that a relationship between two objects has been defined in the Reference Model for one model type, does not mean it will be automatically available in another model type. The relationship must be explicitly modelled for every model type.

Before creating the Reference Models you must also decide if you want to include user-defined symbols or derived-model types (see Chapter 12). These must be created first and both the custom symbols and the derived model types included in the set of Reference Models.

You may be thinking that creating all these models sounds like a lot of hard work. It certainly requires some thought and effort, but it is a lot simpler than creating a Filter from scratch. For instance, you may use an *EPC*, *EPC (column display)*, *EPC (row display)* and *Function allocation diagram* all with the same objects, symbols and connections. Once you have created the Reference Model for the basic *EPC*, you can copy the objects and connections into the other models to rapidly create their definitions.

The Reference Models also give you a very visual indication of the definition of your process or enterprise architecture structure which is much easier to maintain than manually configuring a Filter definition. You can make the connection types and attributes visible using attribute placements. You can also create a range of more complex Filters by merging basic Filter definitions (see Section 14.4).

 Expert Tip – when creating Reference Models it doesn't matter whether you create *occurrence* or *definition* copies of objects and models as the Filter generation will be looking at the types of the models and objects not their actual occurrences. However, it is recommended you create *occurrence* copies because you can then inspect all the relationships of a particular object type in the *Properties Bar*.

14.3.2   Attribute Selections

Any attribute that *is maintained* (i.e. has a value set for it) in the models, objects or connections in the Reference Database will be included in the Filter definition.

The *Name*, *Identifier* and *Type* attributes are enabled for all Filters and cannot be disabled. In addition, the *Time of generation*, *Creator*, *Last change* and *Last user* attributes have their values set by ARIS and hence will automatically be entered into the Filter although you can manually deselect them later.

Object Attributes

The easiest way to define the attribute selections for objects is to create one or more Reference Models containing all the object types in your Filter (e.g. in an *EPC* for simple process modelling Filters) and then:

1. Select each object in turn and enter a "y" into each attribute you wish to use (or an appropriate character or list selection for non-text attributes),

2. Select all objects and Right-Click > Properties [Format / Attribute placement (objects)],

3. Click Add,

4. Tick the *Only show maintained attributes* box in the *Add Attributes Dialog Box*,

5. Select all the maintained attributes in the *Add Attributes Dialog Box* and click OK,

6. With all the added attributes still selected in the *Placed attributes* list, put a tick in the *Placement* box to the right of the object,

7. Select *With attribute name* and *Alignment* as *Left* in the *Representation* area,

8. Click OK.

You will now see all the maintained attributes (the ones you selected plus the automatically maintained attributes) displayed alongside the objects in your Reference Model (Fig. 14.17). This gives you an immediate visualisation of the attributes you have selected.

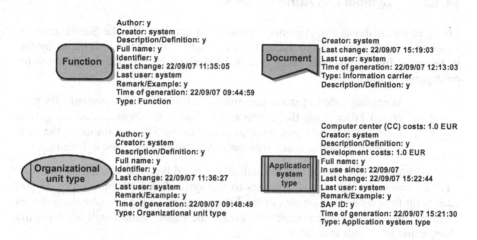

Fig. 14.17 EPC (attributes) Reference Model

Connection Attributes

Follow exactly the same procedure as described above for object attributes, placing the attributes above or below the connection.

Model Attributes

For model attributes, we again ensure the attributes we wish to be included in the Filter are maintained with an appropriate value. This time we have to select one example of each model type (you will already have examples created for object and connection definitions) and populate their attributes. If you wish you can make the attributes visible inside the model using the Insert > Model attribute command from the *Main Menu*.

Unfortunately this is a more tedious procedure than with object and connection attributes as you have to select and place each attribute individually and there is no quick selection of maintained attributes.

 Expert Tip – if you have a common set of attributes for each model, once you have created the attributes placements in one model, you can select them all and copy and paste them into other models. They may not immediately be visible if the attributes are not maintained, but they will appear once a value is entered in the attribute.

14.3.3   Symbol and Attribute Order

The specific attributes and symbols (whose order can be set in the *Select attribute order* and *Select symbol order* dialog boxes of the *Filter Wizard*) will be set by the Reference Models, but their order cannot be defined in the models and must be configured manually later.

Warning – do not make any manual changes to an automatically generated Filter using the *Customize* option in the *Select processing type Dialog Box* if later you want to generate the Filter again using the *Create from a database automatically*. Any manual changes will be lost.

Once you are sure you have automatically created the final version of your Filter, you can make the manual changes to the symbol and attribute order. If you later want to update other aspects of the Filter, you will have to make the changes manually because if you automatically create the Filter again it will not have the change that you made manually.

Expert Tip – if you merge a Filter that has object and attributes orders which have been changed from the ARIS default, these will override the default order in the final Filter.

An alternative to manually changing the symbol and attribute order is to merge into your automatically created Filter another Filter that has the attribute order defined. To create a '*symbol and attribute order reference filter*':

1. Automatically create your main Filter as described above; leave the object and attributes orders unchanged,
2. Take a copy of your automatic Filter (Right-Click > Duplicate) and label it "symbol and attribute order reference filter",
3. Delete all the *Assign connection types* selections (Right-Click > Deselect all),
4. Make the required changes in the *Select attribute order* and *Select symbol order* dialog boxes,
5. Save the Filter.

If you now want to change your main Filter, make the required changes to the Reference Models, automatically generate a new Filter and merge this with the *symbol and attribute order reference filter* to create the final Filter. In this way you can update you automatically generated Filter without losing the manual configuration settings.

Of course, if you remove models, symbols or attributes from the Reference Models you also need to manually remove them from the *symbol and attribute order reference filter* otherwise they will still exist when you merge the two Filters. Similar if you add new models, symbols or attributes to the Reference Models, you also need to add them to the *symbol and attribute order reference filter*, otherwise their order will not be affected when you merge the Filters.

This procedure for setting symbol and attribute order is not ideal, but it is easier than maintaining large numbers of manual changes.

14.3.4   Creating the Filter from the Reference Models

Once we have created the Reference Models, the hard work is done. To create the Filter:

1. In the **Conventions** group, Right-Click > Ne<u>w</u>,
2. Select Cre<u>a</u>te from a database automatically in the Select processing type Dialog Box and click <u>N</u>ext,
3. Enter the <u>N</u>ame and <u>D</u>escription for the Filter in the Create filter dialog box. Click <u>N</u>ext,
4. Select your Reference Database in the Select Database dialog box,
5. Click <u>F</u>inish.

 Warning – before creating a new Filter automatically from a database, reorganise the database to remove any objects or relationships that may have been deleted, but whose definitions are still in the database (select the database in the Administration Module and Right-Click > <u>R</u>eorganize).

The new Filter will be created. You can inspect it by selecting the Filter in the **Conventions** group and Right-Click > <u>E</u>dit. In the Select processing type Dialog Box, accept the default <u>C</u>ustomize option and you can step through the dialog boxes described in Section 14.2 to view the settings.

You can also manually make any changes you wish, but it is best to change the Reference Model and update the Filter by editing it and selecting Cre<u>a</u>te from a database automatically in the Select processing type Dialog Box. The Filter will now be overwritten by the new settings generated from the Reference Models.

14.4   Merging Filters

You may often need to create a number of Filters to support your organisation that provide increasing numbers of models, objects and connections. Alternatively you may want to make a range of specialised models (e.g. UML models) available in addition to your standard Filter.

You could create different Reference Model databases to generate each Filter. However, if the more complex Filter just represents additions to your standard Filter, an easier way to do this is to create separate Filters and merge them together to create a more complex Filter. For instance, you may have a basic process modelling Filter and a UML Reference Filter which can be merged with the process modelling Filter to provide a process modelling Filter that also has UML models.

To merge two or more existing Filters:

1. In the **Conventions** group, Right-Click > New,
2. Select Merge filters in the Select processing type Dialog Box and click Next,
3. Enter the Name and Description for the Filter in the Create filter dialog box. Click Next,
4. Select the Filters you wish to merge in the Select filter dialog box,
5. Click Finish.

The configurations defined in each Filter will now be added together to create the new Filter. Settings such as the Select attribute order and Select symbol order override the ARIS Method defaults.

 Expert Tip – you can also merge new configurations into an existing Filter directly from a Reference Database. Select the Filter, Right-Click > Edit, and select Create from a database automatically in the Select processing type Dialog Box. In the Select database Dialog Box, select the database you want to add in and tick the Add filter contents box and click Finish. New configuration settings will be generated from the Reference Model and added to the selected Filter.

14.5   Applying Filters

Now we have created our new Filter we can apply it when we open existing databases. To login to an existing database using a specific Filter:

1. Select an unopened database in the Explorer Module,
2. Right-Click > Log in,
3. Enter User name and Password in the Enter user data Dialog Box of the Login Wizard,
4. Select the required Filter in the Select filter and language Dialog Box,
5. Click Finish.

To change the default Filter to be used for logging into all databases:

6. Select View > Options [Login] from the Main Menu,
7. Click on the browse button to the right of the Filter field in the User defaults area,
8. Select the required ARIS Server from the Server drop-down box,
9. Select the required Filter from the list, Click OK twice.

The selected Filter will now appear as the default Filter in the Select filter and language Dialog Box of the Login Wizard. It will also be used when a database is opened directly by double-clicking on a database name in the Explorer Module when you are using the default User name and Password.

14.6 Exporting and Importing Filters

14.6.1 Exporting a Filter

Filters are stored in the *Configuration Database* and, like Templates, are not saved when you use the database Backup command. To save a Filter you can export it in XML format as an ".amc" file:

1. Select the Filter in the right-hand pane of the **Filter** group,
2. Right-Click > Export,
3. Choose a directory on your hard disk to save the file.

   ARIS Method changes are also stored in Filters (see Section 14.6.3).

 Expert Tip – you can backup a *Configuration Database* by using the Backupconfig command in the ARIS Admintool (see Chapter 10 and Appendix A).

14.6.2 Importing a Filter

To restore a previously exported Filter:

1. Select the **Filter** group in the *Administration Module*,
2. Right-Click > Import,
3. In the *Import filter Dialog Box* click the Browse button,
4. Select an ".amc" file from your hard disk,
5. Click Open,
6. Click all the *Overwrite* checkboxes in the *Import filter Dialog Box* (Fig. 14.18),
7. Click OK.

   The Filter will be imported into the **Filters** group overwriting any previous Filter with the same GUID.

 Expert Tip – if you wish to import a Filter, but don't wish to overwrite an existing Filter that has the same GUID (even though it may have a different name), remove the tick from the *Overwrite filter* checkbox (Fig. 14.18). The imported filter will now be created with a new GUID.

ARIS Method changes are also imported with Filters (see Section 14.6.3).

14.6.3   Method Configuration

In Chapter 12 we looked at configuring the ARIS Method (e.g. changing connection type names, creating user-defined symbols, etc). These changes are applied at the server level and saved in any Filter created on the server.

When you import a new Filter onto a server, all of the Method changes saved in the Filter will be applied to the server. The changes will add to or overwrite any existing method changes. If you wish to import a Filter, but don't wish to import various categories of Method changes (see Table 14.3), remove the ticks from the four boxes in the *Method configuration conflicts* area of the *Import filter Dialog Box* (Fig. 14.18).

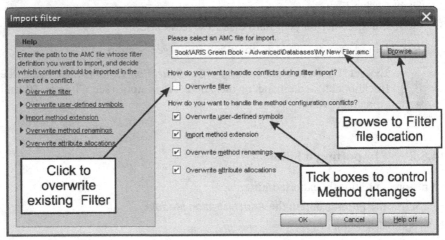

Fig. 14.18 Import Filter Dialog Box

 Warning – if you want a Filter to save Method changes so they can be imported later you must ensure all the items that have been changed or added are selected at least once in the Filter.

 Warning – if you rename an attribute type group, at least one of the default attributes in that group must be selected in the Filter otherwise the new name will not be imported. If the only selected attribute is one from another group that has been reallocated, the attribute type group name will not be changed.

 Warning – importing Filters from different servers with different Method definitions can create unexpected results. Before importing a Filter it is recommended you export one of your existing Filters so as to capture your current Method settings. You can later import that Filter to restore your Method if required.

Bug – in ARIS 7.02, the *Overwrite method renamings* option seems to have no effect and local name changes in the Method are not overwritten unless a specific name change has been stored in the Filter.

Table 14.3 Import Filter Method Configuration Conflict

Term	Meaning
Overwrite user-defined symbols	Overwrites an existing user-defined symbol in the Configuration database with a symbol with the same GUID from the imported Filter.
Import method extension	Imports Method changes from the imported Filter that: • Rename attribute type groups, • Rename attribute types, • Rename connection types, • Rename model types, • Rename object types, • Rename symbols. **Note:** User-defined model types and user-defined symbols are imported irrespective of this setting.
Overwrite method renamings	Overwrites any name changes made locally in the Method with the default, original, name from the Filter. Distinct from *Import method extension* which overwrites any local names with names specifically changed and saved in the Filter. Only valid when *Import method extension* is ticked. **Note**: See Bug above.
Overwrite attribute allocations	Overwrites the allocation of attributes to specific attribute type groups with those from the imported Filter. Only valid when *Import method extension* is ticked.

Chapter 15   Defining and Using Templates

This chapter looks at how to use the Administration Module to define Templates and how they can be applied to set the appearance of models, objects and connections.

15.1   Introduction to Templates

The appearance of the symbols representing individual objects in a model can be changed by altering their settings in the *Object properties Dialog Box*. You can make changes to the appearance of an individual object symbol or select a number of symbols and make changes to them all (Right-Click > Properties [*Format / Object appearance*]). Similarly, we can change the appearance of connections (Right-Click > Properties [*Format / Connection appearance*]) and we can also add attribute placements to symbols and connections (Right-Click > Properties [*Format / Attribute placement (objects)*] or Right-Click > Properties [*Format / Attribute placement (connections)*]).

It is not good modelling practice to use the appearance of objects and connections to represent aspects of the process you are modelling, for instance marking all Functions done by a particularly department in blue. It is better to model everything using objects and relationships. However, creating an acceptable 'look and feel' for your models can be vital in obtaining acceptance from users and establishing a corporate image. Furthermore, it is useful to be able to change the appearance of your models to suit different publishing media (e.g. for printing or to display on the Internet).

If you frequently wish to change the appearance of one or more object or connection types in a model, or create a standard 'look and feel' for certain types of model, you can define a range of *ARIS Templates*. You can then apply a predefined Template to objects, to the entire model or set it as a default for all newly created models.

Templates can be used to preset:

- Symbol appearance properties,
- Symbol attribute placements,
- Connection appearance properties,
- Connection attribute placements,
- Model background colour.

Templates only affect the appearance properties of the symbols and connections specifically selected in the Template; all other properties remain unchanged. Thus a number of Templates can be applied in succession to build more complex appearance changes from a basic set of simple changes. For instance, it is particularly useful to be able to apply different styles of attribute placements on top of an existing look and feel.

Warning – you should not alter the colour of an object's symbol to represent something significant in modelling terms; for instance, to indicate those Functions carried out by a particular department. The colour of the symbol is not stored as part of the object definition and cannot be easily reported on or analysed. Establish relationships to other objects instead.

15.2   Fonts and Languages

Normally, the Font Formats and Languages used to display attribute placements are defined in the ARIS database. However, Templates are defined independently from databases and can be used in any database so the *Administration Module* allows Font Formats and Languages to be defined for specific use with Templates and Filters. These are stored in groups within the **Conventions** sub-group of the **Configuration** group.

When a Template is applied to a database, the Font Formats and Languages will be copied into the database and used for the appearance property settings.

Warning – Font Formats have their own unique GUIDS, so when a Template is used in a database, the Font Formats will be copied into the database, even if there are already identical Font Formats with identical names already defined in the database. The Template Font Formats will be appended with a number (e.g. small font (1)).

Before creating a new Template, check that the Languages and Font Formats you require are available. If not follow the instructions below.

Add New Languages

To add a new Language for use in Templates or Filters:

1.   Select the **Configuration / Conventions / Languages** group in the *Administration Module*,
2.   Right-Click > New > Language,
3.   Select the required Language from the *Create language Dialog Box*.

The right-hand pane of the *Administration Module* should update to show the new language.

Add New Font Formats

To add a new Font Format for use in Templates or Filters:

1. Select the **Configuration / Conventions / Font formats** group in the *Administration Module*,

2. Right-Click > Ne**w** > **F**ont formats,

3. Select the Language for which you want to set the Font Format (you can also check the **A**ccept font changes for all languages box to change the fonts for all languages),

4. Enter a **N**ame for the Font Format in *Create font format Dialog Box*,

5. Click on the Change **f**ont Button,

6. Choose the font settings in the *Change font Dialog Box*.

The right-hand pane of the *Administration Module* should update to show the new Font Format.

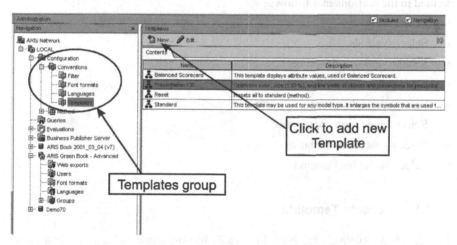

Fig. 15.1 Administration Module (Templates)

15.3   Creating a New Template

A Template is defined using the *Template Wizard* in the *Administration Module* so as to apply a common '*look and feel*' to specific types of model. Only a Configuration Administrator (e.g. a user with the Configuration password – see Chapter 10) can create and manage Templates.

To create a Template:

1. Open the *Administration Module*,

2. Double-click on the **Configuration** group in **Local** or on an ARIS Server,

3. Double-click on the **Conventions** group,

4. Select **Templates**.

The right-hand pane of the *Administration Module* will now show a list of current Templates (Fig. 15.1). You can select a Template and use the *Right-Click Menu* to Edit, Delete, Duplicate or Rename an existing Template. It is often useful to use an existing Template as your starting point by using the Duplicate command and then Edit.

To create a new Template:

- Right-Click > New > Template or click the New Button at the top of right-hand pane of the *Administration Module*.

The *Template Wizard* will now appear with the following dialog boxes described in the sections that follow:

- Create template,

- Select symbols,

- Select symbol appearance,

- Place symbol attributes,

- Select connection types,

- Select connection appearance,

- Place connection attributes,

- Select model background.

15.3.1   Create Template

The *Create template Dialog Box* (Fig. 15.2) has the usual fields to enter a name and a description for the Template. The *Filter* field allows you to apply a Method Filter to restrict the range of symbol and connection types that appear in the lists on other dialog boxes. The choice of Filter is not stored as part of the Template and has no effect on the models or objects on which the Template is applied, but it does making creating the Template easier. The *GUID* (the unique identification for the Template) will initially be set to zeros, but once the Template is saved, the actual GUID will be visible if the Template is subsequently edited. Click Next to go to the next dialog box.

 Warning – when editing an existing Template, beware of selecting a *Filter* that is more restrictive than the Filter which you used to create the Template. Any previously selected symbol or connection types not defined in the chosen Filter will be deleted from the Template.

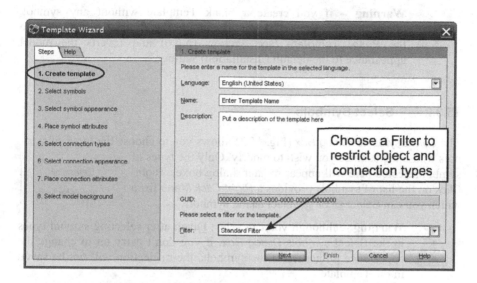

Fig. 15.2 Create Template Dialog Box

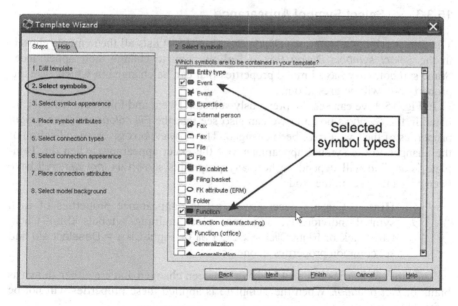

Fig. 15.3 Select Symbols Dialog Box

Warning – if you create a blank Template without any symbol, connection or model background colour settings, this is equivalent to the **Reset Template** (see Section 15.6.6) and reverts the model appearance to the default (installation) settings.

15.3.2   Select Symbols

The *Select symbols Dialog Box* (Fig. 15.3) allows you to choose the types of symbols whose appearance you wish to modify. Only the types of symbol selected here will appear in later dialog boxes. Right-Click on the list of symbols provides a *Right-Click Menu* from which you can Select all or Deselect all the symbols.

| Select all |
| Deselect all |

 Warning – although you can select Finish after selecting symbol types in the *Select symbols Dialog Box*, if you don't carry on to change the appearance properties of the symbols, their selection will not be saved in the Template.

Click Next to go to the next dialog box.

15.3.3   Select Symbol Appearance

The *Select symbol appearance Dialog Box* (Fig. 15.4) lists all the symbols chosen in the *Select symbols Dialog Box* and allows you to change their appearance. Some symbols may have limited properties that can be changed in which case the property box will be greyed out.

In Fig. 15.4 we can see the previously selected Event and Function symbols are listed in the *Symbols* box and we can also see that the *Fill colour* and *Line weight* properties of the Event have been changed. The *Preview* box gives an indication of the changes to the symbol appearance, but the exact appearance when the Template is applied will depend on how any properties shown as *[not defined]* have been previously set in the model.

 Hint – it is not necessary to set the appearance properties of each symbol individually. You can select multiple symbols (Shift-Click, Ctrl-Click or Right-Click > Select all or Right-Click > Deselect all) and set common properties in one go.

The other properties in Fig. 15.4 have not been changed and are either shown as blank or *[not defined]*. When the Template is applied these properties will not be affected.

The effect of the various symbol appearance properties is shown in Table 15.1.

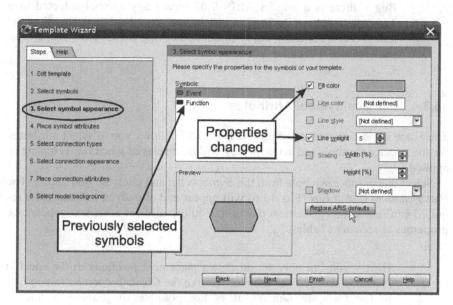

Fig. 15.4 Select Symbol Appearance Dialog Box

Table 15.1 Symbol Appearance Properties

Command	Action
Fill color	Choose the background colour of a symbol. Click on the property box to display the *Choose color Dialog Box*.
Line color	Choose the outline colour of a symbol. Click on the property box to display the *Choose color Dialog Box*.
Line style	Select the style of the outline of the symbol from *Solid*, *Dashed* or *Dotted*.
Line weight	Choose the weight (i.e. thickness and intensity) of the symbol outline by clicking on the up and down controls.
Scaling	Choose the current symbol *Width* and *Height* as a % of its default by clicking on the up and down controls.
Shadow	Puts a shaded outline around the symbol to give it a more three-dimensional appearance.
Restore ARIS defaults	Resets the symbol appearance properties to those set by the ARIS Method.

Bug – there is a bug in ARIS 7.02 where any symbol selected in a Template will have its *Sh*a*dow* property reset to the default (*No shadow*) unless it is specifically set to *Shadow*. Leaving the *Sh*a*dow* property as *[Not defined]* will cause it to be reset.

15.3.4   Place Symbol Attributes

The *Place symbol attributes Dialog Box* (Fig. 15.5) allows you to select attributes for the selected symbols and set how they will be displayed when the Template is applied.

Select one or more symbols from the *Symbols* list and click the *A*dd button. The *Place attribute Dialog Box* (Fig. 15.6) will appear and allow you to choose the required attribute and its placement position. You can also set other text appearance properties as shown in Table 15.2.

 Hint – you can only set attributes placement positions to the specific locations shown by tick boxes. Unlike the *Object properties Dialog Box* in the *Designer Module*, it is not possible to provide X and Y coordinates for the attribute location. You can however, manually move attribute positions after applying the Template.

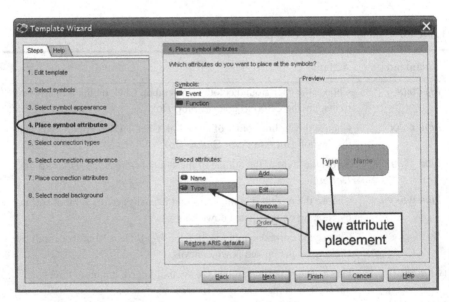

Fig. 15.5 Place Symbol Attributes Dialog Box

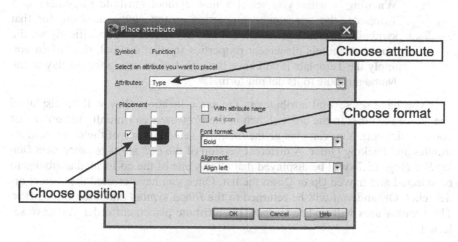

Fig. 15.6 Place Attribute Dialog Box

Table 15.2 Symbol Attribute Placement Properties

Command	Action
With attribute name	Displays the attribute name as well as its value.
As icon	Some special attributes have icons associated with them that can be displayed instead of their value (e.g. the *Existence* attribute). Checking this box will display the icon.
Font format	Selects the font for the attribute display. Note: the fonts in the list are those that have already been pre-defined by the ARIS Configuration Administrator and placed in the *Conventions/Font formats* folder (see Section 15.2).
Alignment	Sets alignment for attributes with multiple lines of text (*Align left*, *Align Right*, and *Centred*).

Once you have set all the required properties, click OK and you will be returned to the *Place symbol attributes Dialog Box*. The *Preview* area will update to show the attribute placements you have selected.

You can modify an existing *Placed attribute* by selecting it and clicking Edit. The *Edit attribute placement Dialog Box* will appear with a similar appearance to the *Place attribute Dialog Box*, but without the option to choose the attribute type. You can select and edit several attribute placements at once and you can delete a placement using the Remove button. Clicking the Restore ARIS defaults button will remove all attribute placements except for the default display of the *Name* attribute.

Warning – when you select a new symbol attribute placement in a Template, the appearance properties of the *Name* attribute for that symbol are reset to the ARIS default. So, unless you specifically set the *Name* attribute's placement properties for that symbol, then when you apply the Template it will have the effect of reverting the display of the *Name* attribute to its default format.

If you have set several attributes to the same location, they will be displayed one above the other in the order shown in the *Preview* area (initially the order that you added them). You can change the order by selecting one of the co-located attributes and clicking Order. A different version of the *Edit attribute placement Dialog Box* (Fig. 15.7) will be displayed that allows one of the co-located attributes to be selected and moved Up or Down the list. Once you have created the correct order, click OK and you will be returned to the *Place symbol attributes Dialog Box*. The *Preview* area will update to show the attribute placement order you have selected.

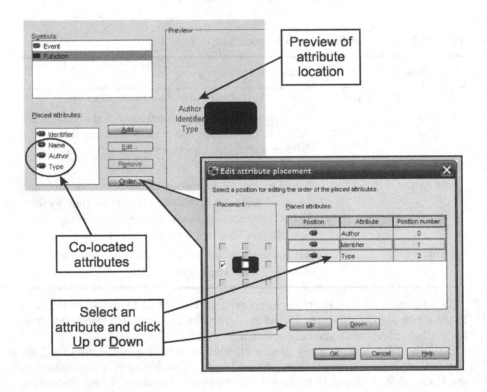

Fig. 15.7 Edit Attribute Placement (Order) Dialog Box

Warning – attribute placement settings for any given symbol or connection are not additive. You must specifically set all the attributes you wish to be visible when the Template is applied. All previous attribute placements for the symbols or connections selected in the Template will be reset.

If you only want your Template to modify the appearance of symbols, you can now click Finish to save the Template (but see the warning about the ARIS 7.02 bug in the next section). Otherwise, click Next to continue and set the connection appearance properties.

15.3.5   Select Connection Types

The *Select connection types Dialog Box* (Fig. 15.8) allows us to choose for which connection types we wish to set the connection appearance properties. For more information on any of the connections types, select it and click the Information button. The *Information on connection type Dialog Box* (Fig. 15.9) will show between which symbol types the connection type can be made and in which model types it occurs.

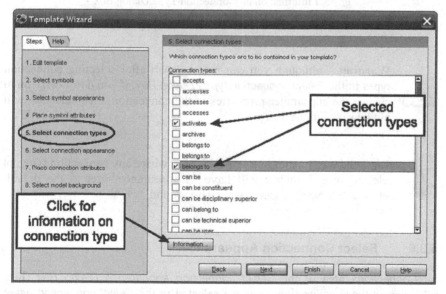

Fig. 15.8 Select Connection Types Dialog Box

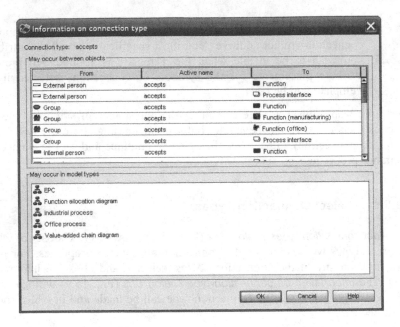

Fig. 15.9 Information on Connection Type Dialog Box

Warning – although you can select Finish after selecting connection types in the *Select connection types Dialog Box*, if you don't carry on to change the appearance properties of the connection, their selection will not be saved in the Template.

Bug – there is a major bug in ARIS 7.02, where any connection type not selected in a Template will have its appearance reset to the default settings. See Section 15.6.2 for a workaround.

15.3.6   Select Connection Appearance

The *Connections* area of the *Select connection appearance Dialog Box* (Fig. 15.10) shows those connection types we selected in the *Select connection types Dialog Box* and the various property boxes allow you to change the connection appearance (see Table 15.3). The *Preview* area gives an indication of the changes to the connection appearance, but the actual appearance of a connection after the Template is applied will depend on the previous settings in the model of any properties not specifically set by the Template.

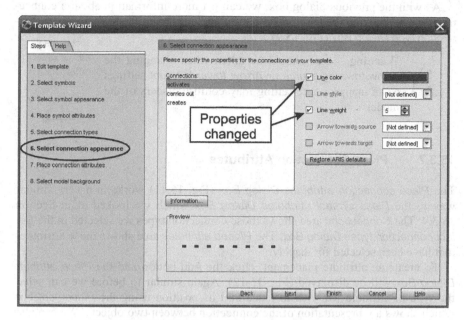

Fig. 15.10 Select Connection Appearance Dialog Box

Table 15.3 Connection Appearance Properties

Command	Action
Line color	Click on the property box to choose the line colour of a connection from the *Choose color Dialog Box*.
Line style	Select the line style from *Solid, Dashed* or *Dotted*.
Line weight	Choose the weight (i.e. thickness and intensity) of the line by clicking on the up and down controls.
Arrow towards source	Allows selection of different line ending styles (e.g. arrows) to be defined for the source object end of the connection. Selecting **ARIS default** will apply the style defined in the ARIS Method.
Arrow towards target	Allows selection of different line ending styles (e.g. arrows) to be defined for the target object end of the connection. Selecting **ARIS default** will apply the style defined in the ARIS Method.
Restore ARIS defaults	Resets the connection appearance properties to those set by the ARIS Method.

As with the previous dialog box, we can get more information about a connection type by clicking the Information button and displaying the *Information on connection type Dialog Box* (Fig. 15.9)

> **Warning** – care should be taken when changing the *Arrow towards source* or *Arrow towards target* settings as an inappropriate setting may confuse readers of the model.

15.3.7   Place Connection Attributes

The *Place connection attributes Dialog Box* (Fig. 15.11) works in a very similar way to the *Place symbol attributes Dialog Box* which we looked at in Section 15.3.4. The *Connections* area shows those connection types we selected in the *Select connection types Dialog Box*. The *Placed attributes* area shows those attributes that have been selected for display.

To create an attribute placement. click the Add button and the *Place attribute Dialog Box* will be displayed (Fig. 15.12). Again similar to before we can select the type of attribute we wish to place and its position using the *Placement* box which shows a representation of the connection between two objects. We can also set the appearance properties described previously in Table 15.2. Clicking the Restore ARIS defaults button will remove all attribute placements.

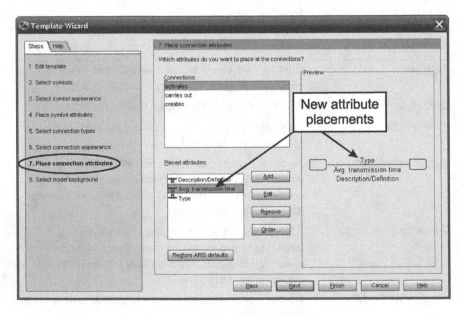

Fig. 15.11 Place Connections Attributes Dialog Box

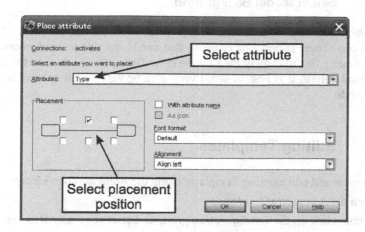

Fig. 15.12 Place Attribute (Connections) Dialog Box

Click OK and you will be returned to the *Place connection attributes Dialog Box*. The Placed attributes box now shows the attribute placement just added and the *Preview* area has been updated to show what the connection with look like.

As with the *Place symbol attributes Dialog Box* you can Edit, Remove and Order existing *Placed attributes*.

If you don't want your Template to define the model background colour, you can now click Finish to save the Template. Otherwise, click Next to continue to the final dialog box.

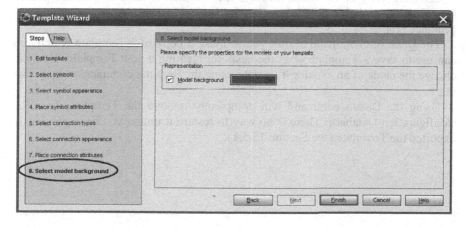

Fig. 15.13 Select Model Background Dialog Box

15.3.8   Select Model Background

The *Select model background Dialog Box* (Fig. 15.13) is the simplest of all the dialog boxes. There is only one property that can be set: *Model background*. Click on the property box to display the *Choose color Dialog Box* and select the required background colour. It is best to avoid very dark or very bright colours for model backgrounds.

15.4   Editing Templates

We can view and edit existing Templates using the *Administration Module*:

1. Open the *Administration Module*,
2. Double-click on the **Configuration** group in **Local** or on an ARIS Server,
3. Double-click on the **Conventions** group,
4. Select **Templates**.

The right-hand pane of the *Administration Module* (Fig. 15.1) shows a list of current Templates. *Right-Click* on a Template to select one of the following editing commands:

*   Edit,
*   Delete,
*   Duplicate,
*   Rename.

Selecting the Edit command displays the *Template Wizard* and allows you to step through the dialog boxes described in Section 15.3 to change the various appearance properties.

The Duplicate command allows you to make a copy of a Template which you can use to save a Template or as the basis for creating a new Template. You can change the name of an existing Template using the Rename command or by pressing F2.

Using the Delete command will completely remove the Template form the Configuration Database. There is no way to restore it unless you have previously exported the Template (see Section 15.5.1).

15.5 Exporting and Importing Templates

15.5.1 Exporting a Template

Templates are stored in the ARIS Configuration Database and, like Method Filters, are not saved when you use the database Backup command. To save a Template you can export it in XML format as an ".act" file:

1. Select the Template in the right-hand pane of the **Templates** group,
2. Right-Click > Export,
3. Choose a directory on your hard disk to save the file.

15.5.2 Importing a Template

To restore a previously exported Template:

1. Select the **Templates** group in the *Administration Module*,
2. Right-Click > Import,
3. In the *Import template Dialog Box* click the Browse button,
4. Select an ".act" file from your hard disk,
5. Click Open,
6. Click all the *Overwrite* checkboxes in the *Import template Dialog Box*,
7. Click OK.

The Template will be imported into the **Templates** group, overwriting any previous Template with the same GUID.

 Expert Tip – if you wish to import a Template, but don't wish to overwrite an existing Template with the same GUID (even though it may have a different name), then remove the tick from the *Overwrite template* checkbox. The Imported Template will now be created with a new GUID.

15.6 Applying Templates

Now we have created a Template we can manually apply it to a model, to selected objects in a model or make it the default Template for models.

15.6.1 Applying a Template to a Model

To apply a pre-defined Template to a model, make sure no objects or connections are selected and do either of the following:

- Format > Apply template,
- Right-Click > Format > Apply template.

Now select the Template from the list in the *Apply template Dialog Box* (Fig. 15.14).

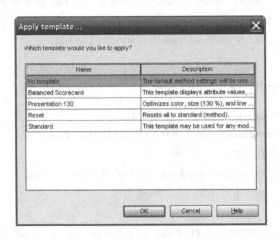

Fig. 15.14 Apply Template Dialog Box

The Template will be applied to the object symbols and connections in the model. Templates only affect those symbols and connections for which settings have been defined and several Templates can be applied in an additive manner to create an overall desired effect. As a result the precise effect of applying a Template will depend on what existing appearance properties were set prior to applying the Template.

 Hint – if the effect of applying a Template is not what you expected you can easily revert to the previous appearance by selecting Edit > Undo (CTRL + Z).

 Expert Tip – attribute placements for any given symbol or connection are not additive. After a Template is applied, any previous attribute placements for the symbols or connections selected in the Template will be reset.

The Template only affects the symbols and connections selected at the time the Template is applied, any new items created will adopt the style of the current model Template (see 15.6.3).

Question – why does a change I have made to a Template in the *Administration Module* not have any effect when I apply it to an open model?

Answer – it is recommended you refresh the database (<u>V</u>iew > <u>R</u>efresh or F5) before applying a Template to an already open model.

15.6.2 Applying a Template to Objects and Connections

If you select one or more objects or connections and apply a Template as described above, then only the appearance properties of the selected items will be updated. This can be a useful way of ensuring the desired effect is what you want and for building up complex appearance settings. The only difficulty with selective application of Templates is that it is difficult to reproduce the same effect at a later date.

 Bug – there is a bug in ARIS 7.02, where any connection type not selected in a Template will have its appearance reset to the default settings. If your Template just changes symbol settings, you can overcome this problem by selecting all the objects in the model and then applying the Template.

15.6.3 Setting the Current Model Template

If you wish a Template to be applied to a model, so all new objects and connections will take on that style:

1. Ensure nothing in the model is selected,
2. Right-Click > P<u>r</u>operties [Format / Representation],
3. Click on the Change Button adjacent to the *Current template* field,
4. Select the required Template from the *Select template Dialog Box*.

This Template will now be applied to the model and all new objects and connections will take on the Template appearance properties.

If you want the model properties, including the Template settings, to apply to all new models of the same type, tick the *U<u>s</u>e as default Checkbox* in the Properties [Format / Representation] *Dialog Box* and select *For this model type* in the *Use as default template Dialog Box*. Alternatively you can choose *For all model types* to apply it to new models of all types in the database.

15.6.4   Setting the Default Model Template

If you want a Template to be used for all new models:

1.   Select <u>V</u>iew > <u>O</u>ptions [*Model / For new models / Representation*] from the *Main Menu* (Fig. 15.15),

2.   Click on the Change button adjacent to the *Current template* field,

3.   Choose a Template from the *Select template Dialog Box*.

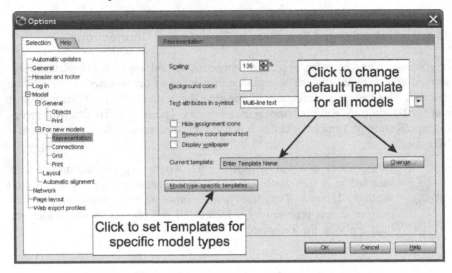

Fig. 15.15 For New models / Representation Dialog Box

This Template will now be applied to new models of all types. If you want to restrict the Template to just certain model types (e.g. *EPCs* and *FADs*):

1.   Select <u>V</u>iew > <u>O</u>ptions [*Model / For new models / Representation*] from the *Main Menu* (Fig. 15.15),

2.   Click on the <u>M</u>odel type-specific templates button.

The *Select model type-specific templates Dialog Box* will appear (Fig. 15.16). The *Model type* field on the left-hand side lists any model types for which a Template has been set and the right-hand *Template* field shows the associated Template.

To add a new model type, click on the <u>A</u>dd button. The *Select new model type Dialog Box* will present a list of all the model types for you to choose from. Select a model type and click OK and it will be added to the *Model type* field and the *Template* field will be set to the Template set in the *Current template* field of the [*Model / For new models / Representation*] *Dialog Box*.

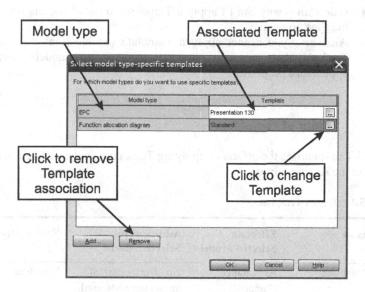

Fig. 15.16 Model Type-Specific Templates Dialog Box

You can change the Template by clicking on the browse button (three dots) at the right of the *Template* field and selecting a different Template from the *Select template Dialog Box*. You can delete a Template association by selecting it and clicking Remove.

Using this approach you can build up a complete list of Templates to apply to any particular model type. *Model type-specific templates* settings override any setting in the *Current template* field.

To summarise: any model type that doesn't have a Template specifically set will use the Template in the *Current template* field, while any model types listed in the *Select model type-specific templates Dialog Box* will use the specific Template associated with them.

 Warning – setting the Template fields in the *View > Options [Model / For new models / Representation] Dialog Box* only applies to new models that are created. They have no effect on existing models. To change an existing model you must specifically apply the Template to that model.

 Expert Tip – to apply a Template to a number of models at the same time, use the *Find* command (see Chapter 5) to produce a list of models, select the required models and Right-Click > Format > Apply template.

Question – why can't I apply a Template to list of objects returned by the *Find* command?
Answer - you cannot apply a Template to objects as it is only the symbols that represent their occurrences in models that have appearance properties.

15.6.5   Effect of Templates

Table 15.4 summarises the effects of applying Templates in the different ways described in the sections above.

Table 15.4 Effect of Templates

Command	Effect on Selected Model	Additions to Selected Model	New Models
Apply Template	Appearance changed	No effect – current model template used.	No effect
Model Properties / Current Template	Appearance changed	Appearance changed – new template used	No effect
View > Options [For New Models / Current Template]	No effect	No effect	Appearance changed for all new models.
View > Options [For New Models / Model Type-specific Templates]	No effect	No effect	Appearance changed for all new models of the same type.

ARIS 7 – in ARIS 7 it is now possible to create user-defined model types based on existing ARIS models (see Chapter 12). For instance you can create different *EPC* model types, each with different objects, for different layers of a model hierarchy. Using the *Current template* fields you can apply different Templates to these user-defined model types to fully customise the look and feel of the models in your enterprise process architecture.

15.6.6   Special Templates

Three special Templates are provided in ARIS:

* *No template,*
* *Reset,*
* *Standard.*

No Template

Applying the Template with the name *No template* has no effect on the objects and connections currently in a model. However, if it is selected as the current model Template (see Section 15.6.3) or the default model Template (see Section 15.6.4), then the effect is not to apply a Template and any new objects and connections added to the model will have the default appearance defined in the ARIS Method.

Reset

Applying the *Reset* Template to the model sets the appearance properties of the objects and connections to the default defined by the ARIS Method. It can also be used as the current model Template (Section 15.6.3) or the default model Template (Section 15.6.4) so any new objects and connections added to the model will have the default appearance defined in the ARIS Method.

The *Reset* Template is similar to *No template* with the exception that it can also be applied to the existing objects and connections in a model.

Standard

The *Standard* Template has been predefined by IDS Scheer to give a suitable format for presenting models on the Internet. On installation, the current model Template (Section 15.6.3) and the default model Template (Section 15.6.4) are set to the *Standard* Template.

You can make changes to the standard Template, but it is better to define your own base Template and change the default settings to use your Template.

Chapter 16   Administration Reports

This chapter describes the ARIS Reports that are valuable for carrying out
database and user administration tasks.

16.1   Introduction

There are a number of ARIS Report (see Chapter 10 for more on running Reports)
that are useful in managing users and databases. These are summarised in Table
16.1 and described in detail in the following sections.

Table 16.1 ARIS Administration Reports

Selected Item	Report Name	Description
Database	Copying users and user groups	Makes copies of selected Users and User Groups within the same database.
Database	Database information	Provides information on the Function Privileges of Users and User Groups and database Languages and Font Formats.
Database	Replace font formats	Replaces every use of a selected font in the database with a different font.
Database	Replace object types	Replaces every use of selected object types in the database with a different object type.
Database	Replace symbol types	Replaces the symbols being used to represent occurrences of a particular object type with a different symbol valid for that object type.
Group	Consolidate objects	Consolidates objects by performing the equivalent of the Find and Consolidate commands.
Group	Export relationship matrix	See Chapter 4.
Group	Output group information	Displays the *Path* and *Description/Definition* attribute of the selected group along with Users and User Groups that have Access Privileges assigned to the group.

Selected Item	Report Name	Description
Group	Replace text attributes	Find and replace a text string occurring in an attribute value of any of the sub-groups, models, objects or connections in that group.
Group	Transfer groups and users	Transfer the group structure (and any associated Users and User Groups) to another database.
Model	Format models	Set the model appearance properties of the model (equivalent to manually using the *Model properties [Format] Dialog Box.*

All of the reports can be found in the **Administration** *Category* of the *Select Report Dialog Box* (see below).

Warning – many of the administration Reports (e.g. **Replace object types**) have significant effects on the database and the results cannot be undone. You are strongly advised to make a backup copy of your database before running these reports.

16.2   Copying Users and User Groups Report

This ARIS Report is run on a database and makes copies of selected Users and User Groups within the same database. This is useful for creating a new User or User Group with the same Function Privileges or Access Privileges as an existing User or User Group. To run the Report:

1. Login into the database as a **system** User,

2. Select the database name,

3. Right-Click > Ev<u>a</u>luate > S<u>t</u>art report,

4. Select the **Copying users and user groups** Report in the *Select report Dialog Box* of the *Report Wizard* and click <u>N</u>ext,

5. Click <u>F</u>inish in the *Select output setting Dialog Box.*

Question – I have selected the Users and User Groups I want to copy, why can I not see an Ev<u>a</u>luate > S<u>t</u>art report when I Right-Click?
Answer – the selection of specific Users and User Groups is made from dialog boxes display by the Report. You must select the database name to run the Report.

When the Report runs, the *Copy user or user group Dialog Box* will be displayed (Fig. 16.1). Tick one or both of the *Copy user* or *Copy user group* checkboxes and select the appropriate User or User Group from the drop-down boxes. You can only select one User or one User Group at a time (one of each) unless you select (**All**). Click OK and the Report will create duplicates of the chosen User and User Groups with the same Function Privileges, Access Privileges and User Group associations. The names of the new Users and User Groups will be the same as the originals, but with a sequence number appended (e.g. **User4** becomes **User4_1**). You can then rename them to something more appropriate.

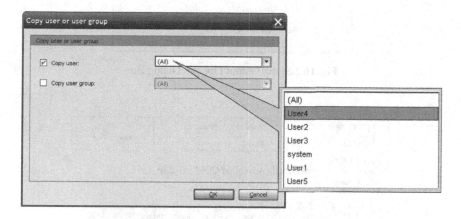

Fig. 16.1 *Copy User or User Group Dialog Box*

16.3   Database Information Report

This ARIS Report is run on a selected database and provides information on the Function Privileges of Users and User Groups, and the Languages and Font Formats used in the database. To run the Report:

1. Login into the database as a **system** User,
2. Select the database name,
3. Right-Click > Evaluate > Start report,
4. Select the **Database information** Report in the *Select report Dialog Box* of the *Report Wizard* and click Next,
5. Choose the *Output format* you want in the *Select output setting Dialog Box.*
6. Click Finish.

The Report displays the *Select output options Dialog Box* (Fig. 16.2). Select the checkboxes for the items you wish to display. Click OK and a Report will produce an output similar to that shown in Fig. 16.3.

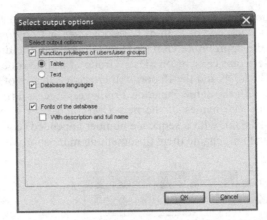

Fig. 16.2 Select Output Options Dialog Box

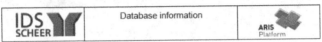

Server: LOCAL
Database: ARIS Green Book - Advanced (2007_10_22)
User: system

Function privileges of users/user groups:

User group	User	Show user management	User management	Change management	Database management	Database export	Method changes	Prefix management	Font format management
Product_ Group_A									
	User4								
	User3								
	system	X	X	X	X	X	X	X	X
	User1	X							
Product_ Group_B									
	User4								
	User2								
	User3								
	system	X	X	X	X	X	X	X	X
	User1	X							
Product_ Group_C									
	User5								
	User4								
	User3								
	system	X	X	X	X	X	X	X	X

Fig. 16.3 Database Information Report

16.4 Replace Font Formats Report

This ARIS Report is run on a selected database and replaces every use of a particular font with a different Font Format.

To run the Report:

1. Login into the database as a *system* User,
2. Select the database name,
3. Right-Click > Ev<u>a</u>luate > S<u>t</u>art report,
4. Select the **Replace font formats** Report in the *Report Wizard Select report Dialog Box* and click <u>N</u>ext,
5. Click <u>F</u>inish.

The Report displays the *ARIS Report (Select font formats) Dialog Box* (Fig. 16.4). Choose the *Old font format*, the one you want to replace, and then choose the *New font format* you want to replace it with. Click <u>O</u>K and all uses of the original Font Format will be updated. The original font is not deleted and is still available if you wish to use it in future.

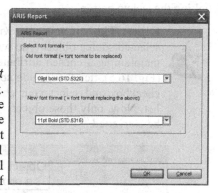

Fig. 16.4 ARIS Report (Select Font formats) Dialog Box

16.5 Replace Object Types Report

This ARIS Report is run on a selected database and replaces all the selected object types used in the database with a different object type. It modifies every object definition that is based on the selected object type so that it is now based on the new type. As you might expect, this is a complex (and drastic) operation and, as well as selecting source and target objects, you also have to choose the symbol and connection types to be used.

To run the Report:

1. Login into the database as a *system* User,
2. Select the database name,
3. Right-Click > Ev<u>a</u>luate > S<u>t</u>art report,
4. Select the **Replace object types** Report in the *Select report Dialog Box* of the *Report Wizard* and click <u>N</u>ext,
5. Click <u>F</u>inish.

The Report displays the *Change object types Dialog Box* (Fig. 16.5). In the left-hand *Source object type* box select the type of object you wish to replace (e.g. *Application system*). In the right-hand *Target object type* box, select the object type you want to replace it with (e.g. *Application system type*). Click the Add selection button and the source and target object types will be shown in the *Selected changes* box:

"Application system -> Application system type"

You can now choose another source and object type and add them to the box in the same way. If you change your mind you can delete an entry by selecting it and clicking the Delete button.

 Expert Tip – if you only wish to replace some of the objects of the selected source object type with the target type, you can mark them by maintaining a chosen attribute. In the *Change object types Dialog Box* (Fig. 16.5), tick the *Include source objects with maintained attribute only* checkbox and select your chosen attribute in the *Attribute* drop-down list. Now, only those objects with the selected attribute maintained will be converted.

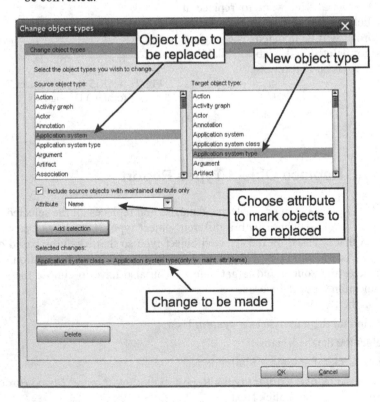

Fig. 16.5 Change Object Types Dialog Box (1)

Click OK and a second *Change object types Dialog Box* (Fig. 16.6) will be displayed. The left-hand *Source object type (source symbol type)* box shows the different symbol types available in the ARIS Method for the source object while the right-hand *Target symbol type* box shows the valid symbols that can be used for the target object.

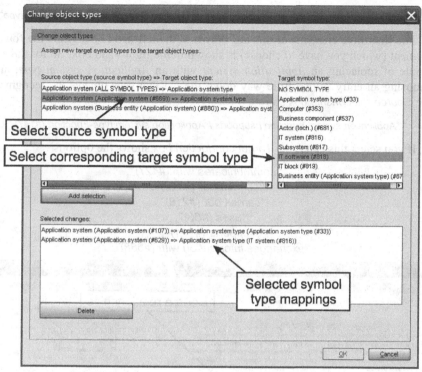

Fig. 16.6 Change Object Types Dialog Box (2)

Select a symbol type for the source object and a corresponding symbol type you want to use for the replaced target object type. If you select the first entry in the source list (***ALL SYMBOL TYPES***) and an appropriate target symbol in the right-hand box, then all the source objects will be replaced with a target object using the selected symbol. The *Selected changes* box will now show:

"*Application system (ALL SYMBOL TYPES)*
=>Application system type (Application system type (#33))"

Alternatively, if you have different occurrences of the source object using different symbol types (often different model types use different symbol types for the same object type), you can select each specific source object symbol type and associate a specific target object symbol type to it (you will need to do all of them). Once you have correctly assigned the source and target symbol types, click OK.

Just when you may have thought the Report was ready to run, a third *Change object types Dialog Box* (Fig. 16.7) is displayed. This time the left-hand Source relationship box shows all the possible relationship types between the source object type and all other object types allowed by the ARIS Method. The format of this box looks rather complicated. It can be understood as:

"*Source relationship / source connection type / target relationship / target connection type*"

The first three elements of this are shown in the left-hand box, while the fourth element (which you have to choose) is shown in the right-hand box. So for the example of replacing an *Application system* with an *Application system type*, and choosing an entry from a little way down the list that uses objects we recognise, the *Source relationship* box shows:

"*Application system-Function / supports / Application system type-Function (#147)*".

If you select this entry, the *Target connection box* shows the options:

"*communicates with (#427)*",
"*has member (#420)*",
"*carries out (#218)*",
"*uses (#60)*",
"*supports (#221)*",
"*exchanges information with (#668)*".

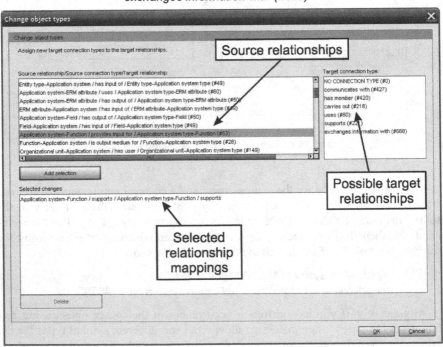

Fig. 16.7 Change Object Types Dialog Box (3)

So what does all this mean? It is saying that one of the 'source' relationships between the chosen source object (the *Application system*) and a *Function* object type is the *supports* connection type. It then asks, for the 'target' relationship between the target object (the *Application system type*) and the *Function* object, which 'target' connection type would you like to use? The *Target connection box* then shows all the possible connection types valid in the ARIS Method. The numbers after the two entries (e.g. #147 and #221) are ARIS reference numbers for the connection types.

So for every relationship between your chosen source object type, and all other object types used in your database that are connected to it, you need to choose an appropriate target connection type to replace it with. In complex databases there could be a large number of objects and relationships so you need to complete this dialog box with care. If you don't want to replace a particular connection type that occurs in your database (i.e. leave it unconnected), select the **NO CONNECTION Type (#0)** option.

Once you have chosen all the connection types, click OK. The Report will run and replace the object types, symbols and connections. If there are any definitions you omitted to select, another version of the *Change object types Dialog Box* (Fig. 16.8) will be displayed, warning you of the changes that have not been made.

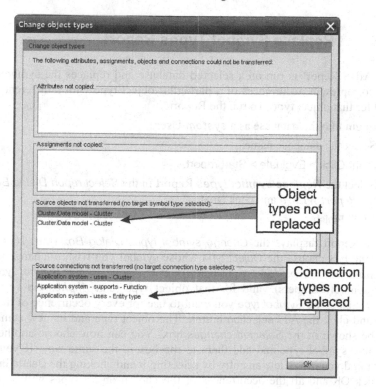

Fig. 16.8 Change Object Types Dialog Box (4)

Warning – some object pairs have multiple connection types with the same name (but different reference numbers) so you need to be sure to select the correct one, or select them all if you are not sure.

Expert Tip – although in principle you can replace any object type with any other object type, in practice you will only be able to find sensible target relationships when the target object type is a similar sort to the source object type (e.g. *Application system* and *Application system type*).

Expert Tip – if you try this Report with some sample objects which you don't bother to rename, you may expect an *Application system* object called "***Application system***" would be replaced with an *Application system type* object called "***Application system type***". The type of the object will in fact be changed, but of course the name is just an attribute so it will remain as it was. Hover your mouse over the symbol to show the *Type* attribute to confirm the object type has in fact been changed.

16.6   Replace Symbol Types Report

This ARIS Report is run on a selected database and replaces the symbols being used to represent occurrences of a particular object type with a different symbol valid for that object type. To run the Report:

1. Login into the database as a **system** User,
2. Select the database name,
3. Right-Click > Eva̲luate > S̲tart report,
4. Select the **Replace symbol types** Report in the *Select report Dialog Box* of the *Report Wizard* and click N̲ext,
5. Click F̲inish.

The Report displays the *Change symbol types Dialog Box* (Fig. 16.9). In the left-hand box choose the *Object type* whose symbol you wish to change (e.g. *Application system type)*. The right-hand box will now list the *Symbol types* (and their symbol numbers) valid for that object type (e.g. *Application system type (#33))*. Select the *Symbol type* you want to use for every occurrence of that object type and click the Add selection button. The object type and its new symbol type will be shown in the *Selected changes* box. You can now choose another object type and symbol type and add them to the box in the same way. If you change your mind you can delete an entry by selecting it and clicking the Delete button.

Click OK and all the occurrences of the chosen object types will be replaced with the chosen symbol.

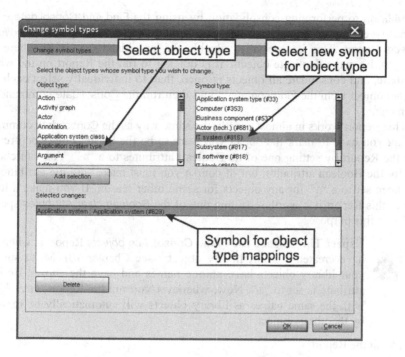

Fig. 16.9 Change Symbol Types Dialog Box

Warning – the *Change symbol types Dialog Box* will show all the valid symbols allowed by the ARIS Method, however the Report can only replace object occurrences with symbols which are allowed in the current Method Filter and that have the same connection types as those used in the model. If you choose symbols that are not valid in the current Method Filter, a warning message will be displayed and the symbols will not be replaced.

Expert Tip – although the Report will replace object occurrences with the chosen symbol, the appearance of the symbol will be affected by any Templates applied to the specific model the symbol appears in. The result may be that the size, colour and line properties of the new symbol will be those applied by the Template to the original symbol and hence the new symbol may not appear as you expect.

16.7   Consolidate Objects Report

In addition to performing consolidation by using the <u>F</u>ind and <u>C</u>onsolidate commands (see Chapter 10), you can also perform the same task using the *Consolidate objects* Report. This is especially valuable for large databases, where there are likely to be many duplicate objects. It is quicker to run the Report on the whole database, and consolidate all objects at once, than to individually select each duplicate object from the <u>F</u>ind command and then run the <u>C</u>onsolidate command on each one.

This Report works in almost exactly the same way as the <u>C</u>onsolidate command except you have to mark the object you want to be the master object before you run the Report by setting one of its Boolean attributes to a "1". You can choose any of the Boolean attributes, but of course you must make sure the attribute has not been set to a "1" for any objects for some other reason. If you make a lot of use of this Report it is worth renaming one of the *Boolean User Attributes* specifically for this purpose.

Expert Tip – a good use of the *Consolidate objects* Report is when you have created a set of library objects (see Chapter 10). Make sure all your library objects have unique names and have the chosen Boolean attribute is set to "1". Now, whenever you run the Report, any objects with the same names as library objects will automatically be replaced by the library object.

To run the Report:

1.   Login into the database,
2.   Select a database group (or **Main Group** to consolidate the whole database),
3.   Right-Click > Ev<u>a</u>luate > S<u>t</u>art report,
4.   Select the **Consolidate objects** Report in the *Select report Dialog Box* of the *Report Wizard* and click <u>N</u>ext,
5.   Choose the *Ou<u>t</u>put format* you want in the *Select output setting Dialog Box*,
6.   Click <u>F</u>inish.

The *Output format* setting in the *Select output settings Dialog Box* does not affect the running of the Report, but determines the format of the log file (see below).

Question – why can I not see the *Consolidate objects* Report when I select a database?
Answer – the *Consolidate objects* Report can only be evaluated for Groups.

When the Report runs, the *Consolidation of objects with identical names Dialog Box* (Fig. 16.10) will display similar options to the *Consolidation Wizard* (see Chapter 10). The main difference is that the *Master object* drop-down list allows you to select which Boolean attribute you have used to mark the master object. In addition, a very useful option is the *Create log file* checkbox which provides a list of which objects have been consolidated (Fig. 16.11) in the document format selected in the *Select output settings Dialog Box*.

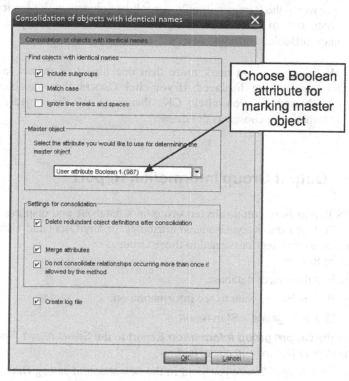

Fig. 16.10 Consolidation of Objects with Identical Names Dialog Box

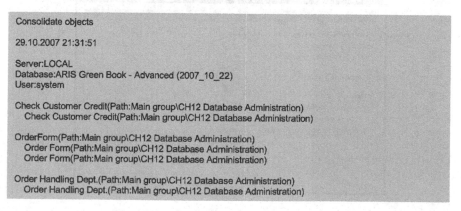

Fig. 16.11 Consolidate Objects Report Log File

Question – why do I get a message in the log file "Unable to find objects for consolidation" when I know there are definitely objects with identical names in the group where I ran the evaluation?
Answer – the Report will only consolidate objects with identical names when one of them has been marked as the *'master'* by setting the chosen Boolean attribute to a "1".

Warning – if you mark more than one object as master, a warning message will be displayed. If you click Cancel, the consolidation will be aborted. If you click OK, then one of the objects will be automatically chosen as the master.

16.8   Output Group Information Report

This ARIS Report is run on a selected group in a database and displays information on its *Path* or *Description/Definition* attributes, or any Users and User Groups that have Access Privileges assigned to those Groups.

To run the Report:

1. Login into the source database,
2. Select the group you want to see information on,
3. Right-Click > Evaluate > Start report,
4. Select the **Output group information** Report in the *Select report Dialog Box* of the *Report Wizard* and click Next,
5. Choose the *Output format* you want in the *Select output setting Dialog Box*,
6. Click Finish.

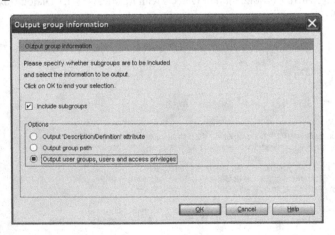

Fig. 16.12 Output Group Information Dialog Box

The Report will run and display the *Output group Information Dialog Box* (Fig. 16.12). Choose whether you want to *Include subgroups* and then select which option you want to display. Click OK and the Report will display an output similar to that shown in Fig. 16.13.

Output group information

Server:LOCAL
Database:Access Rights Example Database (2007_10_03)
User:system

Group	User group	User	Access privileges		
			Read	Write	Delete
Product Processes					
	Product_Group_C				
		User5			
		User4			
		User3			
	Product_Group_B				
		system	X	X	X
		User4			
		User3			
		User1			
		User2			
	Product_Group_A				
		User4			
		system	X	X	X
		User3			
		User1			
Product A					
	Product_Group_C				
		User5			
		User4			
		User3			
	Product_Group_B				
		system	X	X	X
		User4			
		User3			
		User1			
		User2			
	Product_Group_A		X	X	X
		User4			
		system	X	X	X
		User3			

Fig. 16.13 Output Group Information Report

16.9 Replace Text Attributes Report

This ARIS Report is run on a selected database group and allows you to find and replace a text string occurring in the attribute value of any of the sub-groups, models, objects or connections defined in that group. This is very useful for making widespread changes to attributes across the database, for instance to change the name of a process owner or product.

To run the Report:

1. Login into the database as a **system** User,
2. Select the database group,
3. Right-Click > Ev<u>a</u>luate > S<u>t</u>art report,
4. Select the **Replace text attributes** Report in the *Select report Dialog Box* of the *Report Wizard* and click <u>N</u>ext,
5. Choose the *O<u>u</u>tput format* you want for the log file in the *Select output setting Dialog Box*,
6. Click <u>F</u>inish.

The Report will run and display the *Find/Replace – Options Dialog* Box (Fig. 16.14). The two buttons at the top of the dialog box allow you choose whether you want to replace the values in attributes across the whole database (*Database-wide*) or just in the select group (*Selected group*) and whether to *Include subgroups*. In the *Replace attributes in* area you can then choose whether to replace the values in attributes of one or more of *Groups*, *Models* or *Objects* in the selected group. If you selected the *Database-wide* option you can also change the attributes of *Relationships*. Now click <u>O</u>K.

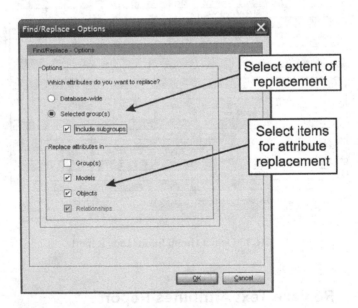

Fig. 16.14 Find/Replace – Options Dialog Box

The *Find/Replace – Attribute selection* Dialog Box (Fig. 16.15) allows you to select in which attribute you want to make the replacement (select the *In the attribute* option and choose the specific attribute from the drop-down list) or select *In all attributes*.

Click *OK* again and the *Find/Replace Dialog Box* (Fig. 16.16) allows you to enter a text string to search for in the *Find what* field and the text you want to *Replace with*. You can choose whether to search based on matching the case of the text strings and you can also choose

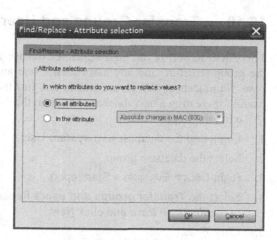

Fig. 16.15 Find/Replace – Attribute Selection Dialog Box

to create a log file of the changes that have been made. Click the Replace all button and all the selected attributes of the chosen items will have the *Find what* text string replaced with the *Replace with* text string. If you selected the *Create log* option, the log file will be created using the document format chosen in the *Select output setting Dialog Box*.

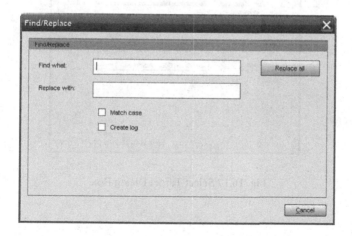

Fig. 16.16 Find/Replace Dialog Box

16.10   Transfer Groups and Users Report

This ARIS Report is run on a selected database group and allows you to transfer the group structure and any associated Users and User Groups to another database. No models or objects are transferred, just the structure, so this Report is very useful for creating a new database based on the structure of an existing database.

To run the Report:

1.   Login into the database as a *system* User,

2.   Select the database group,

3.   Right-Click > Ev*a*luate > S*t*art report,

4.   Select the **Transfer groups and users** Report in the *Select report Dialog Box* of the *Report Wizard* and click *N*ext,

5.   Click *F*inish.

The Report will run and display the *Select target Dialog Box* (Fig. 16.17). Choose the *Server* and *Database* where you want the group structure to be transferred to and click *O*K.

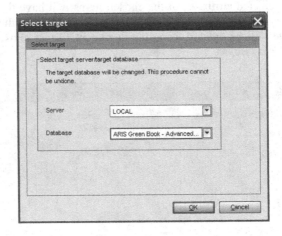

Fig. 16.17 Select Target Dialog Box

 Warning – the Report will try and log into the target database using the same User account as you used to log into the source database. It is best to use the *system* account to ensure the Report has the correct privileges. If the password of the *system* account in the target database is different to the source database, you will be prompted for a *Username* and *Password*.

In the *Conflict resolution Dialog Box* (Fig. 16.18) you can choose how to handle any conflicts with Users and User Groups that may already exist in your target database. Click <u>O</u>K again.

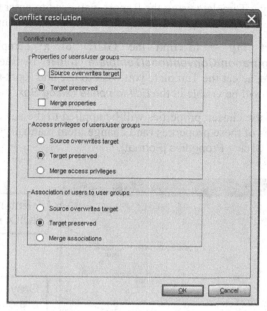

Fig. 16.18 Conflict Resolution Dialog Box

 Expert Tip – it is strongly recommended that you make a backup copy of the target database before running this Report.

16.11   Format Models Report

This ARIS Report is run on one or more selected models and allows you to set the same model appearance properties that you can manually set in the *Model properties [Format] Dialog Box*. To run the Report:

1. Login into the database as a *system* User,

2. Select one or more models,

3. Right-Click > Ev<u>a</u>luate > S<u>t</u>art report,

4. Select the *Format models* Report in the *Select report Dialog Box* of *Report Wizard* and click <u>N</u>ext,

5. Click <u>F</u>inish.

The Report will run and display the *Set model options Dialog Box* (Fig. 16.19) where you can set the model appearance properties as you would normally. The one exception to using the manual *Model properties [Format] Dialog Box* is that, if you want to apply a Template using the Report, you need to enter the GUID of the Template into the *Set model options Dialog Box* rather than its name.

 Expert Tip – to find the GUID of a Template: open the *Configuration/Conventions/Template* folder in the *Administration Module*, select the Template you wish to use and Right-Click > <u>E</u>dit. The GUID will be visible in the *Edit template Dialog Box*.

Click <u>O</u>K and the chosen properties will be applied to the selected model. You can see the values of these properties (and change them manually) by selecting the model and Right-Click > Prop<u>e</u>rties [Format].

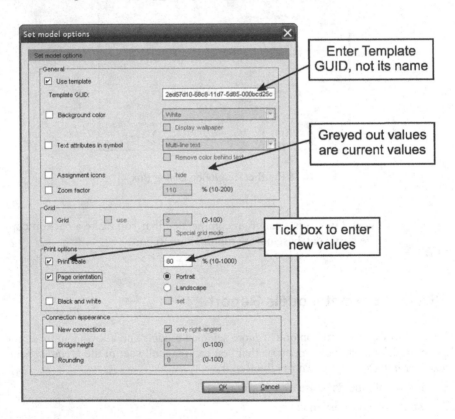

Fig. 16.19 Set Model Options Dialog Box

Chapter 17   Model Verification

This chapter looks at how to verify that your process models conform to the ARIS Method, they follow good modelling practice and they are logically consistent. It describes the ARIS tools that aid verification including Semantic Checks, the Find command and the Consolidate command.

17.1   Why Verify?

Verification is the procedure for ensuring your models are logically consistent, conform to agreed standards and meet the specification. Verification is 'inward looking'; it is about checking your models make sense individually, they fit into a logical structure and are consistent when viewed as a set. Verification is not concerned about whether the models actually do what the customer actually intended; only that they meet the specification.

Validation, on the other hand, is 'outward looking'; it ensures what you deliver is fit for purpose, that is to say it meets the customer's actual needs as opposed to meeting the specification they gave you.

Verification is an important step which should be performed before validation. Validating models are fit for purpose is a difficult task and it is made doubly difficult if the models are not logically correct, they contradict each other or use different methods of representation. Following validation it is often necessary to make changes to the models. If the models are not consistent and don't share the same standards it can be difficult to understand how and where the changes should be made.

The result of verification should be a set of models that can be clearly understood, are not ambiguous, and that form the basis for validation and subsequent implementation. Use of the ARIS Method, and your own modelling conventions, is fundamental to achieving this. Conforming to the Method as closely as possible will help ensure the models are consistent and can be understood by anyone who is familiar with ARIS.

17.2   What Should be Verified?

In this book we have been looking mainly at process models so this chapter refers mostly to *EPCs* (and to a lesser extent *FADs*), but the basic principles apply to all models.

We can divide those aspects of our models that should be verified into several categories:

- Checks on individual models,
- Checks on the database,
- Checks on multiple models,
- Checks on model structure and linking.

In general, you should undertake verification in that order. For instance, there is no point in checking model structure and linking before you have ensured that individual models are logically correct.

17.2.1   Checks on Individual Models

Models should be checked to ensure:

- There is no duplication of Functions, Events and Rules,
- There is no replication of common resource objects,
- Decisions, branches and loops are modelled correctly,
- The model conforms to the ARIS Method,
- Trigger and outcome Events are modelled correctly,
- Object relationships are correct,
- Attributes are populated correctly,
- The model conforms to corporate modelling conventions.

17.2.2   Checks on the Database

The database should be checked to ensure:

- There are no significant objects with the same name,
- There are no inappropriate object occurrences,
- The group structure is sensible and consistent,
- Model naming standards have been followed,
- There are no unnecessary or duplicate models,
- There are redundant generated models,
- Objects are located in appropriate groups,
- Security and access restrictions have been correctly implemented.

17.2.3   Checks on Multiple Models

Models should be checked to ensure:

- Multiple object occurrences are necessary and correct,
- Common linking Events have correct occurrences,
- Common resources are represented by the same objects,
- Model assignments are correct.

17.2.4   Checks on Model Structure and Linking

The hierarchy of models should be checked to ensure:

- Model hierarchies are consistent and synchronised,
- The Function hierarchy is correct,
- The Event hierarchy is correct,
- Model Generation produces valid end-to-end process models.

17.3   Tools for Verification

ARIS has a number of tools, summarised in Table 17.1, that can help with verification. Some of these are described in the chapters referred to, while others are described later in this chapter. The *Compare* and *Animation* facilities are currently only available in *ARIS Toolset* and are not described in this book.

17.3.1   Animation

Animation is a useful technique for verification and validation. It is included in *ARIS Toolset*, but is not available in *ARIS Business Architect*.

17.3.2   Compare

The Compare command is used for comparing variants of objects and models, and comparing their attributes. It is only available in *ARIS Toolset* and is not described in this book.

Table 17.1 ARIS Verification Tools

Tool	Use in	Operation
Animation (not covered in this book)	(only available in ARIS Toolset)	Allows a 'walk-through' of all process paths to ensure the decision logic is correct. Useful for verification and validation.
Compare (not covered in this book)	(only available in ARIS Toolset)	Allows comparison of attributes for models or objects, and their associated masters and variants.
Consolidate (see Chapter 10)	Explorer Module	Allows two or more individual objects to be consolidated into a single object with controlled aggregation of attributes.
Find Models and Objects (see Chapter 5)	Explorer Module	Finds objects and models within the database group structure. Search by name or by the values of populated attributes.
Find Objects with Identical Names (see Chapter 5)	Explorer Module	Finds objects within the database group structure with the same name.
Identifiers (Section 17.3.5)	Explorer Module	An attribute which provides a semi-unique label for each object, model and group. Allows easy identification of duplicates.
Macros (Section 17.3.9 and Chapter 9)	Design Module, Explorer Module	Macros allow modelling tasks to be configured and run automatically. Macros can use pre-existing Reports or Semantic Checks.
Object Occurrences (section 17.3.6)	Designer Module	Use the *Occurrences Tab* and *Attributes Tab* to identify duplicate objects in a model.
Reports (Section 17.3.8 and Chapter 16)	Designer Module, Explorer Module	Standard Reports for checking object occurrences, relationships, populated attributes, etc. User-defined Reports can be produced for checking project-specific aspects.
Semantic Check (Section 17.3.7 and Chapter 9)	Design Module, Explorer Module	Checks for verifying model structure, conformance to the ARIS Method, attribute population, etc.

17.3.3   Find Objects with Identical Names

The *Objects with identical names* option in the *Find Dialog Box* (select a group and Right-Click > *F*ind) searches ARIS groups to find sets of objects with identical, or very similar names. The results of this search can be used as the basis for consolidating these duplicate objects into a single object (see next section). The *Objects with identical names* option is described in detail in Chapter 5.

17.3.4   Consolidate

Often, you may inadvertently create replicas of objects, particularly resource objects (e.g. *Organizational unit types*, *Application system types*, etc). For instance, in one model we may create an *Organizational unit type* object called "*Sales Department*" and then in another model we also want to refer to the "*Sales Department*", but forgetting we have already defined an object, we create a new one and we give it a slightly different name, for instance: "*Sales Dept.*".

The verification procedure described in Section 17.4.1 should identify these two different objects representing the same entity. Having found them we want to make sure we just use one of the objects and delete the redundant one. We can do this manually or by using the Consolidate command (see Chapter 10).

17.3.5   GUID and Identifiers

Each ARIS item (e.g. group, model, object, etc.) has a *Global Unique Identifier* (GUID) defining its uniqueness. An item's GUID can be viewed by selecting it in the *Explorer Module*, Right-Click > Properties and viewing the *Properties [Information]* *Dialog Box*. The GUID is shown in the *GUID* field.

GUID:

```
af1b7ac0-1b57-11db-0ea1-dff18f0e518e
```

Inspecting the GUID is always the final arbiter for deciding if an object is truly unique. However, the GUID can only be viewed from the *Properties [Information]* *Dialog Box* and, because of its length, it is not practical for everyday use. Instead we can use the *Identifier* attribute.

The use of the *Identifier* attribute is one of the most useful tools for aiding the verification procedure. The *Identifier* is a standard attribute for all ARIS items. Its value can be entered manually and is displayed like any other attribute. However, it has a special operation making it useful for verification. If we configure the database selecting the option *Assign identifiers when creating new database items* (see Chapter 10), then each time we create a new object or model, ARIS will automatically assign a value to the *Identifier* attribute. The value will be an alphanumeric prefix followed by a numeric index that counts up automatically for each new item (e.g. *STD.123*, *STD.124*, etc.). If applied consistently, every item in the database will have a unique *Identifier*.

Warning – identifiers are only unique within a particular database and then only if applied correctly. If models and objects are merged from another database, then duplicate identifiers may be applied to different items. This is especially true if the standard identifier (**STD**) has been used.

Just like any attribute, the *Identifier* attribute can be viewed in the *Properties [Attributes] Dialog Box*. For objects and relationships, the *Identifier* can be quickly viewed in *Attributes Tab* in the *Designer Module*. By selecting objects one after another and inspecting the *Attributes Tab* you can quickly check whether objects with the same name are in fact the same object.

Question – why when I view the *Attributes Tab* in the *Designer Module* can I not see the *Identifier* attribute?
Answer – if the *Identifier* attribute is not visible, click on the <u>M</u>ore attributes button and select the *Identifier* from the *Insert attributes Dialog Box*.

17.3.6   Object Occurrences

The <u>F</u>ind command with the *Objects with identical names* option (Section 17.3.3) is valuable for finding objects in a group, or throughout the entire database, with the same or similar names. However, it is good practice to check individual models as you develop them to make sure there are no duplicates, rather than have to work through a huge list later.

You can view all the object occurrences in a model by looking at the *Occurrences Tab* of the *Navigation Bar* when using the *Designer Module* (Fig. 17.1).

Hint – the *Occurrences Tab* of the *Navigation Bar* in the *Designer Module* shows all the object occurrences in current model while the *Occurrences Tab* of the *Properties Bar* shows all the occurrences of the object selected in the current model, in all models in the database.

You can sort the list alphabetically or by object type by clicking on the column headers. If you sort the list alphabetically you can quickly spot object occurrences with the same or similar names. We would expect resource objects (e.g. *Organizational unit types*) to have many occurrences based on the same object definition, while Functions and Events should normally have unique occurrences.

If you identify two object occurrences with the same name, you can check whether they are occurrences of the same object definition, or replicas with the same name, by selecting the object and viewing the *Identifier* attribute in the *Attributes Tab* in the *Properties Bar* (Fig. 17.1). By having both bars open you can quickly select suspect objects and check their *Identifiers*. You can also visually identify duplicate object occurrences that have similar, but not identical, names (e.g. "*Sales Department*" and "*Sales Dept.*").

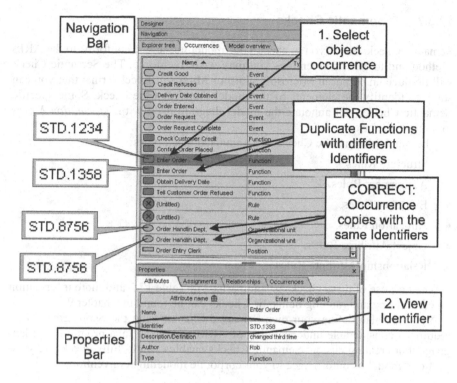

Fig. 17.1 The Occurrences and Attributes Tabs

If you find two duplicate resource objects (e.g. an *Organizational unit type*) you can delete one of them and replace it with an *occurrence copy* of the remaining one. If you find duplicate Functions or Events, delete one of them, make a definition copy of the original one and change the name to something that distinguishes it from the original object. You will need to check the attributes of the objects you are deleting (and those remaining) in case there is different information that needs to be aggregated.

An alternative to manually making the changes is to use the Consolidate command. However, you cannot select object occurrences in the *Designer Module* and run Consolidate, you need to identify all the object definitions to consolidate in the *Explorer Module* or use the Find command.

 Expert Tip – to find the location of an object definition in the *Explorer Module* for a object occurrence in the *Designer Module*, select the object occurrence and Right-Click > Go to > Occurrence in Explorer.

 Warning – although the *Identifier* attribute gives a useful indication of whether object occurrences refer to the same object definition, they can be misleading at times and the only way to be sure is to inspect the *GUID* of the object in the *Properties [Information] Dialog Box*.

17.3.7   Semantic Checks

Semantic Checks allow you to check your model to see if it conforms to the ARIS Method and to other conventions you may wish to enforce. The Semantic Check will produce an output in Microsoft Word or Microsoft Excel format that you can study to identify the elements of the model that failed the check. Some specific Semantic Checks will annotate the model diagram itself with *Information Marks* to indicate the error.

The standard Semantic Checks are organised in six types:

- Structure Rules,
- Assignment Rules,
- Existence Rules,
- Allocation Rules,
- Object Attribute Rules,
- Relationship Attribute Rules.

The purpose of these checks is summarised in Table 17.2 and more information on configuring and running Semantic Checks can be found in Chapter 9.

You may also define your own Semantic Checks using the *Script Editor*. This requires a considerable understanding of ARIS and of the Java programming language, but creating custom Semantic Checks enables you to fully check every aspect of a model's conformance to your corporate modelling conventions.

Table 17.2 Types of Semantic Check

Semantic Check Type	Operation
Structure Rules	Checks the structure of object connections in a model (e.g. are there objects without connections or Rules with multiple inputs and multiple outputs, etc?).
Assignment Rules	Checks the models assigned to objects conform to certain rules (e.g. Events attached to a Function are the trigger and outcome Events in the assigned *EPC*).
Existence Rules	Checks whether all the objects in the selected model exist in a selected target model (e.g. are all the *Organisational unit type* objects used in the *EPC* included in the selected *Organizational chart*?).
Allocation Rules	Checks that relationships are made between specified objects (e.g. do Functions have an *Organizational unit type* assigned to them?).
Attribute Rules	Checks that specified attributes of models, objects and Relationships have values in them.

17.3.8   ARIS Reports

The ARIS Report facility generates documented Reports in various formats including Microsoft Word and Microsoft Excel. The Semantics Checks described in the previous section are examples of ARIS Reports specifically designed for verification. In addition to the standard Reports, it is possible to create your own Reports using the *Script Editor*. By creating custom Reports it is possible to undertake very specific and very extensive analysis of your models and objects. Configuring and running ARIS Reports is described in Chapter 9. Chapter 16 gives some example of Reports for Database Administration.

17.3.9   ARIS Macros

When using ARIS Reports or Semantic Checks, the respective wizards will ask you to make a number of selections to choose the type of Report or Semantic Check, the output format and other details. Each time you run a check or a report, it is necessary to define all the information again. However, instead we can use Macros to pre-define this information and allow the report or check to be run at the touch of a button.

Macros can be configured so they can be started manually, by including them as menu entries or toolbar buttons, or to be run automatically when some ARIS event occurs (e.g. a new model is created or a model is saved, etc). Thus Macros can be used to enforce modelling conventions, for instance by triggering a Semantic Check each time a model is saved.

 Warning although the use of macros to automatically trigger Semantic Checks seems quite appealing at first, the continued triggering of Macros when models are saved can be very irritating to users and should be implemented sparingly.

17.4   Verification Checks

In the sections below we will look at those tools and techniques you can use to carry out the checks suggested in Section 17.2. You will need to experiment to find which best suits your company and project and then create your own verification checklist to use as a corporate or project standard.

17.4.1   Checks on Individual Models

Ensuring each individual model is methodologically correct and consistent should be the cornerstone of all your modelling work. It is best to get into the habit of continually checking the correctness of your models as you go along. In that way, you will learn to quickly recognise and correct errors as you make them, rather than relying on detailed checks after completion. Your final checks will then only need to identify the few remaining subtle mistakes, rather than giving you long lists of errors to correct. It is much easier to interpret the results of Semantic Checks when there are only a few errors.

Typically the majority of modelling errors are caused by the following types of basic mistake:

- incorrect naming of objects,
- duplication of objects,
- incorrect modelling of decisions,
- failure to follow the *Event-driven process chain* method.

As we shall see below, it is easy to check for each of these conditions, so there is no excuse for creating models with these types of errors.

No Duplication of Functions, Events and Rules

Every Event, Function and Rule in an *EPC* should be unique. There should be no occurrence copies of any of them within a single model. To check for erroneous occurrence copies, use the *Occurrences Tab* of the *Navigation Bar*, described in Section 17.3.6. If you find any occurrence copies you will need to create a new object and replace the occurrence copy with it. Alternatively you can make a definition copy of one of the objects and change its name to something that distinguishes it from the original object. To locate the object in the model, you can select the object in the *Occurrences Tab* and then the *Modelling Window* will scroll so that the object occurrence is visible. Remember to delete the object that is no longer required from the model. You will need to check the attributes of the objects you are deleting (and those remaining) in case there is different information maintained that needs to be aggregated.

The situation is slightly different with Rules. By default, the names of these are "*OR*", "*AND*", etc. Ideally you should change the name so as to describe exactly what the Rule does, but most people will find it too much work to do this. If so, you have to accept that all the Rules in the model will have the same name, but this is not normally a problem.

No Replication of Common Resource Objects

Whenever we allocate a common resource to a Function (e.g. *Organizational unit type*, *Application system type*, etc), we want to ensure it is an occurrence of the same object. In that way we can perform analysis of resource allocations

It is very easy to accidentally create replicas of resource objects; that is, to create a new object with the same or similar name to an existing object representing the same 'real-word' entity. Using the *Occurrences Tab* of the *Navigation Bar* to find replica objects is described in Section 17.3.6.

If you find duplicate resource objects, delete one of them and replace it with an *occurrence copy* of the remaining one. You will need to check the attributes of the objects you are deleting (and those remaining) in case there is different information maintained that needs to be aggregated.

Decision, Branches and Loops are Modelled Correctly

One of the most common mistakes people make when modelling with ARIS is to incorrectly model decisions. However, the principles are very simple:

- Decisions are taken by Functions,
- Functions that take decisions are always followed by Rules (*XOR*, *OR*),
- Rules show the valid combination of paths that follow a decision,
- Events following Rules indicate the actual outcomes of decisions,
- Rules cannot have both multiple inputs and multiple outputs.

Follow these principles and you shouldn't go wrong. Wherever an *XOR* or an *OR* has more than one output, it represents a decision. Therefore, it must be preceded by a Function that makes the decision and it must be followed by Events representing the different outcomes. The only other use of an *XOR* or an *OR* is to combine trigger Events or process branches. In this case, the Rule has multiple inputs and only one output. Visually inspect your model, looking for Rules with multiple outputs, and check to see if they meet the conditions above.

The *No XOR/OR after event possible* Rule in the *Structure Rules* Semantic Check will find these types of errors, but it is good practice to be able to spot them visually.

The Model Conforms to the ARIS Method

Process models (*EPCs*) should conform to the *Event-driven process chain* method. That is, the Events and Functions should always follow in sequence. You should not normally connect Functions together without the intervening Events. In high-level conceptual diagrams you may take some liberties with these rules, so as to produce more abstract views, but if you do this in detailed process models it defeats the objective of using the ARIS Method.

You can visually check models quite quickly. Start at the first trigger Event and follow each path of the model. Ignore the Rules and just check that Events and Functions alternate. It doesn't matter how complex the model, or how many combinations of Rules there are; Events and Functions should always alternate. If they don't, then you have modelled something incorrectly and you will need to examine the model in detail to find the cause of the problem.

The *Structure Rules* Semantic Check will help find many of these types of errors, but it is quicker to visually find the worst of them beforehand.

Trigger and Outcome Events are Modelled Correctly

All *EPCs* should begin and end with Events. You can easily check this visually and also by using the *Each path must begin and end with an Event* Rule in the *Structure Rules* Semantic Check.

The trigger and outcome Events may represent things in the external world, or they may be links to other process models. Check all the external Events only have occurrences in the current model, and in sub-process models assigned to Functions connected to the Events. Use the *Occurrences Tab* of the *Properties Bar* to do this. Linking Events, on the other hand, should also have an occurrence in the other linked model (see Section 17.4.2).

You should also check that process paths which appear to terminate in an Event which is a 'dead-end' are correct and they should not in fact be linked to other models. It is worth annotating 'dead-end' Events with an attribute placement to make it clear that this is deliberate.

Object Relationships are Correct

Check each Function in the *EPC* to ensure it has the appropriate resource objects connected to it and the connections have the correct relationships. The modelling standards for the project should define the minimum set of Functional allocations that should be made for each Function. You can do this visually or by using an ARIS Report.

Attributes are Populated Correctly

It is important to set standards defining which attributes should be populated and what they should contain. If you don't do this, your ability to perform later analysis and simulation may be limited. You can check attributes have been populated using the *Object Attribute Rules* Semantic Check.

It is more difficult to check the actual values of the attributes. You could use the *Script Editor* to create a custom Semantic Check, but it may be easier to visually check values using an ARIS Report.

17.4.2   Checks Across the Database

Once you have ensured each of the models in your database passes the checks described in Section 17.4.1, you can look for consistency across the database. The extent to which you do this will depend on the nature of the project. If you have created complex model hierarchies and wish to use Model Generation, then it is important to ensure database consistency.

There are no Significant Objects with the Same Name

From an ARIS perspective, it is valid to have objects with the same name because the uniqueness of objects is ensured by the GUID. However, from a modelling perspective it can be confusing, and it is better that Functions and Events should always have unique names. This makes verification much easier. For instance, the Events representing the outcome of a decision are often labelled "*Yes*", "*No*", "*Valid*", "*Invalid*", etc. Objects with these labels may occur in many different models, leading to numerous objects with the same name. It is better to make the labels more specific (e.g. "*Delivery Not Required*", "*Customer Data Invalid*", etc). If you really are desperate to think of specific names, then append a sequence number (e.g. "*Order Rejected [1]*" and "*Order Rejected [2]*").

The situation is slightly different with Rules. By default, the names of these are "*OR*", "*AND*", etc. Ideally you should change the name so as to describe exactly what the Rule does, but most people will find it too much work to do this. If so, you have to accept that all the Rules in the database will have the same name, but this is not normally a problem.

To check for duplicate names use the _Find_ command with the *Objects with identical names* option described in detail in Chapter 5 and then manually change the name of one of the objects.

There are no Incorrect Multiple Occurrences

In the previous section we checked for multiple occurrences of Events and Functions within the same model. We now need to check across models. Functions rarely have occurrence copies in different *EPCs*. Similarly, the internal Events in a model (i.e. those that are not trigger or outcome Events) should not have multiple occurrences in *EPCs* at the same level of the process hierarchy.

The only way to check for object occurrences across the entire database is to use the *Occurrences of objects* Report. Select some or all of the objects of a particular type (e.g. all the Functions or all the Events) in the *Explorer Module* or using the _Find_ command and run the Report. Depending on the complexity of your model structure you may need quite a lot of skill in interpreting the results and deciding if the occurrences are valid. If you are able to run the Report on sub-sets of objects (i.e. all 'linking' Events or all 'internal' Events), this will make interpretation much easier.

In large databases it may be appropriate to run these tests across sets of models rather than across the whole database. This relies to some extent on having the group structure arranged such that you can partition the database into appropriate sections.

The Group Structure is Sensible and Consistent

The correct operation of ARIS itself does not in any way depend on the structure and arrangement of groups, or how the models and objects are distributed within them. However, in order to make database management easier, and also to allow access control in multi-user server implementations, it is necessary to have some sort of structure. Standards for group structure and naming should be defined at the start of each project (see Chapter 10), and frequent housekeeping will be needed to ensure the standards are maintained. Typically, you may wish to have all your resource objects (e.g. organisation, systems and data) in separate groups so as to form libraries. You can check whether this has been done by using the Find command to find all objects of a particular type. If they are not in the correct group, you can select the offending objects from the *Find Dialog Box* and cut and paste them into the appropriate group in the *Explorer Module*.

Model Naming Standards Have Been Followed

When using complex model structures it is sensible to establish some standards for modelling naming, and at the verification stage you should check these standards have been followed. Models can be renamed without affecting the operation of ARIS, but new models created as assigned models usually take the name of the object to which they are assigned and are best left with these names.

There are no Unnecessary or Duplicate Models

When databases have been in use for some time, they often collect a variety of test models, alternative approaches, 'what-if?' models and generated models. The relationships defined in these models may duplicate or even conflict with those defined in the core database models. The availability of all these models may confuse users of the database, make database management harder and may compromise analysis. It is important to periodically go through the database and remove irrelevant and out-dated models.

Wherever possible, you should avoid having the same relationships defined in more than one model. If you have created such models, perhaps using Model Generation, to show different views of the database, then make sure they are clearly labelled as such. Place them in a special group and periodically review whether they should be kept permanently or just generated when required.

Undertaking this check is a manual process and requires an understanding of the database structure and the purpose of the models. However, if you create a fully linked model structure using model assignments, as previously suggested, you can then check to see if models are assigned to objects. If models exist that are not assigned to objects, then they are not part of the structure. This gives you an indication the model may not actually be required and is a candidate (but make sure first) for deletion!

There are no Unnecessary Generated Models

See above.

Objects are Located in Appropriate Groups

See above.

Security and Access Privileges Have Been Correctly Implemented

Where several users are using the same database on an ARIS Server it is important to check Access Privileges have been implemented correctly. Setting up these privileges is a job for the Database Administrator and Server Administrator (see Chapter 11), but it is the purpose of verification to test these.

Access Privileges are controlled in ARIS on a group basis. Users have Access Privileges (*read, write* and *delete*) to objects and models in certain groups, so it is important to make sure the objects and models are in the correct groups. For instance, all users should have read access to groups containing library objects (e.g. *Organizational unit types*), but should not have *write* access to be able to change them. If a library object has accidentally been left in a group with full Access Privileges, then anyone can change or delete it.

Verification should initially check that objects and models are in the correct location (as described above), and also check Access Privileges. The person undertaking verification should be given several different test accounts with different Access Privileges so they can check the appropriate operations are available from each account.

17.4.3   Checks on Multiple Models

Having checked that individual models are correct and the database itself is correct and consistent, we can start to look at the relationships between models and inter-model consistency. These are the most complex checks to carry out as they have to be done manually and require considerable knowledge of the database structure.

Multiple Object Occurrences are Necessary and Correct

We may have already done these checks for the database in Section 17.4.1. However, with complex model structures (particularly using variant hierarchies) it will be too complicated to undertake these checks for all the models. Instead you will need to choose related sets of models and consider the object occurrences in these models.

Unfortunately, there is no easy way to select a set of models and identify the multiple object occurrences in those models. The only way to approach this is to ensure your directory structure is organised so as to group appropriate models in the same group hierarchy. You can then use the Find command to locate all the objects in that group structure, select the objects and run the *Occurrences of objects* Report.

Common Linking Events Have Correct Occurrences

In previous checks we have ensured that common linking Events had occurrences in other models. At this stage we now need to check the occurrences are in the correct sets of models. For instance, to make sure a linking Event is the outcome Event of one model and the trigger Event in another model. This is largely done manually by inspecting the Event occurrences and opening the models to check the usage of the Event.

If you have created a model hierarchy with variant sub-processes, as described in Chapter 8, checking linking Events is more complex. Linking Events will occur in all the variant sub-process models. You need to work through the models carefully to check the linking is correct. The final check is to use Model Generation to assemble appropriate combinations of models.

Common Resources are Represented by the Same Objects

We have already discussed how resource objects should be represented by occurrence copies of the same object; checks at model level and database level should have ensured this is the case. You will probably need to make some additional checks across related models to ensure objects with seemingly very different names are not actually representing the same 'real-world entities'. This must be a manual check, but you can use the various ARIS Reports to list the different resource objects used in models.

Model Assignments are Correct

When establishing a model hierarchy it is important to ensure the correct models have been assigned to objects. In addition, where these assigned models represent sub-processes, make sure the trigger and outcome Events from the high-level models have been copied down into the sub-process model.

The *Assignment Rules* Semantic Checks can be run on selected objects to check model assignments. Two useful rules in this group are:

- *Function with assigned process (checks events),*
- *Function with assigned FAD.*

The *Function with assigned process (checks events)* Rule checks that the trigger and outcome Events of a Function in a high-level model are also the trigger and outcome Events in the sub-process model. Where the Events in the high-level model are connected to the Function via Rules, then all the related sub-process models are also checked.

The *Function with assigned FAD* checks to see that a *Function allocation diagram (FAD)* assigned to a Function has an occurrence copy of the same Function within it.

17.4.4   Checks on Model Structure and Linking

We have checked our individual models, and checked that related models are consistent and link together. Finally, we need to check that all the models fit together correctly into the intended model structure. With simple structures, this will be an easy task; with complex structures it is likely to be more involved.

Model Hierarchies are Consistent and Synchronised

You should check the decomposition of Functions (and Events if you have used *Event diagrams*) is sensible and consistent. There are no hard and fast rules. The main tests are:

- Does the hierarchy add value?
- Is there significant extra detail added at the next level?
- Does the detail of the Events match the detail of the Functions?
- Is the detail structurally relevant?

If the next level of the hierarchy doesn't add much extra detail, or adds too much detail, then the levels of decomposition are probably inappropriate. Check if the Events shown are structurally relevant (i.e. do they make a difference to the process flow?). If not, is it useful to have them for indication purposes or should they be removed?

The Function Hierarchy is Correct

Generating a *Function tree* from a hierarchy of *EPC* using Model Generation is described in Chapter 6. Check that it generates the *Function tree* correctly and the hierarchy seems appropriate. This is a good check to compare the way one particular process decomposes into sub-processes with the way another process does. Check if the levels of detail look consistent.

The Event Hierarchy is Correct

If you have a fully decomposed Event hierarchy you can generate an *Event diagram* from the hierarchy of individual *Event diagrams*. Check if the levels of detail look correct and consistent. Check if all the detail is actually required.

Model Generation Produces Valid End-to-End Process Models

Many of the checks in previous sections were aimed at ensuring models connect together correctly. The final check is to use the Model Generator to assemble combinations of models into end-to-end processes. If the results of Model Generation show isolated blocks of processes, then the linking has not been done correctly. If the result shows models connected in unexpected ways, then either linking has not been done correctly, or there is accidental linking through inappropriate use of occurrence copies.

If you do find significant errors, you can select models in pairs or in small groups in order to generate the end-to-end model in a step-by-step way to identify errors. You may also need to go back and repeat some of the earlier tests to ensure the correct use of common linking Events and occurrence copies.

Generating end-to-end models using Model Generation is described in detail in Chapter 6.

Appendix A   ARIS Admintool Commands

Command	Syntax / Description
Backup	backup <dbname>|all <archivedir> [<alternatename>]
	Saves a database <dbname> as an adb file in a directory <archivedir>.
Backupconfig	backupconfig <archivedir> [<alternatename>]
	Saves the ARIS configuration data such as filters, templates and charts in an acb file in a directory <archivedir>.
Configadminpassword	Configadminpassword <password> <oldpassword>
	Sets the password of the CFGADMIN user to <password>. In the interactive mode, <password> must not be specified because the user has to enter it.
Copy	copy <fromdbname>|all <todbname> [:<server>] [/<siteadminpassword>][/<dbadminpassword>]
	Copies a database from <fromdbname> to <todbname>. Optional on server <server>. When copying all databases, <server> must be specified.
Createdb	createdb <dbname>
	Creates a new ARIS database with the name <dbname>.
Dbmspassword	dbmspassword <password> <oldpassword>
	Sets the password of the DBMS user to <password>. In the interactive mode, <password> must not be specified because the user has to enter it.
Delete	delete <dbname>|all [force]
Download	download [logs|configs|accounting|all] <dir>
	Downloads files from the ARIS Site to the specified directory <dir>.
	Deletes the database <dbname>. When entering the 'force' option, the database will be deleted even if users are currently logged in.
Exit	exit
	Exits the interactive mode.
Help	help [<command>]
	Displays an overview of all commands or help for a specific command.

Command	Syntax / Description
Interactive	interactive
	Runs the program in the interactive mode.
Kill	kill <sessionid> | all
	Closes the connection <sessionid> of the current server.
List	list [all]
	Lists all of the server's registered databases. By default, only the databases of the current schema context will be listed. When entering the 'all' option, all databases will be listed.
Maintain	maintain <dbname> | all
	The 'Maintain' command initiates the maintenance of the specified database. Maintenance is specified according to the database system, i.e. a fixed set of maintenance tasks will be performed depending on the database system.
Monitor	monitor
	Display of all server activities in progress, such as backup, XML export etc.
Password	password <password> <oldpassword>
	Sets the password of the DBADMIN user to <password>. In the interactive mode, <password> must not be specified because the user has to enter it.
Rename	rename olddbname> <newdbname> [force]
	Renames the database from <olddbname> to <newdbname>. When entering the 'force' option, the database will be renamed even if users are still logged in.
Reorg	reorg <dbname> | all
	Semantically reorganises the <dbname> database by deleting all objects not found in models or ABC tables.
Restore	restore <archive> | <archivedir> [<dbname>] [overwrite]
	Restores a database <dbname> from an adb file <archive>, or restores all adb/bdb files from a directory. The 'overwrite' option is allowed for backup files of the current version only.
Restoreconfig	restoreconfig <archive>
	Restores the ARIS configuration data such as filters, templates and charts from an acb file <archive>.

Command	Syntax / Description
Schemacontext	schemacontext <new schema context>
	Changes the schema context of the current server. Thus it is possible to save ARIS Business Optimizer databases. Possible values are 'aris' and 'bo'.
Server	server <server> [<siteadminpassword>]
	Changes the current server.
Sessions	sessions [byuser | bypid | bydatabase]
	Displays all database connections of the current server.
Siteadminpassword	siteadminpassword <password> <oldpassword>
	Sets the password of the SITEADMIN user to <password>. In the interactive mode, <password> must not be specified because the user has to enter it.
Statistic	Statistic <dbname> | all
	Displays the number of objects in the specified database.
Status	status [<server>]
	Displays the statuses of program, network, and connection to a server <server>.
Version	version
	Displays the versions of the programs and libraries in use.

Key

command	command name or command switch (e.g. "all")
<value>	value to be entered
<value> <value>	two values to be entered (separated by a space)
[<value>]	optional value
<value> | Command	alternative entries (e.g. enter a value or a command switch)

Glossary

ARIS	Architecture of Integrated Information Systems.
ARIS Method	The implementation of the ARIS concept in the ARIS Platform by use of a special product like *ARIS Business Designer* or *ARIS Business Architect*.
ARIS Platform	The range of ARIS products including *ARIS Business Architect*, *ARIS Business Designer*, *ARIS Toolset*, etc.
'as-is'	The current processes operated by an organisation.
Attribute	ARIS modelling information stored for ARIS items (e.g. models, objects, relationships, databases, etc).
BPM	Business Process Modelling.
Business Process	The definition of the tasks, and the sequence of those tasks, necessary to deliver a business objective.
Business Process Architecture	A hierarchical structure of process description levels covering the whole organisation from a business process point of view.
Business Process Management	A systematic approach to managing and improving an organisation's business by the active, coordinated management of all aspects of the specification, design, implementation, operation, measurement, analysis and optimisation of business processes in order to effectively and efficiently deliver business objectives.
Connection	On an ARIS model diagram, the line connecting two objects denoting an ARIS relationship.
Database	A collection of related ARIS models representing a significant business area.
Diagram	The visual representation of an ARIS model.
EPC	Event-Driven Process Chain.
FAD	Function Allocation Diagram.
GUID	ARIS Global Unique Identifier.
IT	Information Technology.
Item	A thing that can be manipulated in the folder structure in the *ARIS Explorer Module* or *ARIS Designer Module*.
LAN	Local Area Network.
Method Filter	A Filter applied to ARIS databases that limits the range of models, objects, relationships and attributes that can be used and displayed.

Model	An ARIS diagram of a particular type (e.g. a *Event-driven process chain*) visually representing the objects and relationships stored in the underlying ARIS repository.
Object	An ARIS representation of a real-world entity (e.g. task, organisation, system, data item, etc).
Occurrence	The graphical representation in a model of an object definition.
PC	Personal Computer.
Properties	The totality of all information known about ARIS items (e.g. models, objects, relationships, databases, etc.)
Relationship	An ARIS representation of the interaction between real-world entities represented by ARIS objects.
Server	A file storage system on a PC or networked file server holding a set of ARIS databases.
Structurally Relevant	Objects that describe the flow and logic of a process model (e.g. Events, Functions and Rules).
Symbol	A graphic used to denote the occurrence of an ARIS object on a model diagram.
Template	A pre-defined format for the graphic appearance of models, symbols and connections that can be applied to many models in one operation.
'to-be'	The future, target, processes to be operated by an organisation.
UML	Unified Modelling Language.
URL	WWW Universal Resource Locator.
XMI	XML Metadata Interchange
XML	eXtended Markup Language
VACD	Value Added Chain Diagram.
WAN	Wide Area Network.
WWW	The World Wide Web (or Web).

Subject Index

Page numbers in **bold** refer to more significant discussions of topics with multiple references.
Page numbers in *italics* refer to figures illustrating the topic.
Entries starting with a lower case letter refer to ARIS relationships (e.g. "activates")